EDGAR R. TREXLER

HIGH
EXPECTATIONS

Understanding the ELCA's Early Years, 1988–2002

D1097166

Augsburg Fortress
Minneapolis

HIGH EXPECTATIONS

Understanding the ELCA's Early Years, 1988-2002

Scripture quotations are from New Revised Standard Version Bible, copyright © 1989 Division of Christian Education of the National Council of the Churches of Christ in the United States of America. Used by permission.

On the cover: Venetian glass mosaic, *Rondel*, by David J. Hetland, commissioned for the entrance to the Lutheran Center in Chicago, the churchwide office of the Evangelical Lutheran Church in America. Copyright © 1989 by Hetland Ltd., Fargo, North Dakota. Used by permission.

Editors: Scott Tunseth and James Satter
Cover design: David Meyer
Text design: James Satter

Library of Congress Cataloging-in-Publication Data

Trexler, Edgar R.
   High expectations : understanding the ELCA's early years, 1988-2002 /
Edgar R. Trexler.
   p. cm.
ISBN 0-8066-4575-X
1. Evangelical Lutheran Church in America—History.
2. Lutheran Church—United States—History—20th century. I. Title.

BX8048.3.T745 2003
284.1'35'09—dc21

2003005548

The paper used in this publication meets the minimum requirements of American National Standard for Information Sciences—Permanence of Paper for Printed Library Materials, ANSI Z329.48-1984.

Manufactured in the U.S.A.

07   06   05   04   03   2   3   4   5   6   7   8   9   10

CONTENTS

ACKNOWLEDGMENTS

"Expect great things from God,
attempt great things for God."

William Carey, English missionary, 1792

I n *High Expectations* I have attempted to write a contemporary account, journalistic and analytical in style, of the early years of the Evangelical Lutheran Church in America. Specifically, it covers the years from 1988 to 2002, 15 years in all. In a sense, this is a sequel to my book *Anatomy of a Merger* (Augsburg, 1991), which gave an account of the deliberations that brought the ELCA into being from its predecessors—the Lutheran Church in America, the American Lutheran Church, and the Association of Evangelical Lutheran Churches. Together, the two books cover a significant part of U.S. Lutheran history in the last quarter of the 20th century.

I owe many debts of gratitude for this book. First, my thanks to the Evangelical Lutheran Church in America for asking me to edit *The Lutheran* magazine from 1988 to 1999 (and the LCA's *The Lutheran* from 1978 to 1987). These opportunities provided both the facts and the vantage point for the observations that are included in this book. A large number of the quotes in the book come directly from the pages of *The Lutheran*. Full documentation for each quote has not been provided, primarily for ease of reading. Additional content for the book has been drawn from the ELCA's official records and my own notes from far more meetings of the ELCA Churchwide Assemblies, the Church Council, the Conference of Bishops, and the Cabinet of Executives than I wish to recall.

ELCA Secretary Lowell G. Almen, a longtime friend and fellow journalist, gave valuable perspective to these pages, and applied his unerring eye to its details. Silvia Chavez, *The Lutheran's* budget and administrative director, tracked down many details (and people). And my wife, Emily, who has lived this history with me, is glad for this volume finally to be out of my system. The quotation at the beginning of this section is her favorite.

As one observer's perspective on the infant Evangelical Lutheran Church in America, as well as grist for future historians' mills, this book is a gift to my church.

EDGAR R. TREXLER
Hendersonville, North Carolina

DEFINED BY THE PAST

"My friends, there will be a new church."

*Bishop James R. Crumley Jr., announcing to the LCA convention
the vote to form the ELCA, August 29, 1986*

When the Evangelical Lutheran Church in America was founded in 1988, it was the capstone of five Lutheran mergers in the 20th century. In this sense, the ELCA was not so much a "new" Lutheran church but rather a church that was in the process of "becoming" for an entire century. It brought together into one Lutheran church 15 churches that were individual entities in 1900, plus four more churches that were created by earlier mergers in 1918, 1930, 1960, and 1962, along with a new church that formed in 1976. During the 20th century, 20 Lutheran churches became one—perhaps a coincidence, perhaps not.

The ELCA represents a majority of the nation's Lutherans—Germans, Norwegians, Swedes, Danes, and Finns—who came to North America as early as 1619. Separated more by distance, language, ethnic roots, and organizational styles than by doctrine, they began to gather into various groups for survival and for evangelism.

By 1900, German Lutherans on the East Coast made up the General Synod (founded 1820), the General Council (1867), and the General Synod of the Evangelical Lutheran Church in the Confederate States (1863, renamed in 1886 the United Synod in the South). In 1918, these churches formed the United Lutheran Church in America. In 1962, the ULCA and the Augustana Church (Swedish background, founded 1860), United Evangelical Lutheran Church (Danish, 1872), and the Suomi Synod (Finnish, 1890) merged into the Lutheran Church in America. When it came into the ELCA, the LCA, based in New York, had 2,874,932 members in 5,834 congregations.

Lutherans with Midwestern roots organized the Ohio Synod in 1818, the Buffalo Synod in 1845, the Texas Synod in 1851, and the Iowa Synod in 1854. All were German in background and came together in 1930 as the former American Lutheran Church.

In 1917, the Norwegian Lutheran Church of America (changed in 1946 to the Evangelical Lutheran Church) was formed by Lutherans who had been in Hauge's Synod (1876), the Norwegian Evangelical Lutheran Church (1853), and the United Norwegian Lutheran Church (1890). In 1960, the ALC, the ELC, and the United Evangelical Lutheran Church (Danish, 1896) formed the American Lutheran Church, the first major U.S. Lutheran merger to bring together Lutherans of German and Scandinavian origins. After expanding in 1963 to include the Lutheran Free Church (Norwegian, founded 1897), the ALC became the second major strain to form the ELCA. At the time, the ALC, based in Minneapolis, had 2,315,726 members in 4, 974 congregations.

The third church in the ELCA merger was the Association of Evangelical Lutheran Churches, founded in 1976, which broke away from The Lutheran Church—Missouri Synod over the LCMS's increasingly conservative interpretation of Scripture. The AELC, based in St. Louis, had 100,496 members in 267 congregations.

The Lutheran landscape for the last third of the 20th century was consumed by merger talk. All Lutheran churches had benefited from the mushrooming membership growth in the 1950s. When the ALC and the LCA were formed, they, along with The Lutheran Church—Missouri Synod, reduced the U.S. Lutheran presence into three major camps. The natural expectation was that Lutherans, who shared common doctrine, would soon find organizational unity. Besides, it was a time for Protestant mergers in the United States. The Congregational Church and the Evangelical and Reformed Church formed the United Church of Christ in 1957. The Methodist and the Evangelical United Brethren churches merged into the United Methodist Church in 1967. The northern and southern branches of the Presbyterian Church, divided since the Civil War, came together in 1983.

Some unexpected roadblocks came along the Lutheran way, however. In the early 1970s, the president of the LCA, Robert J. Marshall, and the general president of the ALC, Kent S. Knutson, discussed the possibility of the two denominations "growing together naturally" in such areas as world missions and the churches' foundations. Marshall and Knutson even sketched possible merged structures and compared them. But when Knutson died in 1973, the rise of David W. Preus to ALC general president (changed to presiding bishop in 1980) derailed further talks because he did not favor merger. Moreover, relationships between both the ALC and the LCA with The Lutheran Church— Missouri Synod deteriorated with the election of Jacob Preus (David Preus's cousin) as its president in 1969. The ALC and the LCMS enjoyed official altar and pulpit fellowship, but the LCMS placed it "in protest" in 1977 and ended it in 1981.

Despite these developments, the ALC/LCA Committee on Church Cooperation in 1975 began to discuss differences in their organizational patterns and evaluating structures. The committee found no substantial differences between the church's theological positions, sociological patterns, and mission statements. Then in 1978, the AELC issued "A Call to Union." This led to the formation of the Committee on Lutheran Unity, with seven members each from the LCA and ALC and two from the AELC. The group first met in January 1979.

After meeting for more than two years, the CLU finally put a proposal before the churches for four types of merged church structure ranging from a federation of the three churches to their merger into a single church. The district and synod assemblies of each church studied the proposals in the summer of 1981. The report in September left no question about the future: 14,308 delegates favored "uniting the churches in some form," while 2,303 favored "retaining the present structures." During the course of the voting, ALC Presiding Bishop Preus announced that he had misjudged the fervor for merger in the ALC and pledged to support it.

The next step was the formation of the 70-member Commission for a New Lutheran Church. The CNLC, as it came to be known, met 10 times—for a week at a time—across the United States from 1982 to 1986. Their merger proposal that formed the ELCA was put to a vote by the three church bodies at their national assemblies on the same day, September 8, 1986. The vote was overwhelming: LCA—611 yes, 11 no; ALC—897 yes, 87 no; AELC—136 yes, 0 no.

Thus the stage was set for the formation of the fourth largest Protestant church in the United States, following the Southern Baptist Convention, the United Methodist Church, and the National Baptist Convention, a black denomination. The ELCA began with 5,288,471 members, 11,133 congregations, and 17, 052 pastors, the second largest church in the Lutheran World Federation (after the Church of Sweden, with 7.4 million members). Lutheran membership internationally exceeds 65 million.

Amid the excitement of the ELCA's Constituting Convention in Columbus, Ohio, April 30 to May 3, 1987, there also came the realization that the dream of one Lutheran Church in the United States had gone as far as it would go for the foreseeable future. With 2.6 million members, The Lutheran Church—Missouri Synod (founded in 1847 of German background), was embarking on a separatist path because of differences in interpretation of Scripture, divergent views on the role of women and disdain for ecumenical relationships. Even though official contacts were retained, it became highly unlikely that rapprochement between ELCA and LCMS would take place.

The nature of the church

The Lutheran merger might have been viewed as easy because it required no new doctrinal statements. But as the early days of the ELCA soon made clear, two items—one ecclesiological, meaning how one understands the nature of the church, and the other emotional—meant that the early years of the new church would not proceed as smoothly as might have been expected. The various organizational differences that characterized the predecessor churches would prove that agreements on paper did not necessarily change "the way we've always done it"

in the minds of both leaders and people in the pew when the
new church was launched.

Chief among the organizational differences was the understanding of the nature of the church. When the merger
commission was meeting, the LCA bishops took extreme exception to what they considered to be a weak statement on the
nature of the church. When the ALC offered to accept, virtually
verbatim, the section from the LCA Constitution about the
nature of the church, the LCA accepted. This section formed
the basis of chapter 3, "Nature of the Church," in the ELCA
Constitution.

The LCA emphasized the oneness of the church, particularly
the interrelatedness of the congregation, the synod and the
national organization. Neither the congregations nor the churchwide organization functioned in isolation. The LCA had a high
view of the clergy, held up ecumenism as a constitutional commitment, and prized the consistency of practice across the church
that came from adherence to the church's constitutions and
bylaws.

The ALC was more congregationally based, with the
national church exercising only those powers ceded to it by the
congregations. Congregations and agencies took more leeway
about observing the church's constitution. A low-church tradition lifted up lay leadership. Ecumenism was appreciated, but it
was not a focus. The congregational attitude was a carry-over
from the days of Norwegian immigration in the 1840s when
settlers came to North American to escape the dominance of a
state church that was top-heavy with hierarchy. "We're kind of
low-church populists," Albert E. Anderson, the late head of
Augsburg Fortress, Publishers, once said.

The AELC reflected the congregational stance of its parent,
The Lutheran Church—Missouri Synod, yet its worldview was
more like that of the LCA than the ALC. The organizational
preferences between the LCA and the ALC created more tensions than might have been expected. Seasoned observers from
both churches were often surprised during the ELCA's early days
at how much leaders from each of the predecessor churches did

not know about the practical ethos of the other. For instance, when controversy arose in the mid-to-late 1990s over adoption of full communion with the Episcopal Church, much of the debate centered over whether a synodical bishop must ordain a seminarian or whether ordination could be delegated to a parish pastor. A pastor of a congregation was a high enough authority to ordain, according to a congregationalist view. The "higher church" view insisted on a bishop doing the ordaining on behalf of the whole church.

Lowell G. Almen, ELCA secretary, often said that the churches that formed the ULCA in 1918 confronted, and largely resolved over the years, issues related to congregationalism. The ecclesial substance of the larger church was directly affirmed in the 1918 ULCA Constitution. This emphasis on the oneness of the church was strengthened by the Augustana Church's entrance into the LCA merger in 1962. But Almen said he was not sure that overcoming congregationalism, apart from a sense of the unity with the larger church, was dealt with by the ALC mergers of 1930 and 1960, and that such issues were not really confronted until the 1988 ELCA merger. They are only slowly being resolved now, he concluded.

The second item to create discord was harder to pin down. Basically, it was a backlash over the emphasis on beginning a "new church." The "new church" phrase, which began as innocuous excitement over the churches finally getting together, soon took on higher expectations of "newness" than could be accommodated. The merger commission was called the Commission for a New Lutheran Church. As it went about its business, it created a number of new realities—a new name, new headquarters, new synodical and regional alignments, new churchwide units, and a new representational system—and, of course, laid the groundwork for new leadership. The merger commission sought information from across the merging churches as to what they would want the new church to be like. The responses came back in such volume that it was impossible for the new church to be everything every respondent wanted it to be. Herein lay the seeds for later contentiousness.

For example, the responses showed a desire for both a women's auxiliary and a churchwide unit devoted to women's issues. The merger commission did not choose one or the other; it approved both. Similarly, various expectations caused the adoption of quotas for clergy/lay, male/female, and minority representation on every board, council, and staff in the new church. The result was the perception that the new church would be all things to all people, whether it could afford "all things" or not and whether "all things" produced a workable structure. When it turned out that the "new" church had shortcomings, high expectations were dashed and grumbling began. The upshot was a kind of emotional, even visceral reaction, to missed expectations. One cannot understand the early years of the ELCA without an awareness of these ecclesiological and emotional influences.

On other issues, there was more commonality among the merging churches. Both the LCA and the ALC had a heavy commitment to world missions and to world hunger appeals. Both were active in the Lutheran World Federation, even providing successive LWF presidents (the ULCA's and LCA's Franklin Clark Fry in 1957 and the ALC's Fredrik Schiotz in 1963). The ALC was more rural and more regional in character because it was the dominant religious group in Minnesota, Wisconsin, and the Dakotas. The LCA was more urban, and had learned to live with religious and cultural diversity because it was not the dominant church even in its areas of concentration. The LCA was more focused on the East Coast. The ALC held more sway on the West Coast, particularly in the Pacific Northwest.

Both churches were active in social ministry and social concerns. The LCA had adopted 17 social statements as teaching statements and to inform the policies of the entire church. The ALC had developed 95 statements and 60 resolutions of concern with various levels of authority. Both churches gave considerable attention to the role of women. Neither was strong in ministries to people of color.

Thus was the context for the legal collapsing of the three predecessor corporations into the Evangelical Lutheran Church in America at 12:01 A.M. CST on January 1, 1988. Considerable Lutheran energy during the last third of the 20th century had been directed toward this consummation. And though the merger began with rousing good will, early tumults arose primarily from the differing ecclesiological styles of the predecessor churches and the inordinately high expectations for the new church.

CHAPTER 1

THE PAINS OF NEWNESS

"It seems a little like the first day of school.
It's tough to get everyone quiet."

*ELCA Secretary Lowell G. Almen, trying to start the "Service of Entrance"
on January 4, 1988, the first official work day of the ELCA*

I t was 8:35 A.M., five minutes after the usual time of opening
for business. But on Monday, January 4, 1988, the tardiness
could be forgiven. Amid excitement and crowding, the headquarters staff of the new church squeezed around the fountain in the
lobby of the Lutheran Center at 8765 West Higgins Road,
Chicago. It was the first official workday of the Evangelical
Lutheran Church in America.

Secretary Lowell G. Almen presided over the "service of
entrance" because Presiding Bishop Herbert W. Chilstrom was
still en route from Puerto Rico where he had installed the
bishop of the Caribbean Synod the day before. After a brief
liturgy, Almen's homily and the singing of "Guide Us Ever,
Great Redeemer," mailroom clerk Hector Baldorioty, the crucifer, led a half-dozen staffers with scissors toward a gold ribbon
stretched across the corridor to the elevators. The staffers
snipped, and the workday began. Some staff members were
already grousing about the open-office concept of cubicles
where they worked. Only the corner offices on each floor had
full walls and doors, and they were reserved for executive directors of churchwide units.

When the new 11-story glass, steel, and concrete headquarters building was purchased by the ELCA nine months earlier
for $27,275,000, its emptiness was symbolic of the massive task
of putting a new church together. Except for the marble
entranceway, the elevator shafts, and the bathrooms, the structure awaited being brought to life. It had no partitioning of
space, no offices, no carpet, no lights, no files . . . and no people.

It took longer for the new church to be up and running than some expected. For months trucks had been backing up to the headquarters of the Lutheran Church in America in New York and Philadelphia, the American Lutheran Church offices in Minneapolis, and the Association of Evangelical Lutheran Churches headquarters in St. Louis. It was natural for staff in headquarters that were closing to spend virtually all their time packing huge amounts of material for shipment to the new headquarters. But there was surprisingly little understanding that the opening of ELCA headquarters would require even more time to unpack the boxes and combine the files from the three churches into reasonably useful order. In most cases, those who had done the packing were not the ones doing the unpacking in Chicago. Missing boxes and files were commonplace; some were never found. Moreover, the old offices had various operating procedures in place, such as places where supplies were stored, or how to requisition furniture, or where the coffeepots were stationed.

Another level of disruption was caused by the fact that the merging churches did not have compatible computer systems. The LCA had an IBM mainframe in Philadelphia, while the ALC utilized a Unisys system. The Transition Team was unable to reach a decision on which system to use and assumed that remote job entry from existing equipment in Minneapolis and Philadelphia would work in the early days of the Chicago operation. Most of the Minneapolis computer employees went to other positions, and temporary workers were expensive, so Almen moved to consolidate the system in Chicago. He signed papers for an IBM mainframe for Chicago at the end of the day on December 31, 1987, after both the New York and Minneapolis offices officially closed, saving about $50,000 by purchasing in 1987 rather than in January 1988. The installation took place in mid-February, and various operational systems were in place by March, but the new system was not fully functional until August of 1988, creating a huge statistical backlog in everything from updating clergy rosters to accounting for financial receipts from synods.

In reality, getting the new churchwide operations up to speed was an enormous task—the delivery of services to 5,288,471 members, 11,133 congregations, 17,052 pastors, 28 colleges and universities, eight seminaries, 275 social ministry organizations, 400 missionaries overseas, and ecumenical relationships at home and abroad. Pension plans and records were consolidated in Minneapolis, as were the inventories and works-in-progress of the ALC's Augsburg Publishing House and the LCA's Fortress Press from Philadelphia.

The churchwide organization actually began taking shape in June 1987 when the ELCA's two officers, Presiding Bishop Herbert W. Chilstrom and Almen, set up makeshift offices at 8735 West Higgins Road. The Lutheran Center building was one of five structures in the O'Hare Plaza complex, which was named for its proximity to Chicago's airport. All early-arriving staff set up shop in the temporary quarters in the 8735 and 8725 buildings on West Higgins Road until the build out of the ELCA headquarters was completed in early December. The headquarters address would soon become a euphemism for the church's headquarters—Higgins Road. It was barely inside Chicago's city limits (the other side of Higgins Road was the suburb of Park Ridge), fulfilling the commitment that the headquarters would be located in the city.

Chilstrom and Almen, along with Office for Personnel Director Chris Stein and a few support staff, began working in the temporary quarters in mid-1987 with a "cattle pen" arrangement of used desks and tables. Phones grew out of the floor in the open space, and people competed for the few available chairs to sit on. Almen recalled more than a year later that on those first few weekends when he would go back to Minneapolis where he was still living, "I would go to what is now Augsburg Fortress, Publishers and beg some boxes of paper clips, file folders, and pens. Then I would haul them back in my suitcase to Chicago so that Bishop Chilstrom and I would have some office supplies to work with, because at that time not even a supply line of paper was in place."

In addition, there were some leftover mandates from the Committee for a New Lutheran Church, including a six-year study of ministry (see page 31) and decisions about ELCA membership in the National Council of Churches and the World Council of Churches (see chapter 5). But those kinds of efforts had to await a headquarters facility and staff that could accommodate such work.

Assembling staff

Bringing staff together proved to be as troubling as monumental. Staffs of the predecessor churches were promised an interview but not a job, whereas those who had never been part of a denominational staff could have multiple interviews. The church's early focus on "newness" mitigated against predecessor staff continuing—even if they were willing to move to Chicago from Minneapolis, New York, Philadelphia, or St. Louis. Some 2,290 applicants competed for 544 executive and support staff positions. Most of the 2,290 applicants put their name in for more than one job, so that the personnel office actually was dealing with 7,740 applications. Executive directors of churchwide units who were selecting staff had to juggle such concerns as inclusiveness goals, fair salaries, and costs.

The personnel office itself was an entirely new entity, with people who had never worked together expected to handle thousands of applications for hundreds of positions in a relatively short time. Dossiers were sometimes misfiled, resulting in applicants' missing out on a chance for a job interview. Hundreds of letters and applications did not receive a prompt reply. Sometimes applicants heard that someone else had been chosen for a job before they were officially notified that they were out of the running. Some responses were framed in formal and impersonal language; some telephone inquiries were poorly handled. Staff in some units had no awareness of how to address clergy in correspondence, yielding a variety of embarrassments that were an early public relations problem for the churchwide office.

The hiring fiasco brought a stinging rebuke from the LCA's Executive Council. Calling the performance of the Office for Personnel "seriously deficient," the letter signed by LCA Secretary Reuben T. Swanson said that "a number of LCA staff persons have been so discouraged by their experience with the Office for Personnel that they have decided to take severance benefits rather than pursue opportunities for employment" in the ELCA. "Thus," he continued, "we have incurred additional financial costs as well as the loss of the experience and commitment of these persons."

Stein said he believed the letter was aimed at "the process" of selecting staff (i.e., quotas) rather than at him or other personnel office employees. Almen said it was "particularly ironic that some of the key leaders on the LCA Executive Council also were on the Transition Team for the ELCA, the group that had established the early personnel operation for what was to become the churchwide office of the ELCA. . . . [The criticism] came as a grave disappointment to those of us in leadership at the churchwide office." The LCA council had not consulted with Chilstrom before leveling the criticism. Chilstrom acknowledged that the personnel office made "serious mistakes" and that some officials used "poor judgment" in the hiring process. Eventually, things improved, but a bitter taste remained both for those who got jobs and those who didn't.

When the ELCA headquarters was fully up and running at the end of 1988, there were 357 executive staff and 233 support staff, a total of 590. Of those, 208 were former national staff. Total staff would decrease to 485 during the financial pressures of the church's first four years. As of August 2002, there were 347 executive staff and 168 support staff working at the Lutheran Center, a total of 515. Of that number, 28.6 percent were people of color, and 62 percent were female. Clergy and rostered laypersons accounted for 26.5 percent.

Lots of negatives

For a variety of reasons, the early years of the ELCA had a kind of dichotomy. In spite of the outpouring of goodwill, prayers, and enthusiasm, the ELCA took on a two-level character —"business as usual" in congregations and growing pains in the churchwide organization. This might have been expected because mergers have meager effect on day-to-day life in congregations, the place where most people experience "church."

As time passed for the ELCA, it seemed that many laypersons were basically positive toward the new church, while many clergy were not persuaded. Letters in the debut issue of *The Lutheran*, dated January 6, 1988, complained that inclusiveness goals were not being met, salaries were too high, and that there was a lack of appreciation for "experienced" staff. Even the logo of the magazine itself came under criticism.

Some synods were experiencing difficulty as well. In the Metropolitan Chicago Synod, Bishop John Tietjen resigned on November 23, 1987, because the synod council refused to approve one of his choices for an assistant. When fiscal responsibility became an issue, the comments of Pastor James Klosterboer, Elkader, Iowa, at the 1989 Churchwide Assembly, were typical of the attitude that was infecting the church. "If the bishops took a $10,000 pay cut, and their assistants a $5,000 pay cut, and the ELCA executive directors a $5,000 cut, it would be easier for them to come to my congregation and talk money."

Some of the tensions came from unexpected sources. For example, Bishop Chilstrom had to issue a memo to the synod bishops, declaring that a letter they received that was allegedly written and signed by him was a hoax. The letter dealt with charges against a pastor in the Metropolitan New York Synod.

Other problems came from more organized sources. Approximately 900 people gathered in June 1990 on the campus of St. Olaf College in Northfield, Minnesota, for an independent theological conference in which critics hurled barbs at the ELCA. For three days during the "Call to Faithfulness" conference, prominent theologians chastised the ELCA for its ecumenical policies, its approach to social involvement, its mission philosophy, the content of its periodicals, its encouragement of inclusive God language and its alleged lack of theological direction. The ELCA's problems, they said, were caused by the church's failure to be faithful to biblical theology and Lutheran confessions.

Carl E. Braaten, professor of systematic theology at the Lutheran School of Theology at Chicago, was interrupted nine times by applause when he described the church as struggling between traditional concepts of evangelization and a new mission philosophy whose proponents contend that words like *humanization, development, liberation, wholeness,* and *justice* are simply different words for salvation.

Paul Hinlicky, then editor of *Lutheran Forum,* hurled an issue of *The Lutheran* to the floor from the high pulpit of St. Olaf's chapel, deploring the publication of a "Viewpoint" piece by an Arizona pastor who advocated "entertainment evangelism."

A second "Call to Faithfulness" conference a year later continued the same criticisms. "There is a pervasive feeling of letdown and betrayal among rank and file of both clergy and laity," said Braaten. He blasted the "various mutations of the gospel that have emanated from synodical offices and church-wide units," accusing the ELCA administration of "buying into a pluralistic theology of religions that reduces Jesus to one of many great religious leaders in history."

Chilstrom attended the second conference and challenged critics to love the church despite its imperfections. He said he hoped his presence would be seen as an affirmation of independent movements, which he said have played a significant role in the life of the Lutheran church from the beginning. He cautioned, though, that that such movements are healthy only if grounded in the Pauline admonition to "let all that you do be done in love."

In 1990, George Forell, visiting professor of systematic theology at the Lutheran Seminary at Philadelphia and a member of the ELCA Church Council at the time, told the ELCA Convocation of Teaching Theologians that the ELCA has two choices—to follow other mainline Protestant bodies in embracing cultural and theological fads, or to hold fast to its own classical theology. Some theologians urged that they not be "wasted resources" in the church. Bishop Michael C. D. McDaniel of the North Carolina Synod said the church needs to "restore bishops and teaching theologians back into play instead of pacing the sidelines." He claimed that the 60:40 ratio of laity to clergy on boards and councils signals the "profound distrust for authority" that underlies the ELCA structure and ensures that decisions will be made by the "theologically illiterate."

In response, Chilstrom said the ELCA has no "magisterium. We depend on assemblies of the church, made up of a mixture of trained and untrained theologians to determine our mission." He acknowledged that this is "risky," but said, "somehow we manage to come back to our moorings."

Still another uproar came when the ELCA, through the Commission for Women, participated in a "Re-Imagining" Conference in Minneapolis, so-called because women were asked to "re-imagine" their religious traditions through feminist lens. Two ELCA pastors were among more than 20 feminist theologians from around the world who spoke or led small groups, some of whom created an uproar because they invoked in prayers the name of Sophia, the goddess of wisdom. The conference shared the goals of the World Council of Churches' Ecumenical Decade: Churches in Solidarity with Women.

The Pastors of Large Congregations Conference, a loose-knit grouping of pastors of congregations with 3,000-plus baptized members also inflicted a few bruises on Chilstrom. The pastors urged him to be a stronger leader, particularly in evangelism and growth, while Chilstrom appealed to them to be more fully involved in the life of the ELCA. Some of these larger congregations were not providing active leadership in synodical or churchwide efforts. In 1995, the conference sponsored a nationwide closed-circuit television program to discuss openly the qualifications needed in the next bishop. At the 2001 assembly, the conference tried to position one of their number, the Rev. Michael Foss, pastor of 9,332-member Prince of Peace Lutheran Church in Burnsville, Minnesota, as a candidate for presiding bishop. He received 32 votes.

As the charges flew back and forth, some stereotypes of the new church came into play. Along the East Coast, the new church was perceived as having a "Midwestern" tilt, causing its detractors to say that the ELCA had moved from a mainline to a "sideline" denomination. One factor in that criticism could have been that for the first time, East Coast Lutherans—the oldest groups in the merger—did not have any of the church's headquarters physically located on their turf. Former ALC members thought their church had left them by moving to Chicago.

There was disagreement about the need for the regional level of bureaucracy that had been built into the ELCA organization. In the West, regions one, two, and three functioned well, pulling together congregations and synods that were spread over wide geographic areas. In the East, where synod territories were smaller, regions were seen as unnecessary and costly.

Among both clergy and laity came the lament, "I don't feel like I belong in this church." Or, "My church has left me." Or even, "The church is going in a direction I can't agree with." Some objected to the new church's decision to impose a quota system on selections of staff and elections to the church's committees and task forces. Others objected to the role of special interests in determining the staffing and programming of the church, particularly minority concerns and women. There was some feeling that competency of boards was compromised by the necessity of quotas. Bishop William H. Lazareth of the Metropolitan New York Synod, who had been a member of the merger commission, said, "We sold out to sociology and ideologized the political views about the church's organization. Things are being done on the basis of hormones more than on the basis of our confessions."

In time, those who felt that it was not aiming its energies at anything in particular applied the word "unfocused" to the church. Rightly or wrongly, Chilstrom became the lightning rod for such criticism. An independent publication, *The Lutheran Commentator*, called for his resignation in 1991. The continued outpouring of complaints over the first two or three years began to sap some of the churchwide organization's energy and morale.

The new church was trying to invent all aspects of itself, and some units functioned more efficiently and effectively than others. Some units created their own problems. Difficulty getting in touch with ELCA units was often cited throughout the church as a lack of customer care. Some units inexplicably didn't answer their phones promptly, or staffers used voice mail so they wouldn't be interrupted. Even though interdependence was a byword in describing the style of the new church, some church-wide units seemed to forget that it applied to them, creating not only uncertainty about programmatic boundaries but betraying trust between units. The Division for Congregational Life planned a social ministry event in Miami, much to the surprise of the church's synods and bishops who did not know about the planning. Out of that event came demands for prior contact before an event was imposed on the programs of synods. On another occasion, DCL staff participated in drafting a resolution that was critical of the curriculum materials being produced by another ELCA unit, Augsburg Fortress, Publishers.

The Conference of Bishops, unhappy with two opinion pieces about homosexuality written by former LCA Bishop James R. Crumley Jr. and former ALC Presiding Bishop David W. Preus that were scheduled for publication in *The Lutheran*, pressured Crumley and Preus to withdraw the pieces against my wishes as editor. I called the action "manipulation," saying it crossed the line to censorship. When I was up for reelection as editor of the *The Lutheran* in 1991, some bishops told their delegations not to vote for me, but the vote was 650-287 in my favor. In 1991, the Church Council complained about the "slant and tone" of the periodical and asked for a review of its content. A year later the council affirmed the magazine, saying that "the magazine has been doing what the ELCA asked it to do . . . which is premised on the exercise of editorial freedom and responsibility" to the church. The council found that "the magazine is attacked by some and praised by others for its perceived independence and, at the same time, attacked by some and praised by others for functioning as a 'house organ.' Perhaps these diverse and contradictory opinions are evidence of an evenhandedness or basic fairness in the magazine's coverage of sensitive issues."

Controversy outside of Higgins Road also came into play, forcing the fledgling church to respond to heated topics before it had enough history to do so with balance and finesse. Chief among these controversies were charges and countercharges over the unauthorized "ordination" of three openly gay seminarians by two California congregations and the later suspensions of the congregations. Clergy sexual misconduct came into the open in the ELCA, as it did in most denominations, with three ELCA synodical bishops and two ELCA clergy staff persons being forced to resign. A controversial human sexuality statement was drafted and then laid aside after a huge outcry (see chapter 4).

Three years of red ink regarding the ELCA's finances caused tensions about programming and loyalties, as well as major layoffs in staff (see chapter 2).

A statement on ecumenism that was planned for adoption by the churchwide Assembly in 1989 was delayed until 1991, as critics, including 34 faculty members from Luther Seminary, St. Paul, Minnesota, objected to the proposed document (see chapter 5). Bishop Chilstrom's own ecumenical journeys overseas were criticized as too frequent.

Confronting divestment

The Board of Pensions faced a major confrontation, because it refused to divest itself from firms doing business in South Africa, citing its legal obligation to maximize income for its members. In 1989, 44 synods and the 1989 Churchwide Assembly passed resolutions demanding divestment of the board's $227.4 million direct or indirect investments in firms doing business in South Africa within two years. Board of Pensions President John Kapanke said the time line put the board in an "almost impossible position."

Voting members were as adamant as the board. "We're not General Motors, we're not IBM, we're not ITT," said Sarah Pye-Ross of Philadelphia. "We're the church. If this is what we want you to do, do it." Pastor Elvin Bjork, Salem, Oregon, said, "Pension funds do not belong to the ELCA but to pension members. We ought not to fight social battles, no matter how worthy, with other people's money." Bishop William H. Lazareth, Metropolitan New York Synod, gave short shrift to pension board lawyers who counseled against divestment. "Prudence is a Christian virtue, not a legal category," he said, "and the church of

Jesus Christ should not have its ethics determined by pagan lawyers. [The South African regime] dehumanizes black people redeemed by Christ's love," and to support it "is to subsidize sin."

At its own board meeting after the assembly, the Board of Pensions continued its hard line. "Why do we think we are wiser than the law that was set up for the protection of [pension] members?" said pension board member Elizabeth A. Storaasli. "I would prefer a schism in the church [rather] than placing my trusteeship at risk. The Church Council and Bishop Chilstrom have a political problem. That's their problem, not ours." One of the board's investment advisors, Kenneth M. Anderson, said the "annual budget of the ELCA is not enough" to cover the risk of lawsuits if the board were to divest.

In a later response to the ELCA Church Council, Kapanke gave a detailed report on the legal risks involved in obeying the assembly's directive. "We know for a fact," he said, that "if we amend the plan, there will be a lawsuit. That is not an 'if'; it is a fact." The Church Council scolded the pension board for "atrocious" public relations and a "belligerent" attitude. "I'm not interested in hearing of the personal risk the trustees are taking, or how much time they've spent," said council member Richard McAuliffe, later named the ELCA's treasurer. "I would rather hear they're struggling to do the right thing."

"We have managed to get ourselves knee-deep in the barnyard," Almen told the council. "It is time for us to quit throwing things at each other from around our feet and find a gate out of the barnyard." He said the assembly had "exceeded its authority" but that the pension board had "forced the assembly like a pressure cooker to blow its top." He especially chided the board for buying additional stock in South Africa-related companies and then two weeks before the assembly sending out a waiver statement to be signed by those who had funds in South Africa-free funds.

The council avoided a head-on confrontation with the pension board by appointing a 19-person working group to prepare a list of advantages and disadvantages of each potential course of action, including the church's commitment to justice in South Africa, and each option's legal and financial implications.

In June 1990, the board gave basic approval to a compromise. Under the plan, South Africa-free investments would be the norm for pension investments. Plan members would have six months to choose where their funds would be invested. If they made no choice, their accounts would be placed in the South Africa-free fund. Final approval of the South Africa-free fund depended on a favorable ruling (later received) from the Internal Revenue Service. By the time that three new South Africa-free funds were set up on July 1, 1991, South Africa had abolished apartheid.

Toward restructuring

Major staff turnovers crimped the development of some units. Within the church's first year, the chief executives of the Division for Outreach, the Women of the ELCA, and the Lutheran Office for Governmental Affairs in Washington resigned. Some of the problems resulted from executives hiring more staff than approved. Some came because of differences in administrative style. No benchmarks or parameters were set for how a unit was to function. Each struck out on its own, usually following the vision of its executive director, who often reflected the style of operation in his or her previous church body. Some executive directors seemed unaware that their early decisions set precedents. The ELCA secretary answered questions about the interpretation of the constitution and bylaws. The Division for Congregational Ministries and the leadership of the Women of the ELCA had disagreements with Augsburg Fortress regarding publishing issues (see chapter 2). The Women of the ELCA had five executive directors in its first 15 years, partially because of differences in understanding of the respective roles of the unit's staff and its board.

Preaching during Church Council worship in April 1988, Chilstrom said, "Thank God for an honest Bible! What was the ministry of Jesus? It was one of constant interruption with irritating problems. I wonder how many times he said to himself, 'If only I didn't have to deal with all these difficulties, then I might be able to get on with the real mission of the kingdom.' I wonder how many times Paul said to himself, 'If only I didn't have to deal with all of these problems. Then I might be able to get on with the real mission of the church!' Do you see what is beginning to emerge? The mission of the church is not carried out in the absence of difficult problems and irritating interruptions. The mission of the church is to be done in spite of—in the midst of—the most trying of circumstances. . . . No, my friends, the problems will not go away. In fact, they could get worse."

As early as October 1989, Chilstrom suggested that the time had come to consider restructuring the church's organization and launched a program known as "Focusing for Mission." "We're not tearing down the workbench, not changing the principles of organization or statement of faith," Chilstrom said, "but if we are to perform responsibly, we need to reorganize, not for the purpose of reducing staff, but for redirecting our limited resources."

Even the process created tension. "This is perceived as a CEO-directed, top-down process," said Larry Rasmussen, a member of the Commission for Church in Society board. "We don't live in an era that accepts top-down change."

Robert Bacher, ELCA executive for administration for whom the restructuring gave a larger role in supervising day-to-day functioning, said that the proposal had grown out of a long process involving input from many groups. "What people are really saying is, 'I don't agree with the results,'" he responded. "I don't think we can be criticized for not having an open process. People have had a shot at it."

As it turned out, reconfiguration resulted primarily in fewer boards and board meetings, and an estimated saving of $400,000 annually. The revamped structure, adopted by the 1991 Churchwide Assembly, telescoped the number of churchwide units from 23 to 18, with six divisions, two commissions, five departments in the Office of the Bishop, and five other units. There were accusations that the merging of the Commission for Finance and the Commission for Church in Society into other units was designed to eliminate their executive directors.

Another "new" issue that affected the ELCA's startup was the imposition of a quota system for selections of staff and elections to assemblies, councils, boards, committees, and task forces. This "representative principle" was mandated by the new church's documents. Everyone had to deal with them. Congregations had to send a male and a female voting member to synod assemblies; the members of a synod's assemblies, board, and staffs were forced to reflect inclusiveness even if the representation didn't reflect that synod's own membership. Quotas were adhered to for national assemblies, boards, and staff. In board elections, assemblies were told what categories had to be filled, forcing certain nominees to be paired against each other.

The basic quota system was 60:40 laity to clergy, 50:50 male to female, and 10 percent people of color or primary language other than English. The intent was to ensure participatory decision-making. It may have accomplished the opposite in the early days of the church. Many people felt left out of the new system. Old leaders were not present or at times felt unwelcome. With much of the grassroots feeling disenfranchised, morale and finances suffered. In governance, quotas tended to bring in people without prior board or committee experience.

The topic produced such prolonged outcries that the 1993 ELCA Churchwide Assembly asked for a review of the church's representative principles. Two years later, the assembly affirmed quotas, noting that the principles "aren't an end in themselves but are a means appropriate to this time in this church's history." Warren Pertee, Baltimore, Maryland, told the assembly, "We should hold up the principles, and not penalize an area that isn't able to uphold them." When critics said that quotas had become another mark of the church, Chilstrom defended them by saying that the church freely took the strategy upon itself, often citing Acts 15 where the early church set up certain regulations for its organization. When Chilstrom was criticized for not including a black person in his group that visited Namibia in 1988, he replied that if every group were to be represented in his travels, he would have an entourage of 15 to 20 people.

What went wrong?

How did the early years become so troubled, especially with the good will that accompanied the ELCA's start? Some pointed to dislodged loyalties and cumbersome structure. Others said the church was too large, too remote, lacking in identity and taken over by ideological power cliques. Some noted that it seemed caught up in women's and sexuality issues. Still others pointed to a loss of evangelistic zeal and reduced new-church starts.

Certainly one issue that was a holdover from the predecessor churches was the understanding of the nature of the church (see the prologue at the beginning of this book). Chilstrom was forced to speak about this topic on a number of occasions, often citing chapter 3 from the ELCA Constitution:

> The church exists both as an inclusive fellowship and as local congregations gathered for worship and Christian service. Congregations find their fulfillment in the universal community of the church, and the universal church exists in and through congregations. This church, therefore, derives its character and powers both from the sanction and representation of its congregations and from its inherent nature as an expression of the broader fellowship of the faithful. In length, it acknowledges itself to be in the historic continuity of the communion of saints; in breadth, it expresses the fellowship of believers and congregations in our day.

In 1992, Chilstrom warned the Church Council that the ELCA must not become a federation of 65 churches, referring to the independent tendencies of some of the church's 65 synods. He cautioned that the ELCA's interdependent expressions—congregation, synod, and churchwide—must not grow to resemble the pattern of the Lutheran World Federation and its autonomous member churches.

Regardless of whatever reasons might be cited, the new church's insistence on "newness" was both its promise and its downfall, at least at the beginning. Being "new" raised expectations to impossible heights, suggesting that the church could do whatever it set out to accomplish. When it was unable to deliver on these expectations, people felt betrayed and began to find fault. The result was a lack of trust that infected the ELCA in many of its early dimensions, a sickness that would last for some years as members challenged its fiscal management, its perceived "liberal" stances on social issues, its alleged lack of evangelistic zeal and the influence of pressure groups that felt the beginning of a new church was a time for them to get their oar in the water. In some ways, the ELCA was a kind of a "wish list" church, because the merger commission tried to give every group as much of what they requested as possible. Consider all this newness:

- New headquarters city, building, and procedures. The décor in the new headquarters studiously avoided evidences of the past.

- Only 26 of the first 65 bishops had ever been a bishop before. In the ALC, only one district boundary remained the same. In the AELC, every synod boundary changed. In the LCA, 18 of 30 changed. The nine Regional Centers for Mission were new to everyone.

- Loss of memory in the churchwide organization was rampant. No officers had held similar positions in the predecessor bodies, and only five of the 21 executive directors had done so. Less than half of the church's 182 executive staff and only 33 of the 233 support staff members came from previous churchwide staffs.

- New funding patterns created havoc, and the projections for the new church's budget gave the new church three years of red ink. There were new patterns for seminary linkages, funding, and governance. There were no social statements since the predecessor church body statements had come forward only as historical documents.

All together, the early disagreements, turmoil, and frustrations were the price of newness.

Finishing a task

The 1993 assembly in Kansas City, called "crabby" by some observers, nonetheless saw the culmination of a major item that was forwarded to the new church by the merger commission—a six-year study of ministry. The unfinished business came because the commission could not find a satisfactory compromise among the varying understandings of ministry in the merging churches. The LCA and the ALC had similar understandings of rosters of ordained clergy and lay professionals. The AELC, growing out of its long tradition within The Lutheran Church—Missouri Synod, had a tradition of parochial school teachers being considered as rostered ministers, both for Internal Revenue Service purposes and with voting privileges in the AELC assembly. The merger commission could not agree on the appropriate status for the various non-ordained persons, who ranged from deaconesses to teachers to church secretaries. Some were paid, others worked for free. Some worked part-time, others full-time. Hence the decision to let the ELCA make the decision.

Because of the turmoil surrounding the ELCA's beginnings, the study actually did not get off the ground until early 1989. In 1991, a task force suggested three options for the church's ordained ministry. The first was a three-fold ministry, composed of ordained bishops, pastors, and deacons (including all lay categories). The second was a two-fold ministry, with an Office of Word and Sacrament for bishops and pastors, and an Office of Word and Service for all lay professionals including deaconesses and associates in ministry. The third option was a single office of ordained ministry—a development of the pattern currently in the ELCA. The one office would include bishops and pastors, while other church workers would have lay status.

The task force chair, John H. P. Reumann of Philadelphia, said the document was "good enough to go out" to the church. "And where it is bad, it will take its lumps."

Among those responding was the ELCA Conference of Bishops which leaned toward the church having ordained ministers of Word and Sacrament and ministers of Word and service who are officially recognized.

A year later, reports coming back to the task force favored the single office of ministry. But the task force surprised some people by recommending the ordination of persons other than pastors—that "approved and called candidates for diaconal ministry shall be ordained as diaconal ministers as part of the office of ministry." Diaconal persons (coming from the Greek *diakonia*, meaning "service") could be deaconesses and missionaries, and could serve in congregations, institutions, and agencies as leaders in education, administration, music, parish nursing, social service, and similar ministries. They would have equal status as clergy, be required to have theological training, would be clergy voting members at synod and churchwide assemblies and would be considered as clergy for tax purposes.

Paul Nelson, director for the ministry study, said the task force chose the word "ordain" for diaconal ministers over alternatives such as "consecrate" to emphasize the one office of ministry. He acknowledged that the "move to recommend that people who serve in this [diaconal] office be ordained for that ministry rather than set apart in some other way was a very bold move, made very soberly, following prayer." The task force approval was 11-3 with one abstention.

On another subject, the task force recommended six-year renewable terms of bishops. At the time, bishops served four-year terms. Another recommendation that the office of bishop "be a distinct form within the one office of ministry" means that "bishops are ordained pastors who are installed to serve as bishops," Nelson said. "We haven't said it's fundamentally unlike being a pastor."

In October 1992, after hearing many reactions from across the church, the task force affirmed its ordination decision for diaconal ministers 12-4. A recommendation through the Division for Ministry went to the Churchwide Assembly in Kansas City in 1993 for one ordination into the office of ministry, with installation being the rite by which ordained ministers are placed into specific ministries of diaconal minister, pastor, or bishop. The recommendation also called for the Associates in Ministry roster to be retained and that lay workers be encouraged to continue training for such ministries. Other laypersons who did not qualify for AIM status would be "grandparented" from the old rosters of their predecessor churches into the roster of associates in ministry.

The report to the assembly said that "ordination to pastoral ministry is for the ministry that centers in proclamation of the word and administration of the sacraments. Ordination to diaconal ministry is for a ministry centering in witness to the word and leadership in serving ministries."

The 1993 Churchwide Assembly in Kansas City basically adopted the report except for an important change—it said "yes" to the creation of a diaconate but "no" to ordination of persons in it. The vote wasn't even close—790-192. The decision means that the ELCA had the following recognized ministries— ordained pastors and bishops, and officially recognized three lay ministries—including diaconal ministers, associates in ministry, and deaconesses. Assembly-goers also approved six-year terms for bishops, but the use of the term "presiding bishop" for the church's chief officer did not come until 1995.

Voting members in Kansas City found many reasons to oppose the ordination of diaconal ministers. Some people felt an ordained diaconate denigrated the ministry of all the baptized. Others objected because it would add another layer to the ministry listings. The Rev. Bryan Leone, Biglerville, Pennsylvania, noted the potential for difficulty in ecumenical dialogues if the ELCA ordained diaconal ministers.

The first diaconal minister to be consecrated was Audrey Forbes on May 19, 1996. She was called by First Lutheran Church, Ellicott City, Maryland. At the end of 2001, the ELCA had 34 diaconal ministers.

A smoother future

It is somewhat remarkable that the ELCA survived its early years as well as it did. Harsh criticism came from within and without, from its seminary faculties, clergy, and bishops as well as the laity. Not only did the church survive its birth, it endured adolescence long before it became a teenager in terms of its years of existence. When he was elected bishop in 1987, Chilstrom said the merger commission had given the new church a "worthy ship." In 1989, he said that "such a big ship would take a long time to turn," but he "was confident that it would right itself." His prediction came true at the 1991 Churchwide Assembly in Orlando. Where the 1989 assembly endured a poorly lit warehouse atmosphere in Chicago, Orlando was bright and comfortable. Maybe the atmosphere played into the picture, but clearly there was a different spirit among voting members. "This was a great coming-together time for this church," Chilstrom said when the Orlando assembly was over. From beginning to end, voting members were upbeat, unfailingly courteous in debate, decisive in decision-making, thrilled over excellence in worship and study of the Lord's Prayer, and anxious to go home with the message of a church come of age.

The next assembly, in 1993, for example, made the ministry decision with very little harsh language. It was a kind of turning point that saw broad-based attacks against Higgins Road quieting down, other than on specific topics (ecumenism, sexuality). The question of faithfulness gave way to theologians, bishops, clergy, and members buckling down for the long haul of making the church work. Stereotypes of "East" and "Midwest" tempered. Quotas became a part of the church's life and, though questioned from time to time, were never seriously discussed again. Finances turned from initial years of deficits to a stable financial base. The church's Office for Personnel became the Department for Human Resources, an effective and, in time, respected unit.

Through it all, the stability of the church resided with the thousands of congregations and millions of members who simply stayed the course where they lived. Their wisdom gave the new church time to settle in, to work out its own procedures and priorities, and to function as the new entity it was, unencumbered by either the viewpoints or the history of its predecessors. More importantly, the weaving together of the threads of most North American Lutheran history into one church body remains part of the ongoing challenge and opportunity of the ELCA.

CHAPTER 2

A MATTER OF MONEY

"The current posture of the church is prudently funded."

*ELCA Treasurer George E. Aker, November 1988, to the Church Council;
the year ended $10.6 million in debt*

"The church had a very, very satisfactory year."

*ELCA Treasurer Richard McAuliffe, March 1999, reflecting on the
ninth consecutive year of the church living within its budget*

The ELCA's early financial fortunes are unwittingly reflective of the two men who served as its treasurers. The first, George E. Aker, came to the ELCA position from Reno, Nevada, after being president of Nevada National Bank and board chairman of the Jersild Knitting Company, a family business in Neenah, Wisconsin. Tall, immaculately dressed and groomed, Aker was a smiling man who generally charmed his way out of tough spots. Unfortunately, his optimism couldn't make very real crises go away. The church was going $10.6 million in debt in its first year. By the end of 1990, the church had experienced three consecutive years of deficits and had depleted $20 million in cash balances, virtually all the funds that came to the ELCA from the merging churches. During those years no churchwide unit received all its anticipated funding.

Richard McAuliffe, the second treasurer, was a no-nonsense man who was given to saying as little as possible about the church's finances. At the same time he made it abundantly clear that the church would live within its means, that it would become solvent, and that it would rebuild its reserves. And it did. In 1999 alone, after eight years of operating with a surplus, the church had sufficient cash balances to fund some $12 million in projects that had been kept on hold during the year.

Unfortunately, the ELCA churchwide organization had another financial troublespot: its separately incorporated publishing house, Augsburg Fortress, Publishers. The publishing house, which does not receive direct financial support from the churchwide budget, began life in the new church on a good financial basis. However, needed upgrades for technology taxed expenses and difficulties in distribution and management during the mid-1990s took a heavy toll on consumer confidence. With sales declining steadily, the publishing house found itself struggling to stay out of the red. In 2001 alone, it lost $6.8 million (see page 52).

A financial hole

As for the ELCA's own financial start, the new church began in a financial hole of its own doing. The constituting convention adopted an initial budget of $112 million with a $4 million income deficit. Compounded by Aker's standard lines that he had "measured confidence" in receipts or that he was "cautiously optimistic," the situation deteriorated year by year—a deficit of $10.6 million in 1988, $8 million in 1989, and $1.4 million in 1990. "Pink slips" forced 39 staff to leave in 1989, six more in 1990, 25 more in 1991, and 19 in 1992 for a total of 89. The 1991 budget included $320,000 in interest payments so the church could borrow funds to cover cash flow problems during the summer income slump. (This was the last year borrowed funds were needed.)

Two factors came together to produce the early financial troubles. Either would have been a problem by itself, but together the fiscal flaws were insurmountable. The first was an over-projection of income that would come to the new church from congregations and synods. The second was under-performance by congregations and synods in sending funds to the churchwide organization.

In reflecting upon one of the most difficult elements of his early leadership, Chilstrom recalled a pre-ELCA meeting in Minnetonka, Minnesota, when "anyone in his or her right mind would have looked at the projected budget figures for the new church and said, 'stop.' But we had to go on in faith."

Minnetonka, a Minneapolis suburb, was the site where 52 LCA, ALC, and AELC staff members struggled for two days in early 1987 over budget reductions, even wondering whether financial realities would swamp the merger. Requests from churchwide units for their beginning budgets ran as high as $144 million. A projection of income from congregations through synods was no higher than $119 million. The Minnetonka participants got each side of the ledger down to about $106 million. Nonetheless, the Transition Team, a 10-person group that oversaw the merger details, added some $6 million in costs and presented the new church with the unbalanced budget. The Constituting Convention adopted it, and the die was cast for the ELCA's early financial crises. The Church Council was expected to make the necessary adjustments in spending to offset the budget deficit. It was a larger challenge than they could solve.

In fairness, the Transition Team worked at a disadvantage. When they began budget planning in 1986, the only firm figures from the three predecessor churches were for 1984. It was almost impossible to use those numbers to extrapolate income and cost figures for a single merged church that would begin operation in 1988. Moreover, the new church adopted a March-to-February fiscal year, meaning that the first year was a 14-month budget, a circumstance none of the planners had ever experienced. The second year was an 11-month budget because it later was determined that a February-January budget was more workable. The result is that it is extremely difficult for the church's financial figures from 1988 and 1989 to be consistent with reports since then.

The ELCA's total income for 1988 was $92.4 million. In addition to income from special offerings, bequests and trusts, missionary sponsorship, and the gift from the Women of the ELCA, and endowments, the figure includes mission support of $64.9 million ($60.9 million in funds sent by congregations through synods to churchwide, plus $4.1 million from former LCA congregations for retiree medical benefits obligations. This practice was continued through 1990. Beginning in 1991, this obligation became the responsibility of the churchwide budget, with the former 6 percent being included in total mission support). Compared with the church's $92.4 million income in its first year of operation, the church spent $103 million, producing a $10.6 million deficit.

A similar pattern occurred in 1989, with $80.9 million in total income, including $65.3 million through mission support, and expenses of $88.9 million, for a deficit of $8 million. In 1990, the last year of the deficits, total income was $80 million ($65.9 million through mission support) against expenditures of $81.4 million. The deficit was $1.4 million.

In 1991, the turnaround year, the ELCA's total income was down to $79.4 million, with $64.8 million from mission support, and spending of $78.6 million. The balance of $768,395 was returned to the reserves to begin replacing the more than $20 million that the church had overspent in its first three years.

The Transition Team was reasonably accurate in projecting the financial giving of members in congregations. Congregational giving rose 4.4 percent in 1988, 7.7 percent in 1989, and 4.8 percent in 1990, reaching $1.5 billion. Congregations forwarded $116.2 million to synods in 1988, $117.2 million in 1989, and $118.6 million in 1990. But the Transition Team could not have predicted that in 1989, synods would forward only $300,000 more to the ELCA, even through synods had received $1 million more from the congregations. In 1990, the pattern was repeated with synods sending to the ELCA only about half of the $1.4 million increase they received from congregations during the year.

Without a doubt, the new church as originally organized was costlier than the combined predecessor churches. The ELCA had 65 synods compared with 53 synods and districts of the merging churches, nine new regional centers, three additional churchwide units and larger governing committees and boards. There was a new headquarters to build out. ELCA seminaries hoped to receive 50 percent of their funding from the churchwide and synodical budgets. By early 1989 the "figure was 37 percent and falling behind," the Division for Ministry reported.

The flow of funds

The single largest reason for the financial fiasco was not poor financial planning, but the differences in how the predecessor churches and the new church handled the flow of funds. The uniting churches had differing patterns of receiving and disbursing funds. Almen later reflected that the merging churches could have been of more assistance to the new church in providing a better introduction of the pattern for mission-support contributions in the new church.

In the ALC, congregations provided to the districts of the ALC what in most instances were called dues, often a per-confirmed member assessment. Benevolence funds were sent directly to the national office for the domestic and international work of the ALC. In the LCA, benevolence funding was similar to that which emerged in the ELCA—namely, contributions from congregations were sent to synod offices, a portion of which was then transferred to the national office.

"It became clear that the treasurers of many ALC congregations had not been prepared adequately for the fact that the funds that had previously been contributed for both district dues and national benevolence now were all to be submitted to the synod office as mission support," Almen analyzed, "with an agreed upon portion to be transferred by the synod to the churchwide organization for the domestic and international work of the ELCA." A study of giving patterns in the late 1980s and early 1990s appeared to show that much of the money that once had been submitted in ALC district "dues" disappeared into congregation budgets and did not become part of the overall mission support in the ELCA, Almen continued.

The Church Council recognized the possibility of fiscal trouble three months before the ELCA's official start date. In October 1987, they reduced the expenditure authorization for all churchwide units to 95 percent of their anticipated budget. This reduced projected expenses from $112 million to $106 million against the hoped-for $108 million in receipts. In January 1988, Aker told the Cabinet of Executives that he had "measured confidence" that the receipts would come from congregations through synods. Because the ALC and LCA were closing their books during the first two months of 1988, early fund flows to the ELCA were minimal. Through March 1988, the ELCA had received $3.5 million. April saw another $4 million come in and May brought another $7 million, for total receipts of $14 million for the church's first five months. However, expenditures for the first five months were $32.4 million, beginning a downward slope that would turn into a roller coaster.

In July 1988, Chilstrom sent a memo to all staff members, asking that they rein in travel expenses. No car rentals unless "absolutely necessary," he wrote, "eat modestly . . . consider staying in private homes when it is appropriate." He was critical of staff using the ELCA's 800-number for receiving personal calls, and made the request: "if you are the last to leave your floor, please turn out the lights."

In September 1988, Aker said that 48 percent of the budget had been met—not quite half of it, with slightly more than half of the fiscal year over. In November 1988, using figures as of the end of August, which showed a $9 million deficit, Aker told the Church Council that "the current posture of the church is prudently funded" for this year. The building that housed the LCA church headquarters in New York had been sold by this time for $15 million, with $4 million of the proceeds being used as "income substitute." (The remainder of the sale proceeds financed the buildout of the Higgins Road headquarters.)

During the same council meeting, James Bergquist, executive director of the Division for Outreach, asked for an additional $1 million to maintain support for existing urban and rural congregations. Rafaela Morales Rosa, a member of the council and pastor of a Hispanic congregation in Worcester, Massachusetts, that was supported by the division finally had heard enough. "You talk about 'out there.' I am the 'out there.' If the check from the ELCA is late, I don't get paid, and my family does not eat. Families invite me to their home to eat because they know the check hasn't come."

Finally the council adopted a motion to continue the 40-50 new congregation starts in 1988, and to take $1 million from reserves so the division could maintain support of urban and rural ministries "at or near the 1988 budget." Even in the midst of a deficit, additional money from reserves was being allocated.

Staff cuts

To counteract the deficits, two things happened. Churchwide expenses, totaling $103 million in 1988 for 14 months, were cut to $88.9 million in 1989, and to $81.5 million in 1990. The reductions came as churchwide units were restricted to spending 95 percent of their anticipated income in 1988, then 93 percent later the same year. Spending restrictions were set at 88 percent in 1989, and then to 82.5 percent in 1990. A hiring freeze began in May 1989, and layoffs that fall totaled 39. In 1990, executive staff salaries were frozen.

Those who were laid off received either two months' notice or two months' separation pay. "We have no choice," Chilstrom said. "Cutting must be done. Both those whose jobs are eliminated and those who remain to carry additional work suffer the consequences." During the announcement of staff reductions, Chilstrom referred to the cuts as "pruning" a tree so that it could produce better fruit. The agricultural term appeared to offend some who lost their jobs.

The staff reductions represented a very painful period and clearly one of disappointment, particularly for some staff who had uprooted their households and families to move to Chicago, only to see the responsibilities to which they were called eliminated in the reorganization. The cuts diminished enthusiasm and creativity among staff who felt that new ideas could not be funded.

The $5.6 million in budget cuts in 1990 reduced the number of new congregations funded through benevolence dollars to four; two-thirds of the ELCA's 330 mission congregations received less support; support for urban ministries dropped from 305 to 222; and 45 of 96 rural ministries received smaller subsidies.

Long-term overseas missionary positions were reduced to 212—60 fewer than in 1988; support of seminaries dropped $600,000; church colleges received $266,000 less; and support of the Lutheran World Federation, the National Council of Churches, and the World Council of Churches dropped 29 percent.

When the ELCA posted its third straight deficit, Chilstrom said, "I feel like the coach of a team that has a third losing season." During the year, he appealed to the bishops to send at least 2 percent more than the amount they had previously agreed to send. "We're with you 100 percent," said Bishop Richard Jessen, Nebraska Synod, "but we can't make the difference for you this year."

At Grace Lutheran Church, Erskine, Minnesota, the congregation council learned about the deficit and one member said, "Why that's only about $3 per member [of the ELCA]. I move we take $3 per member from current expenses and send it to the ELCA." The motion passed unanimously.

Although churchwide units had been told to budget for a 3 percent increase in 1991, they were restricted in April that year to 93.5 percent of expected expenditures, a $5.2 million cut (a total of $10.8 million in cuts over two years). The slashes meant that belt-tightening was no longer an option in most units. Entire programs would be dropped. The first announced casualty was the demise of *World Encounter*, the magazine of the Division for Global Mission (it never returned, even when the church's finances later turned around). Other cuts included $1.2 million in global missions, $990,000 in outreach, $15,000 in support for each region, dismissal of all but one of the worship staff in the Division for Congregational Life and still more reductions in grants to seminaries, colleges and ecumenical agencies. Then 25 more staff positions were eliminated, for a total of 64 staff reductions over two years. Six positions were cut in 1990. Also, 19 more positions were eliminated in 1992. Churchwide staff then totaled 485, one-third less than the combined staff of the predecessor churches and the common agencies, such as the Lutheran Council in the USA and Lutheran World Relief.

Almen estimated in 1991 that the ELCA received about $25 million to $36.7 million less in income than the predecessor churches would have expected that year. In addition to $5 million more being needed to operate the synods and $2.5 million annual cost for regions, additional congregational revenue was being used to fund higher pension and medical costs, increasing maintenance and repair costs of church buildings, and direct funding by congregations of up to $3 million annually for new congregations.

"The candy store of the churchwide organization must close now," Almen told the Church Council in April 1991. "The time has ended when every interest group, every caucus, every concern, every emphasis, every self-proclaimed representative body, every good intention, every noble effort, and every great program could demand to get whatever was wanted, as if there were no limits. . . . The candy store is closed because the resources absolutely are no longer here—and in fact they never were—to operate as if the contents of the candy store do not require money."

Chilstrom surprised the Church Council by pulling out his personal check for $5,000 and presenting it to Aker, proposing it as the first gift of a special churchwide offering in late 1991. Chilstrom then wrote letters to synod bishops, the Cabinet of Executives, and members of the Church Council and boards, inviting them to join him. By year's end, $1.5 million was received in the "love offering."

The special giving, along with underspending of budgets by churchwide units (already reduced to 93.5 percent of their original 1991 budgets) meant that 1991 was the first year the ELCA ended a year with positive numbers, if only by $768,395. More significantly, it was the beginning of a financial turnaround. The church had rebuilt its cash balances and utilized some additional funds that could be disbursed over and above the budget. Between 1996 and 2001, the Church Council authorized the allocation of more than $21.5 million for mission opportunities that the operating budgets of churchwide units were unable to fund. The ELCA does not have an abundance of money, but it is solvent and in 2001 had cash and cash equivalencies of $23.6 million. Church guidelines suggest that the church's reserves total at least 15 percent of the previous year's operating budget.

The 1991 experience emboldened the Church Council to endorse the expenditure of the church's full $93.3 million budget for 1992. The decision marked the first time the ELCA approved a "100 percent expenditure authorization."

"If we put the authorization at less than 100 percent, people will think we expect less than 100 percent," said Loren Mathre, St. Petersburg, Florida. "We should go out there with a positive approach.

At the 1991 council meeting, Robert N. Bacher, ELCA Executive for Administration, said, "It's a judgment call, but the conversations going on in synods give us confidence. Besides, starting lower doesn't mean that we will get more." The strategy paid off. In 1992, the ELCA's total income was $77.6 million, with operating expenditures of $76.3 million.

McAuliffe's arrival

Coinciding with the 1991 turnaround was the departure of George Aker and the arrival of Richard McAuliffe. He had been executive vice president, treasurer, and chief executive officer of Harris Bankcorp & Harris Trust & Savings Bank, Chicago, for 30 years. He had been a member of the Church Council and chair of the council's Finance Committee. He brought a high degree of fiscal responsibility to the churchwide organization, often through simple measures such as having a quarterly meeting with the budget and executive directors of each churchwide unit. Soon the reality took root that each unit would live within its authorized budget, or some serious questions would be raised.

McAuliffe played things so close to the vest that he rarely talked to reporters, and even then only for a sentence or two. After the churchwide organization had its second straight positive year in 1992, he would only say that the "budgeting process is working." In 1995, he said that the budgets for 1996 and 1997 were "realistic and hopeful." In 1996, he became almost verbose, acknowledging that the ELCA's financial health is "improving." But "it's a muted celebration," he continued. "We're looking good mainly because of reduced spending by churchwide units and unexpectedly high income from bequests and investment. We're financially stable because we're not fully in mission. The church has learned to live within its means, but its means is not sufficient to do all the things the ELCA wants to do."

Noting that 1996 was the sixth consecutive year when income topped receipts, McAuliffe called the results "most satisfactory." When ELCA income exceeded expenses by $1.9 million in 1997, he said the church had a "marvelous year." He saved his superlatives that year for reporting that 53 of the ELCA's 65 synods increased their giving in 1997 over 1996. In 1999, he told the bishops that the church had had a "very, very satisfactory" year. By the time McAuliffe retired in 2001, the ship of the churchwide organization had experienced 11 consecutive years of financial balance. The ELCA was clearly on a solid financial course for sailing into the new century.

But the waters stirred again. Although the church's 2002 budget was the first 12-month budget to exceed $100 million ($85 million for operating expenses and $16.5 million for the World Hunger Appeal), new ELCA Treasurer Christina Jackson-Skelton and Charles Miller, Executive for Administration, announced in July 2002 that spending by the churchwide organization for the year needed to be reduced $2.4 million to $82.6 million, with churchwide units asked to plan for a 4 percent spending reduction. The reductions came from an anticipated $1.5 million shortfall in income from bequests and trusts, and $450,000 shortfall in income from interest and investments, both largely the result of stock market declines and lower interest rates. The income projections for 2003 were also adjusted downward by $1.3 million, and the ELCA Church Council set the 2003 spending authorization at $85.3 million.

A major financial liability loomed because of retiree medical benefits. At its formation, the ELCA assumed these obligations of the predecessor churches. Although the ALC had funded its future obligations, the LCA had not. An additional 6 percent needed be collected from former LCA congregations to pay their "unfunded liability." In reality, the 6 percent was not additional funding but an allocation of regular benevolence.

In 1990, the ELCA Church Council directed that $5.8 million be allocated annually from mission support to fund post-retirement subsidies. As retiree medical benefits increased sharply in the 1990s (due primarily to pharmacy increases in excess of 20 percent a year), the $5.8 million became inadequate. An estimate in early 2002 showed the ELCA's annual contribution of $5.8 million, together with existing assets, would provide for only 60 percent of the obligation. Even if continued through 2030, the annual allocation would need to be nearly $15 million to fully fund the obligation.

In November 2002, the Church Council "bit the bullet" and adopted a proposal that the churchwide organization's contribution to the retiree health plan would increase to $6.2 million in 2003, $6.45 million in 2004 and $6.7 million in 2005, followed by annual 1 percent increases.

The details of the financial turnaround for the 1991-2001 decade become evident in an analysis of the church's income and spending (see adjacent chart). In 1992 and 1993, total ELCA income slipped a bit—in 1992 to $77.6 million, and in 1993 to $75.3 million. But then it moved upward, with $76.4 million in 1994 and reaching $81.8 million in 1998 and $86.6 million in 2001, only to slip to $82.9 million in 2002. None of the figures for total income include approximately $12 to $15 million received annually by the World Hunger Appeal (see chapter 6).

Mission support, the contributions to churchwide received from the synods, followed a similar pattern, dropping to a low of $63.1 million in 1993 and 1995, but moving upward to $66.7 million in 1998 and $69.5 million in 2001, then dropping to $68.8 million in 2002. Throughout the life of the ELCA, synods averaged sending to churchwide about 52 percent of funds sent to them by congregations.

The ELCA's dramatic financial moves from 1992 onward were fueled in large part by the disciplined spending of churchwide units. The spending dropped yearly—$76.3 million in 1992 to a low of $71 million in 1995, then going upward yearly to

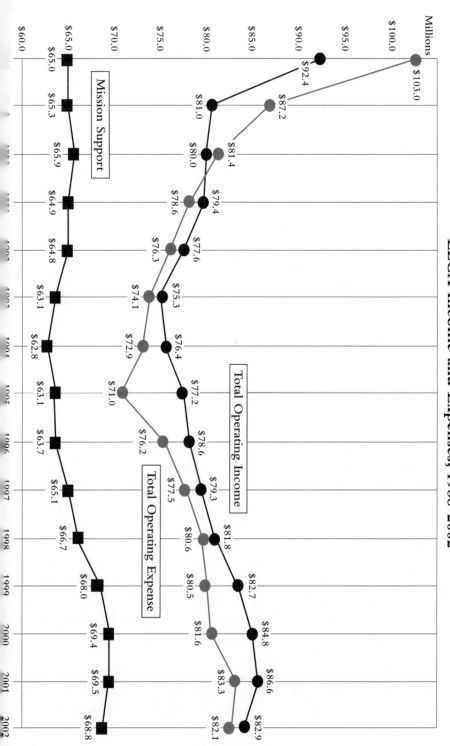

ELCA Income and Expenses, 1988–2002

	Millions														
$103.0	$100.0	$95.0	$90.0	$85.0	$80.0	$75.0	$70.0	$65.0	$60.0						

Mission Support

$65.0 $65.3 $65.9 $64.9 $64.8 $63.1 $62.8 $63.1 $63.7 $65.1 $66.7 $68.0 $69.4 $69.5 $68.8

Total Operating Income

$92.4 $81.0 $80.0 $79.4 $77.6 $75.3 $76.4 $77.2 $78.6 $79.3 $81.8 $82.7 $84.8 $86.6 $82.9

Total Operating Expense

$103.0 $87.2 $81.4 $78.6 $76.3 $74.1 $72.9 $71.0 $76.2 $77.5 $80.6 $80.5 $81.6 $83.3 $82.1

Years: 1988 1989 1990 1991 1992 1993 1994 1995 1996 1997 1998 1999 2000 2001 2002

$80.6 million in 1998 and $83.3 million in 2001, then going down to $82.1 million in 2002. The restraint meant that the church's cash position improved, with $6.1 million going into unrestricted cash in 1995 alone.

Congregational giving strong

Giving by members in congregations, another barometer of the church's financial strength, moved steadily upward starting at $1.1 billion in 1988 and reaching almost $2.5 billion in 2001. Comparing the figures is instructive because of the dramatic increases in total giving in congregations (more than $1.4 billion) compared with the lean years of the ELCA that actually saw ELCA total income drop by $5.9 million between 1988 and 2001.

In 1988, members of ELCA congregations gave $1.1 billion through congregational and special offerings. The giving averaged $379.88 per confirmed/communing member. Congregations spent $989 million on current operating expenses and capital improvements and $95 million in debt payments, and 60 percent of congregations reported no indebtedness.

In 2001, total income among congregations reached nearly $2.5 billion, up 2.7 percent from 1999. A total of $1.66 billion was received in regular, unrestricted offerings, with average regular giving per confirmed member at $526. Of the total income of ELCA congregations, 90 percent was devoted to operating expenses, capital improvements, debt reduction, and other expenses. Another 7.86 percent was contributed for synodical and churchwide mission support, hunger and disaster appeals, missionary sponsorship, Mission Partners and designated causes. Congregations held more than $1.67 billion in savings and investments, endowments and memorial funds, which meant that, for the first time, congregations had more monies in reserves than they received through regular giving. Almost two-thirds of the congregations reported no debt in 2001.

Two other churchwide units came to provide excellent support for the ELCA's many activities. The Mission Investment Fund, a revolving fund that makes loans to new congregations, brought forward funds from the predecessor churches totaled $67 million in 1988. The fund grew rapidly to $251 million by 2001. Approximately 200 congregations were assisted with $76 million in loans in 1988, compared with 501 loans for $21.8 million in 2001. Of this figure, 54 percent went to mission congregations, 40 percent of established congregations, and 6 percent to institutions and congregations. In 2001, 3,226 congregations invested their funds in the Mission Investment Fund, as did 4,729 individuals.

The other unit that channels significant financial resources to the church is the ELCA Foundation, a continuance of predecessor church foundations. The foundation received 613 gifts in 1998, including 164 for life income agreements. In 2002, the foundation received 3,263 gifts, including 478 gifts for life income agreements. Since 1988, the foundation has been received $309 million in gifts, bequests, and new life income agreements, with $168 million distributed to ELCA churchwide, synodical, and local ministries. Some $388 million in expectancies for all ELCA ministries from all sources (deferred gifts, life insurance, bequests, and trusts) await future distribution. In 2001 alone, the giving to the foundation was $31.4 million, the ninth consecutive year of $20 million or more. Of this figure, $10.2 million was in bequests.

The church in its early years, then, had significant financial strength in its congregational life, but not in the areas of ministry beyond the local boundaries. Early deficits at both the synodical and churchwide levels produced a loss of staff morale, a loss of confidence in the churchwide operation by the people in the pew, and a mission pullback (starting fewer new congregations) when church members thought the new church would be more in mission than its predecessors. The handling of funds became another dimension of the many criticisms of the new church that included the lack of evangelism, declining membership, being liberal on issues of sexuality, controversy about the ecumenical goal of full communion, non-sexist language, a general lack of interest in the churchwide organization and a lack of trust that led to vigorous and even brutal criticism of "Higgins Road." But as the century ended, the financial footing was recognized as solid and money issues were not as pronounced, taking some of the criticism away too.

Publisher's red ink

In contrast to the ELCA's movement toward lasting financial equilibrium, Augsburg Fortress, Publishers, the church's publishing house, experienced steadily declining sales, which often led to budget deficits. The publisher is separately incorporated from the church (as is the Board of Pensions) and receives no benevolence income from the churchwide organization. In addition to its financial precariousness, it experienced a decade of organizational and managerial problems, as well as some notable difficulties in working with other units of the church.

Augsburg Fortress was the last of the new church's major units to consolidate from its predecessors, the ALC's Augsburg Publishing House in Minneapolis and the LCA's Board of Publication in Philadelphia. Even in November 1988, 11 months after merger, the board of Augsburg Fortress still was discussing the difficulty of consolidating the two publishing houses into a single unit. Each had owned a building and supported a series of stores or distribution centers across the United States. The consolidated headquarters would be in Minneapolis where Augsburg Fortress added to its space by buying the old ALC headquarters building for $1.1 million in 1987. The Philadelphia building was sold for $6 million in 1990, with the proceeds going to the publishing house. Albert E. Anderson, the publishing house's president and chief executive, was quick to point out that the ALC brought $6 million into the consolidation, whereas the former LCA publishing house brought the Philadelphia property but no cash reserves. (Augsburg Fortress sold its own headquarters in 1996 for $8.25 million and moved into rented quarters elsewhere in Minneapolis.)

The publishing house closed stores in some areas in order to have a single branch store and distribution point in each of the church's nine regions. But the changes took time. In May 1989, Anderson said the consolidation would be completed by the end of that year, two years after the church began operation. Noting at the meeting that it is time to begin planning "what we ought to focus on becoming," Anderson acknowledged that some problems still needed to be worked out. "Complaints have persisted on order fulfillment and shipping out of our Philadelphia location." Stores were closed in Pittsburgh, Philadelphia, Baltimore, and Columbia, South Carolina, all former LCA locations. "There was considerable consternation in the Pittsburgh area," Anderson acknowledged in 1988, "although the criticism is now abating." Much of the difficulty arose because the decision to close the store there was made without consultation with the synods served by the store.

Distribution proved to be an Achilles' heel for the publishing house. In 1995, the nine regional warehouses were consolidated into one distribution center at Grove City, Ohio. Simultaneously, new technology and a computer system were installed and inventory reduced. An anticipated three-week changeover stretched into three months. Customers experienced delays in receiving orders, being billed for material not received, and difficulties with the telephone ordering system. "We have been back-ordered twice," said Pastor Charles B. Riggs, Our Saviour Lutheran Church, Tucson, Arizona.

Marvin Roloff, Augsburg Fortress president, wrote to church leaders acknowledging the problems. "We simply got off balance in this massive change. The telephone system probably caused the most frustration for customers." The delays were a key problem for Augsburg Fortress as it experienced the kind of decline that was affecting many denominational publishers in the 1990s. Lutheran congregations historically were loyal to using their own denominational materials for Sunday school, vacation Bible school, music, bulletins, and a host of other printed literature. As time passed, this loyalty eroded and Augsburg Fortress faced the predicament of sliding sales. When customers experienced service problems from the publishing house, it gave them even more reason to shop elsewhere, and they did.

The decline in sales and overage of inventory combined to spell financial trouble for the publishing house in the early and mid-1990s. It was not until 1997 that Robert McNulty, vice president for finance, could say that for the first time in the 10 years since the merger, the house "is showing an operating profit without puffing inventory." In 1988, Augsburg Fortress lost $1.5 million, primarily from costs of consolidating the two publishing enterprises. In 1989, the house had a $300,000 surplus and a $1.5 million surplus in 1990. But there was a $2 million-plus loss in 1993, a $3.8 million loss in 1994, and $8.1 million loss in 1995, with $5.1 million coming from an inventory write-off of over-stocked materials. Lean years continued, with a $1 million loss in 1999, when 34 of its 373 employees were terminated and voluntary retirement packages were offered to 38 others. The loss in 2001 was $6.8 million, which led to the elimination of 49 more positions that remain unfilled. In 2002, only "display" items were sent to synod assemblies in order to save the company shipping costs. Customers could order items but could not purchase them on site, as had been the practice in the past. For the first nine months of 2002, losses slowed but still totaled $1.8 million.

A shift in leadership

As Augsburg Fortress faced a decade of financial challenges, the transition of leadership in 1992 also proved difficult. Anderson rightly had been revered for his 45 years of experience in Lutheran publishing and was a leading member of the merger commission and a part of its committee that designed the organizational framework for the ELCA. His successor in 1992 was Gary J. N. Aamodt, owner and chief executive office of A-R Editions in Madison, Wisconsin, a publishing house noted for its modern editions of historical music.

"I have a commitment to publishing and a commitment to the church. This position gives me a tremendous sense of integration," Aamodt said in accepting the position. He proved to be an outspoken man who irked many of his fellow church executives time and again. But Aamodt also was technologically savvy and sophisticated. Two years after taking over, Aamodt said that in spite of "Augsburg Fortress's long and celebrated history, it has not been as healthy as many would like to think. Technology is changing the way we do everything in life, and unfortunately Augsburg Fortress is light years behind the rest of the world in this field."

Aamodt's predecessor, Albert Anderson, did not lead the publishing house in keeping up with the computerized advances being made in printing, inventory control, and accounting. While editor of *The Lutheran*, I recalled with astonishment in 1988 being given hand-written financial statements about the magazine's financial health, not computer printouts.

In many ways, Augsburg's lack of technological development made it difficult to make the changes necessary to remain competitive and stable. The high cost of becoming a modern-day publishing enterprise put financial stress on the organization. Aamodt began to make some important changes, but his own demeanor added to the difficulty of moving uphill all the way.

Aamodt remained in his position only until April 28, 1995, when he was abruptly asked by the Augsburg Fortress board of directors to resign, effective two days later. More than a year later, a smoldering dispute between Aamodt and Augsburg Fortress erupted when the two parties filed charges and countercharges in a Minneapolis court.

The dispute focused on the expenditures Aamodt authorized for his benefits, how his implementation of those benefits was financially favorable to him, and the payments he authorized for his resulting tax liabilities. The September 1996 issue of *The Lutheran* reported that Aamodt "accused the publishing house board of breach of contract, fraud and defamation over the terms of his employment in 1992 and his dismissal. The publishing house countered by charging that Aamodt improperly spent more than $500,000 in Augsburg funds to buy an annuity [pension] and life insurance and to pay for personal tax liabilities resulting from those purchases and from a leased Mercedes Benz."

Aamodt told *The Lutheran*, "This is all about promises made and promises not kept, and about a bungling board that had an employment arrangement with me that it did not carry out." In the same issue, *The Lutheran* also noted, the board admitted that it "did not have specific figures on the cost of the benefits when they hired Aamodt." H. George Anderson, later ELCA presiding bishop, was chair of the Augsburg Fortress board when Aamodt was hired.

The suit was settled in May 1997, with the terms remaining confidential. In the July 1997 issue of *The Lutheran*, Aamodt said he was "extremely pleased" with the agreement. "It represents to me both moral and financial vindication." Marvin Roloff, Aamodt's successor, said, "We're glad to know that the dispute is behind us and that the settlement was made in the best interests of the publishing house." No figures of the settlement were made public. Roloff said that although Aamodt's expenditures "cut into our profit line," they were not a major factor in the publishing house's financial woes.

During Roloff's years as president and CEO, the publishing house shut down its presses and outsourced its printing work, implemented new computer systems, centralized its ordering and fulfillment operations, and moved to new offices in downtown Minneapolis.

In September 2002, Beth A. Lewis succeeded Roloff, the first woman president and CEO in the history of Augsburg Fortress or its predecessors. After completing a Florida-to-Minnesota "Asking for Directions" driving tour, she said customers were challenging the company to communicate better, to develop a coordinated marketing strategy, and to earn back their trust.

Relating to other units

Beyond the financial and leadership troubles, and the difficulties in providing timely service to customers, the publishing house at times experienced relational problems with other churchwide units. From the beginning of the ELCA, an "uneasy" relationship existed between the Women of the ELCA and Augsburg Fortress over the publication of *Lutheran Woman Today*. (The Women of the ELCA has units in 7,837 congregations and uses the magazine for program material.) Basically the arrangement with Augsburg Fortress assigned the content of *LWT* to the Women of the ELCA, with production, marketing and distribution assigned to Augsburg Fortress. Over time, the working arrangements between the two parties became strained.

The Women of the ELCA's concerns included maintaining editorial independence, the lack of audience-subscriber data coming from the subscription service hired by Augsburg Fortress, the breadth and scope of the circulation marketing effort, the limited amount of information sharing and the perceived lack of cooperation and consultation of the part of Augsburg Fortress. The publishing house was concerned that *LWT* was "issue driven," as opposed to "customer driven," and indicated that the editorial content-focus of *LWT* was not keeping up with the changing interests and needs of Lutheran women and the expectations they had from a "Lutheran" publication. Augsburg Fortress was also concerned about the magazine's declining circulation (180,000) and that the magazine operated at an annual loss of approximately $150,000, which was absorbed by the publisher.

Analyzing the situation did not provide the basis for agreement, and tensions increased. In September 2000, Augsburg Fortress launched *Sunday/Monday Woman*, a non-denominational, consumer magazine intended to serve women 30 to 50 years of age. The house invested approximately $1.7 million in the development and operation of *Sunday/Monday Woman* from 1999 to 2001, achieving 30,000 to 40,000 circulation. But with forecasts of additional investments being needed before breaking even in 2004 or 2005, Augsburg discontinued the magazine after the November/December 2001 issue.

In February 2001, the board of the Division for Congregational Ministries asked its executive directors to "investigate alternative" means of "publishing, producing, and distributing resources" designed for congregations. Board members expressed concern over the existing arrangement with Augsburg Fortress, saying that the publishing house "has become inefficient and ineffective."

"We are not overthrowing Augsburg Fortress as the publishing house," said Ronald Bruggeman, Omaha, Nebraska, DCM board chair, "but clearly there is a problem. We are genuinely concerned that products may not be developed," apparently referring to the publisher's shaky financial standing. The board also asked the ELCA Church Council to review the relationship between Augsburg Fortress and the churchwide units. ELCA units are to use Augsburg Fortress for producing their materials.

Roloff said he was "deeply concerned" over the actions. The Augsburg Fortress board was frustrated by the lack of specifics in the resolution. "What's their beef?" said Fred Korge, Houston. He termed the resolution "not nice." In Chicago, ELCA Secretary Lowell Almen made it clear to all churchwide units that they were to use Augsburg Fortress for the production of their materials.

With the restructuring in 2001, Augsburg Fortress made rebuilding a relationship of trust with other ELCA churchwide units a company-wide priority. Even so, the future of Augsburg Fortress remains shaky, especially in its financial dimensions. Because every major Lutheran denomination depends upon its own printed material, Augsburg Fortress must return to financial stability and regain creative vitality in order to continue serving the ELCA and the wider church.

In spite of difficulties, the publishing house has some impressive numbers—more than 80 books were published in 2001 under the Fortress Press and the Augsburg Books imprints, along with 500 other publications to further faith development and congregational life. The pew edition of *With One Voice* sold 80,288 copies in 2001. *The Lutheran* continues to have the largest circulation of any Lutheran magazine in the world and is the largest denominational publication in North America. The service call center received nearly 220,000 incoming calls for orders, and the distribution center processed 190,000 orders. Augsburg has joined the technological revolution with online ordering, a sales channel that has increased each year. In January 2002, Augsburg Fortress introduced *ReadyClickGrow*, a Web-based resource that enhances a congregation's ministry by making biblically based materials and activities available to members through their congregation's Web site.

CHAPTER 3

THE STYLES OF LEADERSHIP

"I kept hearing a voice, 'Let George do it!'"

*Herbert W. Chilstrom, first ELCA bishop, announcing the election of the
second ELCA bishop, H. George Anderson, August 1995*

Herbert Walfred Chilstrom—teacher, pietist

Chilstrom is probably the only person in church history who
suggested the name for a new church and then became its first
bishop. While he was a member of the merger commission, he
moved the adoption of Evangelical Lutheran Church in America
as a way to incorporate the key words of all the predecessor bodies into the church's new name. As for his election, he needed
nine ballots to become the first presiding bishop of the ELCA,
and he held the office for eight years, the longest thus far.

The occasion was the 1987 Constituting Convention of the
ELCA in Columbus, Ohio, April 30 to May 3, 1987. David
Preus, ALC presiding bishop, led for the first four ballots, but
Chilstrom moved into the lead on the fifth ballot and stayed
there. (Special rules for that convention permitted nine ballots;
the limit now is five.)

"I feel like many mantels have been sewn together and placed
on my shoulders," Chilstrom told the convention, invoking the
names of current and former leaders in the predecessor churches
that were now coming together in the ELCA.

Chilstrom, 55 when he was elected, is a tall man, nearly six
feet four inches, with a long gait and white hair. He was bishop
of the LCA's Minnesota Synod from 1976 to 1987, possibly the
most important aspect of his being tapped to lead the new
church. When a person embodied the combination of being a
bishop of the East Coast-heavy LCA serving in the Midwest-
heavy ALC, all the political bases were covered. He was a pietist

out of the Swedish tradition whose great-grandparents migrated to Minnesota in the 1850s. One of his favorite items in his home is the small glass bowl that held the water at his baptism. He felt the call to become a pastor at 14.

Chilstrom served a two-point parish in Pelican Rapids and Elizabeth, Minnesota. Afterward, he was a professor of religion and academic dean at Luther College, Teaneck, New Jersey, and came back to serve a large church in St. Peter, Minnesota, near Gustavus Adolphus College. In addition, he earned a doctorate in education from New York University. He is part of a "clergy couple," along with his wife, Corinne, who was ordained in 1985 by the ALC.

Convention-goers who elected Chilstrom bishop may well have remembered his behavior in the merger commission. When the LCA bishops raised a host of questions about the nature of the church during the waning days of the merger negotiations, to the point that some thought the merger was in danger, Chilstrom came to the rescue. Living up to his reputation as a reconciler, he by chance flew back to Minneapolis after that LCA bishops' gathering on the same flight as Lloyd Svendsbye, ALC vice president and a member of the merger commission who had been in New York for a different meeting. For two and one-half hours they talked. By the time they landed in Minneapolis, they determined to bring merger commission members from the Minneapolis area together a week later. They met for two nights, and that reconciling role would not be forgotten when voting time came at the constituting convention.

Most people seemed to recognize that Chilstrom was the best choice to make the merger work even though he may not have been their first choice, said Robert Bacher, who was to become Chilstrom's choice for ELCA Executive for Administration. Preus and James R. Crumley, LCA bishop, were sending mixed messages about their interest in leadership roles in the future, and voters did not see the same creative possibilities with them that they projected on Chilstrom.

Chilstrom obviously had to hit the ground running, closing down one bishop's office in the LCA and opening a new one in the ELCA. He had no chance to ease into his new role because issues kept going off like firecrackers around him—personnel and hiring flare-ups in the new church, irregular ordinations of openly gay persons in San Francisco, and financial troubles that grew worse than anyone imagined they could. Chilstrom was an optimist, keeping a stiff upper lip in responding to criticism, even though forces beyond his control kept him from delivering as well as he would have liked on the hopes he raised. He was telegenic; he liked to preach and teach and to press the flesh. He was a good first "front man" for the ELCA, articulate and personable. And he was compassionate, especially when meeting with folks who had suffered natural disasters of hurricanes, earthquakes, and floods.

An introvert by nature, Chilstrom's leadership style, though, was primarily that of a person making his own decisions. During his early years, his assistants were Bob Bacher, Morris "Bo" Sorenson, and Lita Brusick Johnson. Bacher recalls that the group was known as "Bobbolita." The trio, upon whom Chilstrom depended heavily, represented the three predecessor churches. Bacher (from the LCA) was sought by Chilstrom for his organizational skills. Sorenson was good in smoothing ruffled feathers in formerly ALC congregations. And Chilstrom liked Johnson's spark (she was from the AELC). The close relationship between Chilstrom and the "Bobbolita" group did not transfer to the church's secretary or treasurer. The dynamics of his staff relationships evolved with other assistants when Craig J. Lewis, an African-American man who had headed the Commission for Multicultural Ministries, succeeded Bo Sorenson. Later, Lee Thoni, who had been in the Division for Congregational Ministries, became an assistant. In time, Chilstrom seemed to read more about issues and talk less with staff. To some, including several members of the Conference of Bishops and the Church Council, it seemed that his "kitchen cabinet" became really his wife, Pastor Corinne Chilstrom.

In 1992, when he decided to develop a 10-page single-spaced list of suggestions about the church's finances, he did it in typical style. He anguished alone over a weekend, drew up an analysis and laid it on his staff on Monday "like a thunderbolt" as he left the office to go to the airport for another meeting.

At the same time, his staff talked with him about not provoking some topics, such as the ordination of gays and lesbians. Most people knew that he supported it, but his staff talked him out of saying more because it would be counterproductive. His letter to President Bill Clinton in support of gay people in the military led to hundreds of protest letters.

In the Church Council, he sat at the head table but didn't enter into the discussion very often, rather throwing the council members back on themselves to make decisions. His arena of influence was more out and around the church. The vice president of the church presided over the council. Chilstrom saw his role in the Conference of Bishops as being one of the bishops of the church. He sat among them while the chair of the conference presided. Chilstrom would comment occasionally on issues before the conference, but he might go a whole day at the conference without saying a word. One of the synodical bishops is elected by peers to chair of the Conference of Bishops.

Some people thought that with the bishop presiding over the Churchwide Assembly, the vice president presiding over the council, and the chair of the Conference of Bishops presiding over the conference it meant that leadership was diffused in the church. Probably not. Rather, the division of labor between clergy leadership and lay leadership was a matter of balance and creative tension. The ELCA relies on its bishops, but it also strongly encourages lay leadership.

In his day-to-day workings, Chilstrom could be a puzzle, with staff and other churchwide executives not knowing exactly where he would come out on a given issue or how he would respond to questions. When critics in 1988 clamored for a focus for the church, he pondered and developed a 23-page booklet, *Foundations for the Future*, which called the church back to its biblical and confessional roots. Two years later, he introduced Mission90, and Bible reading and study was at its heart.

"The contents of Mission90 was who Herb was," Bacher said, "personal piety and faith." He was primarily a teacher, and believed that if people were faithful enough to the call of God and paid attention to the proclamation of the Gospel, things would work out." Mission90's sub-theme was "See, Grow, Serve," and focused on small group studies, Bible reading and study, tithing, membership, developing a mission partnership with a local and an overseas congregation, and joining projects opposing injustice, violence, and environmental destruction.

In the midst of continuing calls for clarity of focus in church-wide ministries, the Church Council responded, establishing as funding priorities global mission, domestic outreach and theological education, upon the recommendation of Chilstrom.

His ecumenical and international interest was considerable. He often helped overseas churches celebrate anniversaries—for example, the 100th anniversary of American Lutheran missionaries coming to Madagascar. He ventured into South Africa and Namibia at the height of apartheid, joining Bishop Kleopas Dumeni of the Evangelical Lutheran Church in Namibia to meet with the South African Governor-General in Windhoek, Namibia, to plead for abolition of apartheid. He stayed overnight in a black township and attended a labor union meeting. He went with Presiding Bishop Edmond Browning of the Episcopal Church to England, Norway, Sweden, Denmark, and Finland, to accentuate the full communion efforts of Lutherans and Episcopalians in the United States. He met with Russian Orthodox leaders in Moscow and with oppressed Lutherans in Latvia, Estonia, and Poland. He was a vice president of the Lutheran World Federation. When he retired in 1995, he calculated that he had traveled 796,717 miles for the ELCA, the equivalent of 72 times around the world. He guessed at one time that he spent four of his eight years as bishop away from home.

As chief executive of a church that was conflicted in its early years, Chilstrom naturally became a lightning rod for criticism. But as his successor, H. George Anderson, observed, Chilstrom did "a heroic job in helping the church live through its first eight years. The church's problems were not out of inattention or mismanagement but came because of social issues. He outlasted the financial flap at the beginning." Nonetheless, some of the critics were both sharp-tongued and unfair. An Omaha pastor said, "We are in turmoil with a rudderless ship and gutless leadership." A gentler friend said Chilstrom tried to govern the ELCA the same way he did the Minnesota Synod, except that Minnesota was a matter of overseeing a cultural phenomenon where Lutherans were dominant, the culture was tolerant, and he could ride the crest with his personal touch. "But the ELCA," the friend continued, "is not the same cultural phenomenon, not as friendly or as tolerant. He is the same man, but his turf isn't and he doesn't realize it." He was deeply hurt by the call for his resignation in 1991 by an independent Lutheran publication, *The Lutheran Commentator*. Another independent newsletter, *Lutheran Forum*, gave him less than a passing grade.

The criticisms stung Chilstrom, but he was vindicated when he was reelected to a second four-year term in 1991 by 885-140 on the second ballot. He missed election on the first ballot by nine votes. "This assembly means that the leadership is finally confirmed," said then-Rocky Mountain Synod Bishop Wayne Weissenbuehler. "This election is their first real mandate. Nobody knew each other four years ago, so we didn't know how things would go, but now [the leadership] has been given a second chance. They have a window of opportunity to make this church work." Nonetheless, Chilstrom announced two years later that he would not be available for reelection in 1995. For some people, it also signaled his slowing down. He even referred to himself in the latter part of those two years as "a horse heading for the barn."

Despite the criticism that came his way, he did not choose to respond very often. He had an edge but did not show it much. After he was no longer presiding bishop, he was more confrontal, even though selective. For example, he was a compelling interpreter of the full communion issues with the Episcopal Church and wrote extensively about it. His writings were often influential when used by other spokespeople in the right places. He chided a synod bishop for openly supporting WordAlone, a group that outspokenly opposed aspects of the ELCA's full communion efforts. He also spoke openly in favor of moving toward gay and lesbian ordinations.

At the time of his retirement, Chilstrom was asked what he felt good about during his eight years. First on the list was Mission90, especially his six-part video series, *What Does It Mean to Be a Christian?* He was known as "one-take Herb," because he was so comfortable in front of video cameras that scenes seldom needed to be remade. He felt good about bringing the original churchwide staff together and settling into a sense of community. "The first three years were really difficult," he recalled. He also found satisfaction in bringing the churchwide organization under control, especially the financial troubles. And he felt good about the companion synod program and his leadership role in the Lutheran World Federation.

As for disappointments, he mentioned finances—"somehow we can't seem to move our people to give more than two or three percent of their spendable income." Another disappointment was the lack of interest in Bible studies in parishes. And he regretted that the ELCA "has not been able to convey to our gay and lesbian members that they stand on level ground with us." He was dismayed at the vitriolic anger he sensed in letters that crossed his desk. "It was difficult for me to reconcile that with the fact that these letter-writers are supposedly committed members of the ELCA," he observed. He also wished the church could have made more progress during his eight years in becoming a multicultural church. Chilstrom wanted to be remembered, he said, "as a pastor who preached and taught the gospel of Christ, and as a mediator who brought opposing forces together and worked for resolution." He often commented that he tried to bring a pastoral tone to leadership.

Hugh George Anderson—builder of confidence

The ELCA's second presiding bishop took a different road to the office. Anderson was a towering intellect whose entire professional life took place in academic circles. He was never a parish pastor. Rather, he went directly from seminary and graduate school in 1958 to become professor of church history at Lutheran Theological Southern Seminary, Columbia, South Carolina, and then its president in 1970. In 1982, he became president of Luther College, Decorah, Iowa, another instance of an LCA person becoming a major church figure in the ALC-dominated Midwest. He likely would have been president of the LCA in 1978 but withdrew after a large lead on the first ballot because he "didn't feel an inner call." He was also a potential candidate when the ELCA was formed in 1987, but he felt he could not leave Luther College at that time. When his name was rumored as a possible bishop in 1995, he said he was too old, to which his wife, Jutta, replied, "That sounds like a reverse Jeremiah ["Do not say, 'I am only a boy,' for you shall go to all to whom I send you ..." (Jeremiah 1:7)]. Remembering that twice before when the church considered him and he declined, this time he said, "If the church calls again, I won't stand in the way."

When it became common knowledge that Anderson would accept the position if elected, he went to the Minneapolis assembly as the front-runner. In fact, it was his election to lose. He didn't, being elected 698-334 on the fifth ballot. Anderson was 63 at the time. He is probably the only bishop who had flunked his confirmation exam. In Anderson's home congregation in Alhambra, California, the pastor at the time—future LCA President Robert J. Marshall—was so frustrated with the class that everyone had to take the test over.

A man much shorter than Chilstrom, Anderson continued the gray-haired appearance and gave the ELCA another articulate spokesman. In leadership, he was rather quiet, unflappable, and listened to and depended upon his advisors and staff. He could get to the heart of a question quickly and incisively, bring fresh perspectives to old questions and turn a clever phrase. His style was that of listening and interpreting where the church is, and where it is headed. His built confidence within whatever group he was meeting with, such as being a master presider at churchwide assemblies, working hard to be fair and to give voting members access to the discussion on the floor.

Among his chief talents, thanks to his church history background, was the historical perspective he brought to issues, especially for those of an ecumenical or international nature, or to issues of the ELCA's founding since he had been a member of the merger commission. He could easily see the broad picture of the whole Christian church and often relayed that perspective in meetings. A memorable moment for him was his signing, as a vice president of the Lutheran World Federation, of the *Joint Declaration on the Doctrine of Justification* with the Vatican in 1999. He understood that day in Augsburg, Germany, that he was a historian making history.

When Anderson spoke, listeners knew that he knew what he was talking about. This made him a formidable leader who generated confidence, was solidly orthodox, and was consistently predictable. When he preached, he turned the sermon into a teachable moment. He could handle tough issues and was an expert interpreter of texts. He wasn't a spellbinding speaker, but when a listener got on his wavelength, Anderson was likely to take the listener on a journey into a text that he or she had never considered before. Because he was adopted as an infant, he often used his adoption as a personal description of how God adopts us as his own.

In the Church Council, he would enter into discussions frequently, remarking both on a topic or a procedure that was under review. At the Conference of Bishops meetings, he sat at the head table in contrast to Chilstrom, who sat among the bishops, primarily to be visible as a leader and to be an obvious listener to the bishops.

The bishop's office is always beset by those who have a different viewpoint. In this regard, Anderson could be disarming, often using humor to do so. He also had the ability to disengage his own anger and the other person's anger, not getting caught up in the emotional side of issues. He could stay focused on an issue without slipping into rancor. In those times when controversy swirled around him, such as during the discussions about the full communion with the Episcopal Church, he took the high road and did not try to argue with those who viciously attacked him. Some criticized him for not being more of a take-charge leader, a "here's where we are going, are you with me?" type of leader. Actually, he was sad that he had to lead the church through the full communion discussions, not because he didn't believe in full communion, but because he would have preferred to put his energies elsewhere.

Robert Bacher, the ELCA Executive for Administration, admired him as a "very good administrator, even conceptually." Anderson often reflected that being a college president and dealing with diverse constituencies was good preparation for being the presiding bishop of a church.

When his six years were drawing to a close, Anderson reflected on the satisfactions of his tenure. "The ecumenical agreements rank very high," he said, partly because of their intrinsic significance and partly because of his own background. The church's increase in giving was next on his list, with giving moving upward from an average of about $64 million per year from congregations through synods to a new high of $69 million. When ELCA Treasurer Richard McAuliffe told Anderson that he thought the church had plateaued at the $64 million level, Anderson bet him a steak dinner that it hadn't. Anderson obviously won.

He was pleased that his emphasis on solidarity with people in poverty had taken hold. In fact, he was surprised at the response to it. The thrust began initially as a sermon to the Conference of Bishops, but it struck a note and took on a life of its own, especially "being in touch with such persons and seeing affluence as the trap it can be."

Anderson also was pleased with the response to the "Seven Initiatives" he put forth—not as programs, but as "areas on which we will be able to grow into the future that God is offering us." Congregations were encouraged to implement several of the initiatives in their communities. The initiatives included deepening worship life, teaching the faith, witnessing to God's action in the world, strengthening one another for mission, helping the children, connecting with youth and young adults, and developing leaders for the next century.

As for disappointments, Anderson regretted that "we were not able to do much with evangelism." The church produced materials, he said, and congregations bought them. But "we found that they made a momentary difference—membership would go up a little, then drop back. The core finding in evangelism was that congregations with the right climate were growing regardless of whether they were located in a growing area or not."

Anderson also regretted not being able to mend the problem of interdependence in the church, an issue that also haunted Chilstrom. He said that "conscious efforts by critics to undermine *Called to Common Mission* (full communion with the Episcopal Church) alienated some people, not just from congregations but also toward synods and the churchwide organization. I am sad that I couldn't do more, but whatever I did was perceived as more propaganda from the church's central office."

Being presiding bishop "turned out to be better than I expected," Anderson reflected. Calling it an "all consuming job" he said, "you draw on every experience you ever had and every speech you ever made just to stay afloat." As for criticism of him or of the church, he said, "If you wait long enough, the energy will drain out of groups and extreme positions will lose heat. If we stick to the mission of the church, people understand when you do so, and they have the good sense not to go over to movements that feed on negatives and fear." He was referring especially to the WordAlone movement that vigorously attacked the full communion proposal with the Episcopal Church.

Anderson also said it was a "revealing" job in which he learned a lot about the church and the people in it and its activities and sources of conflict. "I constantly learned from bishops all over the world a deeper discovery of how God works in the world." The six years also taught Anderson "how little any one person is able to do, and how it's the work of the whole church that makes the decisions and gets the work done. It's been the Holy Spirit—God working throughout the whole church—that's made this time so exciting."

He also appreciated the "bonding" with the bishops and ELCA executive staff. He spoke especially of his good relations with Secretary Lowell Almen. When Anderson stepped down at the 1999 Churchwide Assembly, Almen had trouble holding back tears when he offered a tribute to him. The ELCA's first 14 years were characterized by three things, he said:

1. *Sifting*—realizing what the church needed to keep from the past and what structures were not helpful and what baggage needed to be left behind, a discernment process.

2. *Leading*—that the ELCA is respected and the deference that is paid to it, especially in the Lutheran World Federation.

3. *Changing*—living in a fluid culture that requires new energy and new solutions.

Would Anderson, the reluctant nominee for bishop, do it again? "It was a good experience," he said. It gave him a way to pull together his natural interest in church history and ecumenics.

ELCA Church Council—serious, responsible

The formation of the Church Council was a contentious point throughout the merger negotiations, and some of that tension played out during the ELCA's early days. At issue was whether the members of the council should be elected by the Churchwide Assembly (the council is the chief legislative body between assemblies) or whether the council should be made up of representatives elected by each synod or region. The ALC had followed this latter pattern, the LCA the former.

The final decision was that the assembly would elect the 33 members of the council for six-year terms, following the clergy/lay, male/female, minority quotas set up for all church boards, committees, and task forces. In addition, the officers of the church were members of the council, making a total of 37 people who met two or three times a year.

The leadership style of the council varied as members were elected to, or rotated off, the council. Adding to the variety was the unique style of each of the church's vice presidents, unsalaried laypersons who presided over the council. For example, with Christine Grumm of San Francisco, the church's first vice president (who served from 1988 to 1991), the council followed her intense, no-nonsense, driving style, cajoling them with her "now folks" and "any comments" style, and pushing the council toward decisions.

The second vice president, Kathy Magnus of Denver, served from 1991 to 1997. Her election proved to be a test of the church's ability to handle delicate moments. Although she led on all five ballots, she was finally elected by one vote (490-489) over Sylvia Pate, an African American who was serving at the time as interim director of the Commission for Women. Magnus tearfully accepted the office saying, "I hope you will pray for me." Her highly organized style helped the council to move efficiently through large amounts of material and to deal with some difficult situations, such as the uproar over the first draft of a sexuality statement in 1993.

The third vice president is the highest elected African-American in ELCA history, Addie Butler of Philadelphia, who took office in 1997. Her style was more tempered than either of her predecessors. Her strength came as an inspirational leader, sharing her sense of privilege and hope at being chosen to do what she was doing.

In 2002, the Church Council considered changing the vice president's position to a four-year term and providing a stipend. Some felt the six-year term was a larger commitment than potential vice presidential candidates might make. Others suggested that reducing the term would be viewed as a demotion of the office since the church's other three officers are elected to six year terms. In the end, the council made no changes.

Perhaps as a reflection of the general turmoil and malaise in the church, the first Church Council reflected its own ambivalence. The council is the churchwide organization's board of directors, but it did not seem to grasp that significance fully. From time to time it vacillated between micro- and macro-managing. Moreover, the council was conflicted early by the great disparity of background and experience of its members, ranging from those who had never served on any church board or committee to former or future church leaders such as former LCA President Robert J. Marshall, H. George Anderson, Richard McAuliffe, and Kathryn Baerwald, former ALC general secretary. The stature of such persons, who were valuable members of the council because of their backgrounds and experience, intimidated some. At the same time, they also helped keep the council's keel even.

Another obvious factor around the table at early council meetings was the tendency of some members to protect the views and stances of their predecessor bodies, and to continue to hold presuppositions and stereotypes about predecessor churches that were not their own. In the midst of uncertainty about direction and decision-making, the council also moved toward creeping regulations, partly as a result of ELCA Secretary Lowell Almen's tendency to try to nail down as many ambiguities as possible to prevent mischief. But the council came together early in confronting the refusal by the Board of Pensions to follow the directive of the 1989 Churchwide Assembly to find a way to divest pension funds from corporations doing business in South Africa.

As the years passed, the council grew more comfortable with itself and became more congenial as the members shared a common ELCA experience. They gave more priority to their commonness and played down their previous heritages and practices. Gradually there were fewer "big names," and the council became "folk," not intimidated or deferential to their colleagues. By 1995, the council was functioning more smoothly and was better able to serve on behalf of the whole church. They were serious and responsible. One observer noted how impressed he was with how seriously they took their role. More and more, they valued the role of the advisory bishops who had voice but not vote. Often called the "back row bishops" because of the seating arrangement in the room, the warmer relationship was symbolized by the bishops coming to sit among the regular council members.

ELCA Conference of Bishops—collegial, maturing

The Conference of Bishops, though advisory in nature, remains a highly significant element in the church's governance. For one thing, each of the 65 synodical bishops oversees the life and work of the ELCA in a particular geographic territory, averaging about 200 congregations in each synod. The geography differs greatly, however, from the ELCA having seven synods in Pennsylvania and six in Minnesota, to single-state synods such as North Carolina or South Dakota, to synods that encompass several states, such as the Rocky Mountain Synod (which is composed of Colorado, New Mexico, Wyoming, and a small part of Texas). Or there is the Southeastern Synod (which is made up of Alabama, Georgia, Mississippi, and Tennessee).

When the bishops first came together, they, like the Church Council, brought with them the heavy baggage of the practices and priorities of their predecessor church bodies. This eased over time, but some vestiges still remain on topics such as high- and low-church liturgical practices, congregationalism, and their view of the church as a whole. They are collegial but, at the beginning and still to some degree, are searching and probing over the role of the conference. The longer they amassed more common experiences in the ELCA, the more they grew together as friends. They developed ways for mutual support, with bishops using personal stories in the sermons they preached at conference meetings, in speaking freely about issues in their respective synods and in including spouses in one meeting each year.

The finest hour of this mutual support may be their showing solidarity with New York-area pastors and congregations after the events of September 11, 2001. In April 2002, 32 synod bishops were among some 200 pastors from across the ELCA who came together in the greater New York area, including parts of New Jersey, for worship services, including an opening service in Manhattan. The visiting pastors preached in most area congregations. The "Solidarity Weekend" was the brainchild of Bishop Stephen P. Bouman, Metropolitan New York Synod.

As time passed in the life of the ELCA, the conference welcomed seven women as synod bishops. The first woman Lutheran bishop in North America was April Ulring Larson, elected by the LaCrosse Area Synod in 1992. Andrea DeGroot-Nesdahl, Western North Dakota Synod, soon followed her in 1995. A few years elapsed before Margaret G. Payne, New England Synod, was elected in 2000, followed in 2001 by Margarita Martinez, Caribbean Synod, and Carol S. Hendrix, Lower Susquehanna Synod. In 2002, Marie Jerge, Upstate New York Synod, and Wilma S. Kucharek, Slovak Zion Synod, were added.

The bishops figure strongly in the church's governance, because they interpret within their own conference and for the Church Council the viewpoints and the sensitivities of their respective areas. Moreover, they are kind of "spiritual directors" for the synods and advise the council on areas of theological concern. It is in this role that the conference has played major roles on three extremely sensitive issues.

The conference was forced to galvanize quickly because it had to respond to the challenge to the church's ordination procedures by the irregular ordinations of three homosexual people in San Francisco. In March 1988, only two months after the church began, the bishops tested various responses for several days, ending with a consensus statement: "Persons of homosexual orientation who seek to be ordained or who are already ordained will be expected to refrain from homosexual practice."

The statement basically affirmed the pattern in the three church bodies that formed the ELCA. A key word in the statement was homosexual *practice*, as distinguished from homosexual *orientation*. The latter was allowed if the person remained celibate. "Just as heterosexual sex outside of marriage comes under discipline, so will homosexual practice," said Southeastern Iowa Synod Bishop Paul Werger, chair of the conference. In essence, the bishops' statement said, "If married, faithful; if unmarried, chaste."

In 1989, the bishops dealt with the non-sexist language that was being used in place of the traditional Trinitarian formula for baptism. While noting that the phrase "Creator, Redeemer, and Sanctifier" is not a "personal synonym for Father, Son, and Holy Spirit," the conference unanimously declared: "In the name of the Father, and of the Son, and of the Holy Spirit is the only doctrinally acceptable way for a person to be baptized into the body of Christ." At the same time the bishops acknowledged that the "creative use of both masculine and feminine metaphors, analogies, similes, and symbols are highly appropriate and recommended for effective preaching and teaching."

A third area of influence came when the bishops adopted guidelines regarding clergy blessings of same-sex unions. In 1993, they said they saw basis neither "in Scripture nor tradition for the establishment of blessings." Further, their statement said: "We, therefore, do not approve such a ceremony as an official act of this church's ministry. Nevertheless, we express trust in and will continue dialogue with those pastors and congregations who are in ministry with gay and lesbian people, and affirm their desire to explore the best ways to provide pastoral care for all to whom they minister."

In 1995, when Paul Egertson was elected bishop of the Southern California (West) Synod, he acknowledged that he favored the ordination of active homosexuals who were living in committed relationships and that he had participated in the blessings of two same-sex unions prior to his election. When some bishops asked Egertson on the floor of the conference whether he would abide by the conference's injunctions against such blessings and ordinations, Egertson said he would. He added that if he ever felt he must defy church policy and participate in such services, he would resign as bishop. In 1999, after he had announced that he would not be a candidate for reelection, Egertson took part in the irregular ordination of Anita Hill, a lesbian in a committed relationship, in St. Paul, Minnesota. When Presiding Bishop H. George Anderson asked Egertson to honor his promise to the conference and resign as bishop, he did.

That incident, along with concern about the role of some bishops in the full communion discussions, caused the Church Council in April 2001 to adopt a seven-point resolution as "a reminder of the limits in the authority of synodical bishops and of their obligation to undergird the life and well-being of this church."

The statements on ordination of practicing homosexuals, same-sex unions and baptismal language were adopted by the bishops as advice to the church, but they were never challenged during the ELCA's first 15 years. They took on the stature of policy even though they are not. In each case, the conference spoke on a crucial matter at a crucial time. Their theological teaching role at these moments was greatly appreciated and long lasting. At one time the conference struggled with speaking on social issues. They were stung in 1988 by criticism when 38 bishops signed on a letter opposing Nicaraguan Contra aid, a document sent to them by the ELCA Office for Governmental Affairs. The bishops gradually realized that such social statements were not their role. That responsibility lay with the Division for Church and Society.

In a similar vein, the conference faced some early strains over whether the bishops had a magisterial function. Some bishops thought of their role as pastoral, others saw themselves as teachers, and still others favored creating a House of Bishops. But as time passed, the magisterial notion faded.

It took the many discussions over full communion with the Episcopal Church for the bishops as individuals and as a conference to come of age in being able to work through differences. When some bishops asked for the possibility of some leeway for seminarians who conscientiously objected to being ordained by a bishop in the historic episcopate, other bishops who did not favor such exclusions nevertheless agreed to go along with them for the sake of the unity of the church. Bishop Ted Schneider, Metropolitan Washington, D.C., Synod, was one of those who said, in effect, "You who have constituents with problems about the historic episcopate are not where I am, but I understand what you are saying and I will go along with the principle of exceptions." The outcome was a sign of the maturity of collegiality of the Conference of Bishops.

CHAPTER 4

BOOKENDED BY SEXUALITY

"Behold, I am doing a new thing."

Opening words at an unauthorized ordination of a gay man and two lesbians,
San Francisco, January 20, 1990

W ith those words from the prophet Isaiah used as an invo-
cation, clouds of incense and sounds of rhythmic
drumming filled the nave of St. Paulus Lutheran Church in San
Francisco on Saturday, January 20, 1990. An estimated 900 people watched as 42 ELCA clergy, most wearing white albs and red
stoles, along with three associates in ministry and 32 clergy from
other denominations, crowded into the chancel to lay their hands
on Jeff Johnson, 27; Ruth Frost, 42; and Phyllis Zillhart, 32.
It was the first ordination, albeit irregular, of admittedly practicing homosexuals in the ELCA or in its predecessor churches,
although people with a homosexual orientation had been
ordained.

During the two-and-half-hour service, the trio was
acclaimed as "ordained ministers in the church of Christ." In
addition to the traditional ordination vows, the three added
a promise to "be diligent workers on behalf of lesbian and gay
sisters and brothers, supporting our coming out, championing
our rights, challenging society's prejudice, and encouraging our
relationships and marriages."

A shirtless male dancer, with his body painted red and green,
performed a fire dance. During the passing of the peace, worshipers joined in clapping to a steady drumbeat, and a few began
dancing in the aisles.

A cocktail hour and banquet with "big band" music followed
the ordination service. The $100-a-plate event drew 300 support-
ers to the Nikko Hotel ballroom. Proceeds from the dinner,
as well as the offering at the service, netted more than $10,000

for the gay and lesbian ministry at St. Francis Lutheran Church in San Francisco. The church already had two openly gay assistant pastors, James Lokken and Michael T. Hiller.

On the day following the ordinations, Johnson celebrated the Eucharist at First United Lutheran Church, San Francisco, where he was installed as assistant pastor. Frost and Zillhart were installed the same day as assistant pastors at St. Francis Lutheran Church, also in San Francisco. Frost baptized an infant and Zillhart consecrated the communion elements. The two women had been together five years as a couple.

Two days after the service, disciplinary charges against the two congregations were hand-delivered by an official of the Sierra Pacific Synod. A disciplinary hearing would ensue, leading to possible censure, suspension, or expulsion from the ELCA. Each church was charged with "willfully disregarding and violating a criterion for recognition" as a congregation of the ELCA. That criterion is that ELCA congregations "agree to call pastoral leadership from the clergy roster of this church." None of the three homosexual seminary graduates called as assistant pastors was on an ELCA clergy roster or a list of approved candidates.

When he received the papers, John Frykman, pastor of First United, said, "We realize it's a risk, but it's a risk we are willing to run. The congregation had no openly gay or lesbian members. James DeLange, pastor at St. Francis, which serves a neighborhood that is heavily gay and lesbian, called the ordinations a "justice issue."

Days before the ordinations, ELCA Presiding Bishop Herbert W. Chilstrom and Joseph Wagner, executive director of the Division for Ministry, issued statements voicing the church's official rejection of the ordinations, saying they "undermine the unity of the church."

Chilstrom was furious that a supportive letter from retired bishop Krister Stendahl of the Stockholm Diocese of the Church of Sweden, living again in the United States, was read during the service. Stendahl, a former LCA pastor and a chaplain and professor of Harvard Divinity School in Cambridge, and a noted scholar, told the ordinands he was convinced that "it is right for your congregation to proceed in an extraordinary manner and find ways for your ordination." Chilstrom reproached Stendahl for involving himself "in the affairs of another church. . . . If a retired bishop of the ELCA were to inject himself into a difficult issue in the Church of Sweden, our church would surely be embarrassed."

The ordinations were the culmination of two years of rumors about gay ordinations. Not only was the service a first for the ELCA, it came at a time when the young church was vulnerable because the documents about approval of candidates and the expectations of clergy behavior from the predecessor churches were no longer in effect, and the new church's own documents were still being formulated and were untested. Some people felt that the three people and advocacy groups like Lutherans Concerned took advantage of the church's newness to provoke a crisis. Some feared that the ordinations would move the ELCA toward being "soft" on homosexuality.

At the very least, the ordinations unleashed torrents of anger, fear, or support, depending where one stood on the issue. The immediate crisis passed, but the ordinations proved to be the opening salvo of sexuality issues that were to consume the ELCA at various times in its first 15 years. In 1991, with surprising ease, the church managed to hammer out a social statement on abortion. In 1993 came the release of the first draft of a social statement on sexuality that created such an uproar that neither it nor a second draft was ever forwarded to a churchwide assembly. Also in 1993, the Conference of Bishops adopted a statement that there was basis neither "in Scripture nor tradition for the establishment" of blessings of same-sex unions. The expulsion of the two San Francisco congregations from the ELCA in 1995 again caused tempers to flare. Between 1991 and 1997, three synod bishops and two ELCA clergy staff persons were forced to resign over sexual misconduct. Some parish pastors were removed by synod bishops when charges of sexual misconduct against them were substantiated. These were both heterosexual pastors' infidelities and homosexual pastors who declared their homosexual practice publicly. In 2001, the ELCA set a goal of deciding about the proper ordination of gays and lesbians by 2005, along with another statement on sexuality by 2007. The setting of the time line indicated that the ELCA sensed it was ready to deal with a tough issue. Thus the ELCA is a church bookended, in its early years, by issues related to sexuality.

Approved for ordination?

Early in 1988, a report surfaced that the faculty of Pacific Lutheran Theological Seminary, Berkeley, California, had certified three "openly gay" students for ordination. Eleven bishops of western synods backed the seminary's decision, saying that the faculty decision was in line with the predecessor churches' understandings that "to be 'admittedly' homosexual in orientation does not in and of itself preclude ordination. The policy of the church is that practicing homosexuals will not be ordained."

One of the three people was Jeff Johnson, who would be irregularly ordained in San Francisco in 1990. Along with James Lancaster, the two were certified by a commission of the LCA Pacific Southwest Synod in December 1987, before the official start-up of the ELCA. Pacific Seminary faculty members were part of the synod's interview teams. The third student, Joel Workin, was a member of the ALC and certified by the Pacific Seminary faculty.

The question of their certification turned on the words *openly gay*. It was generally interpreted that the terms *openly gay* and *practicing* were synonymous, but the seminary's acting president, Gary Pence, said that was not necessarily true. "Many of us had never thought of these students as openly gay, even in the sense that they had 'come out of the closet' or gone public," he explained. The issue was never settled, although it caused the ELCA Conference of Bishops to declare at its March 1988 meeting that "persons of homosexual orientation who seek to be ordained or who are already ordained will be expected to refrain from homosexual practice."

Between March and June, Workin, Lancaster, and Johnson each were ruled out, one by one, as candidates after each refused to say whether he was engaged in homosexual practice and whether he intended to remain celibate if ordained. As for Zillhart and Frost, their certification had occurred earlier and had expired long before their 1990 ordinations.

In June 1989, a coalition of ELCA clergy and laity in the San Francisco area, led by DeLange and Frykman, said they would initiate a call process for Johnson to serve in a gay and lesbian ministry. In an interview, Johnson conceded that it would be at least "irregular" for a pastor to be called and ordained without a synod bishop's approval. The group also advertised for a "lesbian woman with a master of divinity degree from a Lutheran seminary interested in ordained pastoral ministry." Even though such ordinations would violate ELCA constitutional practice, DeLange cited historical precedent for congregations calling and ordaining, including Martin Luther's support for ordaining candidates when the "papist" bishops were not "true" bishops. The January 1990 service described earlier (page 75) was the outcome of the coalition's efforts.

In addition to the procedural and certification issues of the ordination, theological questions muddied the waters. The ordinations are "valid" theologically, but those "ordained" are not pastors of the ELCA, because the ELCA does not recognize ordinations that are not authorized by a synodical bishop, and because congregations do not ordain. The three "ordained" people remained on lay status in the ELCA. The ELCA bishop did not stop the ordinations because he does not have the authority to intervene in such a manner in the life of a congregation.

In July 1990, after a three-day open hearing, a 13-member discipline panel upheld the charges filed by the Sierra Pacific Synod against St. Francis and First United congregations. St. Francis was suspended from the ELCA for five years, effective immediately, since there was no dispute about Zillhart and Frost not being approved candidates. Some technicalities caused the panel to delay the same punishment against First United for 30 days to see if the church would withdraw Johnson's call or if Johnson would reapply for certification. Fyrkman said First United would not withdraw Johnson's call, and Johnson did not reapply. First United then was suspended also. The ruling stated that if the congregations complied with ELCA guidelines regarding approved clergy within the five years, the suspensions would be lifted.

After the hearing, DeLange, a pastor of St. Francis, said, "We got a fair hearing. We accept the decision." Since neither congregation met the requirements for avoiding expulsion, both St. Francis and First United congregations were dropped from the ELCA roster of congregations on December 31, 1995. After the decision to suspend the congregations, Lutherans Concerned/North America, an association of gay and lesbian Lutherans and their supporters, vowed to identify 25 parishes that are willing to call openly homosexual candidates in violation of ELCA rules. The effort went to no avail.

From time to time in succeeding years, individual pastors were removed from office when it became publicly known that they were practicing homosexuals. In Oakland, California, Ross Merkel was removed from the clergy roster and St. Paul Lutheran Church continued to employ him as a layperson. The congregation was not expelled from the ELCA, but it was suspended from participating in synod assemblies. The congregation could not send representatives to, or have any voice or vote, in synod assemblies.

In April 2001, Anita Hill, a lesbian in a committed relationship, was ordained by Saint Paul-Reformation Lutheran Church in St. Paul, Minnesota. Hill had been employed by the congregation as a lay minister. Mark S. Hanson, at the time bishop of the Saint Paul Area Synod and elected later that year as ELCA presiding bishop, refused to participate in the service. He later censured the congregation and its members were precluded from participating in synod leadership positions. In January 2003, Peter Rogness, new bishop of the Saint Paul Area Synod, removed the penalties but retained the censure. "Clearly, governing documents and guidelines are being applied variously throughout the church as mission needs dictate," Rogness said. The synod assembly in 2002 had requested removal of the censure.

Abortion–option only of last resort

In the midst of the furor about irregular ordinations, a 15-member task force began drafting a social teaching statement on another difficult aspect of sexuality—abortion. By their second meeting in early 1990, they decided to eliminate what they called "extreme" and "absolutist" positions from consideration. Pastor C. Jack Eichhorst, then of Brooklyn Park, Minnesota, said that he "sensed a greater humility before the enormous task of dealing with abortion than I've ever seen before."

Soon the task force agreed that "after viability, every effort should be made to preserve the life of the fetus and the mother." They also agreed that in some pre-viability cases—incest, rape, and a pregnancy that endangers the mother's life—abortion may be a "tragic option." The group appeared to be moving toward a document emphasizing "common ground." "We won't have a minority report," said Pastor Ted Steege, co-chair of the task force.

Most vocal critic of an early draft was task force member James Burtness, Luther Seminary, St. Paul, Minnesota, who said that the draft made "a relentless, muscular drive to a *Roe v. Wade* position. This is not a *Roe v. Wade* task force. This document does not reflect where the task force is." By October, a 20-page "unfinished" draft statement was sent to congregations for discussion and for feedback from 14 hearings. The draft affirmed "a strong moral presumption to preserve life" but noted that "difficult decisions sometimes have to be made in which preserving the life of the unborn may not always be the highest value." During the hearings, the statement was criticized for being "fuzzy" and "murky" and for emphasizing the "sinfulness" of abortion.

At the church's headquarters in Chicago, 50 to 100 letters arrived daily at the Commission for Church in Society's office. On one afternoon, 30 pro-life activists marched and chanted outside the headquarters building. When the task force came together for the final time before the statement was presented to the 1991 Churchwide Assembly, Burtness, who had criticized an early draft, said "the document's significance is that it presents a spectrum—one that is not arbitrary, not fuzzy, and not endless."

At the assembly, debate stretched on for six hours spread over two days. Central to the document is the statement: "Human life in all phases of development is God-given and . . . has intrinsic value, worth and dignity." Thus the "strong Christian presumption should be to preserve and protect life. Abortion ought to be an option only of last resort."

The statement encourages "women with unintended pregnancies to continue the pregnancy . . . in most circumstances." The statement lists three exceptions:

1. Abortion is morally responsible when the continuation of a pregnancy threatens the woman's physical life.

2. Abortion may be morally responsible when a fetus has "extreme abnormalities, which will result in severe suffering and early death."

3. Abortion may be morally responsible "if the pregnancy occurs when both parties do not participate willingly in sexual intercourse. This is especially true in cases of rape and incest" and in "situations where women . . . have no choice regarding sexual intercourse and little access to contraceptives."

The statement opposes abortion when a fetus "is developed enough to live outside a uterus with the aid of reasonable and necessary technology." It also urges adoption "as a positive option for those who feel they cannot provide adequate care for a child."

Voting members at the 1991 Churchwide Assembly roundly rejected amendments that human life "begins at conception" (761-231). Pastor Joy Bussert of Minneapolis, said, "Neither scientists nor theologians have unraveled the question of when human life begins." Joel Hylden of Park River, North Dakota, who repeatedly tried to amend the statement to make it more restrictive, countered, "Scripture is very clear that life begins at conception." An amendment that the ELCA "supports freedom of conscience" in abortion questions also was defeated (865-118).

Laws that would outlaw all abortions, mandate sterilization or deny information about or access to contraception and morally justifiable abortions are opposed in the statement. The document supports laws that prohibit abortions after a fetus is viable, except in cases where the woman's life is threatened.

The assembly took 74 votes on various motions and amendments, rejecting most of them as inconsistent with the document's non-polemical tone. The finished statement was adopted by an overwhelming 905-70 vote.

Jerald Folk, director of the ELCA church-in-society unit at the time, said the drafters deliberate avoidance of "code words, such as pro-life and pro-choice," means that the document "refuses to be co-opted by the left or by the right. It is bold in saying there is a third way." Presiding Bishop Herbert W. Chilstrom, who praised voting members for their patience and tolerance, said the church's position "could lead the whole country out of the morass of extreme pro-life/pro-choice language."

Bishops' misconduct

If dealing with irregular ordinations of a gay man and two lesbians and debate over an abortion statement were not enough stress for the ELCA's young life, sexual misconduct among clergy also came to the scene. Such revelations came slowly at first, then more frequently. Among them were respected parish pastors, such as Stephen J. Cornils, senior pastor of Central Lutheran Church, Minneapolis, the city's "cathedral" Lutheran congregation. Another was Ronald F. Thiemann, an ELCA pastor who was dean of Harvard Divinity School, who was asked in 1999 to resign after university officials found thousands of pornographic images on his school-owned computer. Others were associates in ministry; another was a retired camp director in North Carolina who was jailed for molesting young neighbor children.

A result of the increasing number of allegations was the need for the ELCA to employ in-house legal counsel. Until 1989, the ELCA did not have in-house counsel, and the predecessor churches never had it. When David Hardy became the ELCA's lawyer, he was shocked that he had four cases of sexual misconduct to deal with. At one time as the years passed, he had as many as 20 pending cases. A great deal of his time, sometimes up to 90 percent, was spent in providing legal counsel to synod bishops who were dealing with allegations that were brought to them. Hardy also spent enormous amounts of time sorting out where the legal liabilities would lie when an allegation was made, because lawyers for victims tended to look for "deep pockets" and sue the pastor, the congregation, the synod and the ELCA churchwide organization. Because part of the ELCA presiding bishop's job description is to investigate any allegations against synodical bishops and to ask for the resignations if warranted, Hardy also spent a great deal of time counseling the presiding bishop on such issues. In time, the ELCA added a second in-house attorney, primarily to care for other matters.

After investigation of allegations brought to Chilstrom, the presiding bishop asked Lowell H. Mays, bishop of the South-Central Synod of Wisconsin, for his resignation in January 1991, citing "evidence of alleged past sexual misconduct that is inappropriate for an ordained minister." Mays resigned rather than "engage in a protracted hearing which could be emotionally devastating in an attempt to establish my innocence regarding alleged events of some 20 years ago." Documentation provided by Chilstrom and by the synod's interim bishop after Mays's resignation showed that "formal charges were based on allegations of five women concerning events over a time period from 1971 to 1988." All the women signed affidavits. Mays resigned from the clergy roster nine months later.

In June 1993, Kenneth Zindle, bishop of the Slovak Zion Synod, resigned after Chilstrom charged that "two women who had been supervised by Zindle in the early 1980s . . . described situations where Zindle engaged in inappropriate sexual talk, gestures, and invitations." Zindle acknowledged that several, but not all, of the behaviors occurred. He said that "the absence of due process in this situation and the lack of pastoral care and concern on the part of ELCA officials were as great a shock as the allegations. Seeing no possibility for fairness, justice, or even an acknowledgment of what we believe as Lutheran Christians, I resigned out of disgust." Zindle remained on the clergy roll to serve a congregation in Missouri.

Mark W. Menees, bishop of the North Carolina Synod, resigned in May 1996 after admitting to sexual misconduct with an unmarried adult woman. The relationship occurred over a period of years prior to his election as bishop in 1991. Menees also resigned from the ELCA clergy roster. He had been a pastor in the United Methodist Church from 1971 to 1979, before becoming Lutheran.

A fourth bishop, Ronald K. Hasley of the Northern Illinois Synod from 1988 to 1998, acknowledged in 1999 after his retirement that he "engaged in improper sexualized conduct and contact with several adult women" while synod bishop. He resigned from the ELCA clergy roster.

Two ELCA clergy staff also were forced to resign. Tom Blevins, who was named director of the Department for Synodical Relations in 1991, resigned the clergy roster in July 1993, following the filing of written charges of sexual abuse based on allegations made by an adult woman. Blevins denied the allegations but resigned for the "health and well-being" of himself and his wife. He served as bishop of the LCA Pacific Northwest Synod from 1983 to 1987.

Chris Stein, director of the ELCA Department for Human Resources, resigned in February 1997 after acknowledging that he purchased a massage from the Black Tie Escort Services using an ELCA-issued credit card on two occasions while in Minneapolis on business. Stein, who was removed from the clergy roster, was the ELCA's first employee, beginning his work in Chicago in October 1986.

Issues of sexual conduct at the ELCA headquarters became harder to delineate on December 19, 1992, when a Celebration of Thanksgiving and Blessing was held at Resurrection Lutheran Church, Chicago, for two laypersons, Ed Howard and Fred Wohlin, both employees of the ELCA Division for Outreach.

A clergy executive staff member of the division participated in the service. Since both Howard and Wohlin were lay employees, not clergy, they retained their positions. That incident, along with occasional reports of pastors conducting house blessings of residences occupied by a gay couple, led the Conference of Bishops in November 1993 to declare that there was basis neither "in Scripture nor tradition" for blessing same-sex unions (page 73).

Uproar over a sexuality statement

Even though the irregular ordinations and the sexual misconduct of bishops tore at the fabric of the young ELCA, no single event would upset the constituency more than the first draft of a statement on human sexuality. From the appointment of the task force in 1988 to the unfortunate release of the statement to the press before it was sent to the clergy, coupled with the Associated Press's sensationalized reporting that distorted its content, the entire effort was a series of errors. The Conference of Bishops had misgivings about its content, the presiding bishop wanted changes but did not feel he could step into the work of the task force prematurely, and the ELCA Division for Church in Society was deluged with 8,000 responses after the first draft appeared. (*The Lutheran* received 125 letters that ran 20-1 against the draft). The director of the study, Karen Bloomquist, was asked to step aside. The Church Council spent seven hours discussing how to respond to the outcry, debating whether to release the task force, and appointing an 11-member consulting panel to work with the task force on a revised draft. The council's biggest challenge came in the words of Bishop Peter Rogness, then of the Greater Milwaukee Synod and an advisory bishop to the council: "What signal can [we] send that reinstates trust?" He advocated continuing the study process but acknowledged that "people's trust in the task force has been shaken."

The selection of members of the task force was deemed by some to have a liberal bias, with a news release about an early meeting noting that the group "discussed the need for having an obvious conservative voice on the task force." The release said some members "expressed a fear of a strong conservative voice 'derailing the purpose of the task force.' . . . Others consented to adding a conservative member if the person is 'reasonable' and open to change." An additional member was added to the task force.

The group produced a 50-page study document intended to facilitate conversation in congregational forums, focusing especially on biblical and theological foundations for addressing contemporary issues, such as the first two chapters of Genesis on the creation of male and female, and the "one flesh" concepts of marriage in Matthew 19 and Mark 10. Another section dealt with "specific issues of concern today," including sexual abuse, homosexuality, cohabitation, and infidelity in marriage. The document noted that "studies have increasingly led to the conclusion that sexual orientation is not a matter of personal choice but is established involuntarily." Speaking about teenage couples, young adults living together, divorced people, and older unmarried couples, the study asked, "How shall the church respond to genital sexual activity outside of marriage? Shall abstinence be the only teaching?"

Almost immediately, the Conference of Bishops "registered major reservations" about the study document. They said discussion inspired by the document "will be ideologically skewed and scripturally indefensible in ways radically inconsistent and contradictory to comparable statements of the predecessor church bodies and comparable statements of sister Lutheran churches around the world." The bishops said they were concerned about "the confessional credibility of the final product." Within a month, the board of the Division for Church in Society extended the time of the development of the social statement from 1993 to 1995. "An increasingly clear voice is saying there is more theological and education work to do around these issues," said Bloomquist, the study's director.

The prevailing comment from hearings around the United States was dissatisfaction with the study's treatment of Scripture. "I believe that this was the most offensive part of the study:

the indication that God's will may or may not be as it is written—almost an effort to rewrite the Bible according to man's wisdom in wrappings of loving understanding," said Bruce Swinford of San Diego. Dean of Pacific Lutheran Theological Seminary, Berkeley, California, Timothy F. Lull, asked the task force to prepare a "pastoral" rather than a "dogmatic" statement on sexuality. At the same time, Charles Miller, head of the Church in Society unit, complained that the task force received some "terribly abusive responses that have been unfair to the members who have trying to do their work faithfully."

In spite of the warning signals on the horizon, the division in October 1993 authorized distribution of the first draft of the sexuality statement throughout the church. Some of its key sections were:

Single adults.
Single persons who are tempted to be sexually active are reminded of the importance of a binding commitment and encouraged to assess such factors as the length and depth of the relationship; the degree of trust, intimacy, and commitment; and the effect on other relationships and obligations. Serious questions need to be asked as to whether this is a relationship leading to marriage, and if not, why not.

Teens.
Although we do not condone it, we recognize that sexual activity is prevalent among teenagers. . . . If teenagers still choose to be sexually active, we encourage the responsible use of contraceptives to reduce the risk of unintended pregnancy. Although there is no "safe sex," the use of condoms is encouraged in order to reduce the risk of contracting or spreading sexually transmitted diseases.

Living together.
Many choose to test out their commitment by living together before getting married. Trial or temporary commitments are not sufficient for developing the total trust and intimate sharing enabled by a binding commitment. In some situations there

may be an enduring commitment to one another with a clear intention to marry at a later date. It is the binding commitment, not the license or ceremony, that lies at the heart of biblical understandings of marriage.

Divorce.

When continuing a marriage is likely to be more destructive to those involved than ending it, divorce, which is always tragic, may be the better option. The primary role of the church is not that of passing judgment, but of proclaiming God's intention for the permanence of marriage and compassionately addressing the suffering we inflict through our failures to live up to that intention.

Gays and lesbians.

Of the many biblical passages referring to sexuality, only a few explicitly refer to same-sex activity. The focus is on same-sex acts rather than on persons who are homosexual in their basic orientation. Throughout Scripture, heterosexual assumptions clearly are present. It follows that no passage specifically addresses the question facing the church today: the morality of a just, loving, committed relationship between persons of the same sex.

Among members of our church, three responses are common: 1) To love our neighbor who is homosexual means to love the sinner but to hate the sin. 2) To love our neighbor means to be compassionate toward gay and lesbian persons and understanding of the dilemma facing those who do not have the gift of celibacy. 3) To love our neighbor means open affirmation of gay and lesbian persons and their mutually loving, just, committed relationships of fidelity.

Response 1 needs to be questioned on biblical and theological grounds, indeed, challenged because of its harmful effect on gay and lesbian people and their families. Responses 2 and 3 are strongly supported by responsible biblical interpretation within a Christ-centered Lutheran theological framework.

Meeting a few days after the board of the Division for Church in Society authorized distribution of the draft, the Conference of Bishops received the draft "with appreciation but also with reservations." The bishops questioned how Scripture was interpreted through the document, especially the section that deals with homosexuality and the three responses. The bishops objected to the fact that the first response of "loving the sinner but hating the sin" was challenged. At one point a bishop moved the ELCA to derail the sexuality statement process. The motion lost, partly because several bishops lifted up the "teaching moment" that the statement could provide. A key element in the discussion was Bloomquist's contention that the statement could not be withdrawn because it was already in the mail. As it turned out, delays at the church's publishing house meant that the document was not mailed at the time she spoke.

Response to the first draft was overwhelming and speedy—and mostly negative. But as much as the content stirred up people, so did the method of distribution and interpretation. On distribution, the ELCA's Division for Church in Society had control, but badly mishandled it. The document was given to reporters before it was sent to clergy. When press reports about the document came out, pastors felt blind-sided. They were asked questions by members that they could not answer because they had not seen the document. One humorous photograph showed a sign at a congregation of The Lutheran Church—Missouri Synod in Brandon, Florida, that said, "We are NOT the church you saw on the front page of the paper." In a letter to pastors, Chilstrom said, "A mistake was made, which we regret, when a copy of the draft was given to a reporter before you received a copy of the draft statement." He reminded them that the draft had no official standing in the church, and asked for their partnership when "this church and our society need a helpful word."

Interpretation was quickly out of the ELCA's hands. Aside from releasing the document, the communications office had no preparatory or explanatory news conferences, no interviews with principals in advance of the release, no commentaries on the content, nor any advance warning to the press that the statement was coming. The article by David Briggs of the Associated Press, which ran on October 20, 1993, was probably the most damaging of all the news accounts.

The article began: "Masturbation is healthy, the Bible supports homosexual unions and teaching teens how to use condoms to prevent disease is a moral imperative, says a task force leading the nation's largest Lutheran body into the sex wars."

The remainder of Briggs's article is relatively accurate, but the headlines and first paragraph, which unfortunately are all many readers read, was clearly misleading. The words *masturbation* and *condom*, for example, each appear only once in the draft.

The story appeared in nearly all of the 50 states as well as Canada, the Caribbean, Japan, and the United Kingdom. Every major U.S. television network, as well as the BBC and PBS *McNeil-Lehrer News Hour* carried the story. On the same day as the story's release, October 20, 1993, Miller and Bloomquist wrote in a memo to synodical bishops: "During the past two years, we have become acutely dismayed over how eager the media are to pick up on and do whatever they can to sensationalize whatever the church has to say, no matter how unofficial, about matters of sexuality, especially homosexuality." Chilstrom sent a letter to nearly 20,000 pastors and lay professional leaders a week later.

Callers deluged the ELCA churchwide office and synod offices. Nearly 25,000 people tried to call ELCA headquarters and 5,000 got through. And they were angry! Ruth Kvernen, Portland, North Dakota, said, "Today the headline in our paper read, 'Lutherans' draft expands boundaries of sexuality,' with subheads saying masturbation is healthy, the Bible supports homosexual unions and teaching teens how to use condoms. I don't find anything to support this in the New Testament. Shame on us for wanting to provide a soft pillow of sin without telling the consequences of it.' "

"Well, the national church has done it to us again," wrote Pastor James F. Peters, Racine, Wisconsin. "This time releasing a statement to the Associated Press before it is released to us pastors and to congregations of the church. As a result we are supposed to speak to this statement that has been put forth with the implication that it is an official statement of the church. I am confounded when I am asked to encourage my members to trust those who are our leaders, because some of our leaders have stifled the sense of conversation within the church family and have lost the sense of trust needed in such important studies."

As editor of *The Lutheran* at this time, my editorial response began with these words: "Let's say it up front: The distribution of the first draft of our church's proposed social statement on human sexuality was a disaster." I went on to say that "the sexuality statement as written is mortally wounded."

Bishop Kenneth Sauer, Southern Ohio Synod and chair of the Conference of Bishops, distanced himself from the statement, saying that he had "many strong objections to the report and does not support it in any way." Bishop Guy Edmiston, Lower Susquehanna Synod Bishop, placed quarter-page ads in eight local daily newspapers that said that he and other synod officials "do not support" the draft and would "advocate strongly for the rewriting of this unacceptable first draft." Three Iowa bishops, Curtis Miller, Steven Ullestad, and Paul Werger, said, "The comments of Dr. Karen Bloomquist, as reported by the Associated Press, represent her personal interpretations and conclusions and those of the task force. They do not represent the ethical position of the ELCA."

In Oil City, Pennsylvania, 60 members of Good Hope Lutheran Church met with Northwestern Pennsylvania Synod Bishop Paull Spring. One member asked what happened to the responses that parishioners sent to the ELCA division. "Did the task force even consider what we told them? Others asked, "Where's Bishop Chilstrom? We need more authority [exercised] by him."

Spring was outspokenly critical in writing the executive director of the division, Charles Miller. Spring wrote: "I cannot describe the furor this has created. . . . We have lay officers of congregations resigning from their positions. We have prospective members who have decided not to join our church. We have lay people and pastors more incensed than I have ever seen.

My question is: Do you know what has been done to this fragile church?"

Not everyone was negative. "There are some good pieces in this draft," said Bishop Glen Nycklemoe, Southeastern Minnesota Synod. "I would hope that we would not lose the positive parts of the statement." Bishop Roger Munson, Northeastern Minnesota Synod, said, "I strongly support the report's position against adultery, promiscuity, sexual abuse, prostitution, anti-gay violence, pornography, and the exploitation of sexuality in adverting and entertainment. . . . I also believe this draft will raise a serious question about the normative nature of Scripture. For some it will seem that science, psychology, and ethics have been placed on a par with Scripture for making decisions in life." By February 1994, 131,871 copies of the draft were distributed, and 1,000 responses had been received.

When the Church Council met two months after the release of the draft statement, they turned immediately to damage control and rebuilding trust, saying that they would deal with the content of the statement at their next meeting. After more than seven hours of discussion, the council voted overwhelmingly to name an 11-member consulting panel to work with the task force. The panel would include three ELCA seminary faculty, three parish pastors, two lay members of congregations, two synodical bishops and one council member. The panel would give "advice, counsel, and critique" to the task force and would be mutually accountable to the board of the Division for Church in Society and to the Church Council.

The council acknowledged "that trust in the current task force has been impaired." But it deemed "unwise" any action to disband the task force. At the same time, the council steered away from supporting a revised statement that would come before the 1995 Churchwide Assembly, opting rather to speak of "a possible social statement" at a "future Churchwide Assembly."

Church Council chair Kathy Magnus helped set the tone for the meeting by declaring, "You are not here to please everyone, but you are here to be leaders. This council will be a safe place for differences of opinion." David Johnson, a pastor on the Church

Council from Fargo, North Dakota, raised concern that some ELCA members would leave the church. "These are great people," he said. "The issue raised that we need to answer is: How are we going to 'do church'? From the top down? I hear [from members] 'Chicago is going to do it to us again.' There's a lot of frustration out there. Maybe the Spirit is trying to tell us something."

James Cobb, a council member and pastor in Norfolk Virginia, noted that reactions to the draft statement came in waves "first of anger, then of study, and now of reflection. The process is beginning to work."

Concern over the statement's use of Scripture prompted one California congregation to send its pastor to the council meeting. Pastor John F. Bradosky of Grace Lutheran Church, Huntington Beach, California, said "about 250 members of Grace have met every Sunday recently to study the issues raised in the draft. . . . Those raising concerns aren't just angry. There is a sense of sadness and of betrayal about the direction their church is taking." At St. John Church, Pocahontas, Missouri, about a dozen people, including Pastor John Kiehl, gathered after worship to burn a copy of *The Lutheran* and *Lutheran Woman Today*, which they said "promoted the acceptance of the homosexual lifestyle." More than 1,300 clergy and lay leaders endorsed a document by three faculty members of Luther Seminary, St, Paul, Minnesota, who wrote that the draft's use of Scripture is disturbing.

The Conference of Bishops, meeting in March 1994, approved the process for continuing with a sexuality study, but could not agree on a response to its content. The conference's committee on theological and ethical concerns suggested that the study's three characterizations of the ELCA responses to homosexuality were "neither accurate nor helpful." The committee also suggested that "as church we have neither a definitive word on the biological and/or behavioral origins or nature of homosexuality, nor are we able to say with unanimity what the church's faithful response should be to persons who understand their homosexual orientation to be a given." But the bishops could not agree enough to adopt the committee's suggestions.

"Almost every time we talk about our role in the church, we say we have responsibility to lead and teach the church in ethical matters," said Bishop Jon Enslin, South-Central Synod of Wisconsin. "Yet, dear people, every time we come to the point of doing that, we back away."

When the board of the Division for Church in Society met simultaneously with the human sexuality task force and the consulting panel, tempers flared. The panel said it would consider the statement's first draft as a resource and not the basis for a second draft. Charles Miller, executive director of the division, was directed to hire a project director to replace Karen Bloomquist, who was asked by Miller to step down because of the "too close identification of one person with the statement's development." Miller acknowledged after the meeting that task force members felt "jerked around, manipulated, used, abandoned by some and dishonored." One said that "whoever writes the next document, it's not us. . . . I think the church needs to know exactly where the power is now."

By June 1994, the first draft statement drew more than 8,000 responses, with 64 percent of responses from the laity negative and 15 percent positive. Among clergy, 42 percent were negative and 25 percent were positive. The responses filled more than 80 three-ring binders.

In October 1994, virtually one year after the initial draft, a second sexuality document was mailed to congregations. Miller said, "Many persons will recognize that the second draft is more akin to what is understood to be the teaching of the church. . . . Some will be disappointed in the second draft's direction, and a number will be relieved. But the largest number will be encouraged that they have something to talk about that is not divisive and not boring." Congregations had eight months to respond.

After the 1995 Churchwide Assembly, the Church Council took a new tack on the subject of sexuality and directed the division to begin drafting a "message" on "those areas for which there appears to be consensus within this church." While social statements set official policy and are adopted by the assembly, messages are descriptive of current policy, involve timely issues, aren't the result of widespread deliberation and are adopted by the Church Council.

Ironically, Bloomquist wrote the message—with the help of a 10-member advisory committee. The document "speaks to an anxiety in our church in the face of our not having adopted a social statement" and recognizes "the number of things we can say with a significant amount of agreement." Because there is not agreement on homosexuality within the ELCA, the topic is not addressed in the message. Rather, the message says that "this church can be a place where, as sexual beings, single adults can find guidance for their particular spiritual, ethical, psychological, and social issues." On marriage, the message says that "marriage is a lifelong covenant of faithfulness between a man and a woman. . . . A marriage grows and changes over time through experiences of humor and playfulness, brokenness and healing, failure and accomplishment, forgiveness and renewal. In the growth, changes and disappointments of a marriage, the counsel and support of the church is important." The nine-page message also briefly treats these misuses of sexuality: adultery, abuse, promiscuity, prostitution, practices that spread sexually transmitted diseases, pornography, and sexuality in media and advertising.

In addition to the abortion social statement adopted by the Churchwide Assembly in 1991 and the message on sexuality adopted by the Church Council in 1996, the ELCA Churchwide Assembly adopted several other social statements. These include: The Church in Society, 1991; The Death Penalty, 1991; Caring for Creation, 1993; Freed in Christ: Race, Ethnicity and Culture, 1993; For Peace in God's World, 1995; Sufficient, Sustainable Livelihood for All, 1999.

Another set of messages adopted by the Church Council are: AIDS, 1998; Israeli/Palestinian Conflict, 1989; A Changing Europe, 1990; Homelessness, 1990; End-of-Life Decisions, 1992; Community Violence, 1994; Immigration, 1998; Suicide Prevention, 1999; and Commercial Sexual Exploitation, 2001.

Return to gay issues

Although the development of a social statement on sexuality ground to a halt for a while, conversation began to shift back toward homosexuality and the ordination of gays and lesbians. The Division for Church in Society began "appropriate efforts related to issues of hospitality and justice" for gay and lesbian people as requested by the 1995 assembly. Roanoke College, Salem, Virginia, hosted a day-long debate on homosexuality in the church. A study titled *Pulpit Fiction* found that gay and lesbian clergy in the ELCA are in sexual relationships despite the church's expectation that they remain celibate. The conference at the University of Michigan focused on the role of gay, lesbian, bisexual, and transgendered Lutherans.

"These pastors want to be intimately connected to someone else, and they want that connection to be with a mutual, chaste, and faithful relationship as is the vision of the ELCA for its heterosexual ordained ministers," said Carolyn Riehl, project director. The conference was sponsored by Lutheran Campus Ministry at the university, the gay and lesbian task force of the Southeast Michigan Synod and the Great Lakes Chapter of Lutherans Concerned/North America.

The report was based on stories of 35 ELCA pastors, nine female and 26 male, ages 29 to 73, living in 16 states and educated in seven of the eight ELCA seminaries. Of the 35 pastors, 21 are living in committed, long-term relationships, six of them living in church parsonages. All have served in parish ministry at least once. Former ELCA Presiding Bishop Herbert W. Chilstrom led a workshop at the conference and said, "More and more people are saying a committed relationship would be appropriate."

The Lutheran Youth Organization designated that 1998 was "A Year of Prayer" for homosexual and bisexual youth, although the organization decided not to organize a youth event for gay, lesbian, and bisexual youth in 2000. "We couldn't determine how to create a safe environment" for participants, the board said.

Approximately 60 members of the gay advocacy group, Lutherans Concerned, protested outside the ELCA headquarters in September 1998, smashing a large clay pot that they said symbolized the brokenness of the ELCA over openly gay and lesbian pastors not being allowed to serve a congregation.

The Division for Outreach studied 16 congregations that are intentionally welcoming to gays and lesbians. The report, requested by the 1997 Churchwide Assembly, suggested that the division "develop and distribute . . . a resource on welcoming gay and lesbian people." Among the report's findings:

1. Gays and lesbians look for clergy and laity who model hospitality in their words and actions.

2. Congregations must have strong leadership to be welcoming to gays and lesbians and must care for all members pastorally amid potentially painful conversations.

3. Welcoming congregations must be ready to discuss issues such as blessing ceremonies for gay and lesbian relationships and the ordination of homosexuals.

4. Welcoming congregations tend to be those that have previously learned to deal constructively with conflict.

The Conference of Bishops reacted cautiously to the division's report. "Either we do a lot more work on this piece or we will release a hornet's nest," said Bishop George Mocko, Delaware-Maryland Synod. He challenged such suggestions as a church displaying a rainbow flag to show that it welcomes gays and lesbians. The outreach division's study was part of a joint report prepared for the 1999 Churchwide Assembly by that unit and the divisions for ministry, congregational ministries, and church in society, as well as the Commission for Women. The report outlined steps the units had taken to generate discussion on homosexuality, including a new resource for congregations. Titled *Talking Together As Christians about Homosexuality*

(ELCA Division for Church in Society, 1999), the report covered biblical, scientific, ethical, and other perspectives.

The 1999 Churchwide Assembly decided not to speed up work on the issue, defeating a motion to suspend temporarily disciplinary action against noncelibate gay and lesbian pastors. The action disappointed gay and lesbian advocates, but it also indicated that the issue was back on the front burner and that it might be dealt with in the future in a temperate way. At its 2000 assembly, the Greater Milwaukee Synod, led at the time by Bishop Peter Rogness, voted not to discipline pastors or congregations that chose to bless same-sex unions. This move defied the ELCA Conference of Bishops that said in 1993 that it did not condone such ceremonies. The ELCA did not reprimand the synod for its actions. Neither did the synod have any pastors or congregations that blessed same-sex unions.

In November 1999, St. Paul-Reformation Lutheran Church, St. Paul, Minnesota, sought a procedure to make an exception so that Anita Hill, a lesbian living in a committed relationship with another woman, could be ordained. Bishop Mark S. Hanson, then of the Saint Paul Area Synod, also had sought advice on a possible exception. The council agreed with a recommendation from the Division for Ministry that rejected the proposal because "the way to approach the ordination of gay and lesbian people is to do so through ongoing conversations . . . and not through exceptions."

In April 2001, three California congregations ordained a gay man, Craig Minich, 28. He was ordained as a youth minister by St. Paul and United Lutheran churches in Oakland, California, and University Lutheran Chapel, Berkeley, California. He was a graduate of Pacific Lutheran Seminary. Paul Basting, president of St. Paul, said the congregation was "compelled by God's Spirit to offer what we feel is prophetic leadership to our church by taking this action." Bishop Robert Mattheis, Sierra Pacific Synod, said he would probably censure the congregations. Mattheis had previously censured University Chapel when it called Jeff Johnson, a gay man who was irregularly ordained in 1990.

Also in April 2001, Bishop Charles Maahs, Central States Synod, censured Abiding Peace Lutheran Church, Kansas City,

Missouri, for "willfully violating" the ELCA Constitution by calling and ordaining Donna Simon, a lesbian not in compliance with the church's expectations, to serve as its pastor.

By the 2001 Churchwide Assembly in August, five synods called on the assembly to deal with issues of homosexuality in various ways—to develop a rite of blessing for same-sex union, to suspend the policy that requires celibacy for homosexual clergy and rostered lay ministers, to provide more material on homosexuality and to develop a social statement on human sexuality. The Committee on Memorials, the committee charged with grouping the memorials [overtures] from synods and formulating an initial response for voting members to consider, suggested that the assembly decline developing a homosexuality document or a social statement and affirm continuation of the conversation encouraged by the Church Council. This was consistent with an unspoken strategy that the ELCA had followed for some years, namely, that continued study was the best course of action because decisions pro and con about homosexuality or ordination of gays and lesbians would be too divisive for the church.

But voting members, sensing that the time had come when the church could grapple seriously with the issues, voted overwhelmingly in support of the development of a study document on homosexuality by 2005, and asked for a plan and time line by 2005 that will lead to the church making a decision about allowing gays and lesbians in committed relationships to be ordained and rostered. All the votes were surprisingly strong—the document on homosexuality was supported 899-115, the ordination time line 624-381, and the development of a social statement on human sexuality by 2007 was supported by a vote of 561-386.

The homosexuality study, as proposed by Bishop Robert Rimbo, Southeast Michigan Synod, would "include study of the Lutheran understanding of the Word of God and biblical, theological, scientific, and practical material on homosexuality. It will also address questions related to the blessing of committed same-sex relationships and the rostering of ministry candidates who are in such relationships."

"Our scholars need to tell us what the Bible says and what it doesn't say," said Ronald Rude, Rocky Mountain Synod. "Our scholars seem divided. But there's another question: Does the gospel override the Bible? [On issues like slavery, divorce and women's ordination] the church has said that it does."

During a discussion of possible suspension of the ELCA *Visions and Expectations* statement that now prohibits practicing gays and lesbians from serving in rostered ministries, Herbert W. Chilstrom, former ELCA presiding bishop who was instrumental in drawing up the existing ELCA policies, said sustained study of Scripture and getting to know hundreds of gay people, their partners and families have been critical to his changed understanding of how the church should relate to gay and lesbian people. "I'm haunted by their stories, including those of hundreds of pastors and their spouses about their children and families," he said. "I long for the day, I hope soon, when that policy can be changed, when some of our congregations will have the freedom to bless same-gender relationships, when we give freedom to some of our congregations to call [as pastors] people who have to be in same-gender relationships."

The effort to suspend the *Visions and Expectations* statement failed when the assembly endorsed the homosexuality study and the time line for deciding on ordinations of gays and lesbians. Timothy Lull, president of Pacific Lutheran Seminary, reflected after the vote that "the assembly was hard pressed on the issue because it knew that a change would be a hard road to go, but they also respected the gay folks who were there. I'm not at all sure what the next assemblies will do."

David L. Miller, editor of *The Lutheran*, said, "There seemed to be a groundswell of folk who simply believe that it would be disingenuous to delay a decision longer. We also have enough large synods which are allowing same-gender blessings that they were able to carry the day, and easily."

Charles Miller, then executive director of the Division for Church in Society, said that unit and the ministry unit would seek ways to combine the study leading to the homosexuality document and the social statement. "Social statements take longer," he said, nothing that the social statement should be expected "later rather than sooner."

The ELCA's study and decision making come in the midst of the struggle within other denominations on the same subject, The Presbyterian Church (U.S.A.) voted in June 2001 to repeal a ban on actively gay clergy and lay officers. But that vote still needed ratification from a majority of 173 presbyteries. It failed. The Episcopal Church is still trying to decide how to deal with a decision in 2000 to acknowledge church couples—which implicitly includes both heterosexuals and homosexuals—living outside wedlock. The church also has made a decision not to discipline priests who conduct same-sex unions or bishops who ordain actively homosexual clergy. More conservative churches, including The Lutheran Church—Missouri Synod and the Southern Baptist Convention, have no notable dissent from the church's tradition of regarding same-gender relations as sinful.

In reflecting on the decisions of the 2001 assembly, Presiding Bishop H. George Anderson said, "At the present time, a vote [on acceptance of homosexuality] would divide this church. It is one of a series of issues, such as segregation and women's ordination, even the merger itself, in which we forget how each of these were possibly church-dividing. We always have to challenge others about the faith, for we never fully capture God's truth. We only know what we know at any given time. On slavery, the role of women, and other issues, change comes on the basis of Scripture, and Lutherans ought not act on change until the Word has done its work."

A 13-member task force on the ELCA studies on sexuality began meeting in May 2002. James M. Childs, professor of theology and ethics, Trinity Lutheran Seminary, Columbus, Ohio, is on leave from the faculty to direct the studies. "This is a group that wants to listen to the church, not to go about its own agenda," Childs said. "There is a keen desire to be very good listeners to one another's views." Bishop Margaret Payne, New England Synod, is the task force chair. The ELCA Church Council approved $1.15 million for the six-year project, which will allow the task force to hold 32 hearings across the United

States and Canada. Faculty members from most of the ELCA's eight seminaries are developing a book of essays titled *Faithful Conversation: Christian Perspectives on Homosexuality*, and edited by Childs. The book is tentatively scheduled for publication in 2003 by Augsburg Fortress. The Women of the ELCA is encouraging its 8,000-plus congregational units to participate locally in the study process.

Opposition to the studies began to formalize in October 2002, when 273 members from every state except Hawaii attended a Conference on Christian Sexuality in Kansas City, Missouri. The group adopted an 81-line "Pastoral Statement of Conviction and Concern" that expressed reservations about their continued involvement with the ELCA should the church approve at its 2005 assembly same-sex blessings and ordinations of gay and lesbian people in committed relationships. Stating that "the ELCA is becoming schismatic and sectarian," they said that Lutheran laypersons thus far have heard only one point of view—that of support for changing church policy. Drafters of the statement said that changes in the church's stance would distort the biblical record, appeal to questionable scientific theories, suppress inconvenient data and rely on individual experience rather than on Scripture.

A final thought

Thus has sexuality bookended the life of the Evangelical Lutheran Church in America. Beginning with the challenge to certify gays and lesbians in 1988 and the irregular ordinations of such persons in 1990, the issue then went to the side burner for a number of years, being replaced the devastating effects of the first draft of a social statement on human sexuality in 1993. Then both subjects died down for a while, only to be raised again in the later 1990s that led to the decisions in 2001 that this church should come to a conclusion on ordination issues in 2005.

Not only have issues of sexuality consumed the church for its first 15 years, the same will be true for its first 18 years, and possibly thereafter, depending on the 2005 outcome. As the ELCA looks back over its history in the long haul, future historians will likely note that its first two decades were taken up with issues related to homosexuality. It is safe to say that the issues of ecumenism and full communion with other denominations, particularly with the Episcopal Church, were a sore point for four to six years. Even so, the anger and disagreement about the taking on the historic episcopate in the installation of synodical bishops and the presiding bishop was primarily a clergy issue. But every member of every congregation will have an opinion about homosexuality and the ordination of gays and lesbians. Therein lies the next challenge for the adolescent ELCA.

Presiding Bishop Anderson was almost prophetic when he said in 1997, "We are now 10 years old. We are marking the transition as a church from infancy to adolescence. In infancy, one always worries about survival. By the time you get to adolescence, you are asking, 'What do I want to be?' I think our church has reached that critical point when we can assure ourselves that we will have the strength to go forward and now need to ask ourselves, 'What is God challenging us to do?' "

CHAPTER 5

THE STRUGGLE FOR ECUMENISM

"American Christians in 1900
inherited Church cooperation and in 2000 are
'bequeathing full communion.'"

*Presiding Bishop H. George Anderson at the
1999 ELCA Churchwide Assembly*

E ven though harsh language and organized resistance to ecumenical relationships stretched both the patience and unity
of the young ELCA, the Evangelical Lutheran Church in
America by 1999 completed a series of ecumenical actions that
left it poised to enter the 21st century at the forefront of the
world's ecumenical scene. No other church had adopted official
ties with such a spectrum of Christendom—full communion
with the Episcopal Church, with three churches of the Reformed
tradition, and with the Moravian Church. As a member of the
Lutheran World Federation, the ELCA was a participant in
the signing of the *Joint Declaration on the Doctrine of Justification*
with the Vatican, a document that brought agreement on the key
doctrinal issue that divided the churches and produced the
Protestant Reformation. Quite a track record for a new church's
first 15 years.

The ELCA's ecumenical ventures began in controversy and
continue that way. The tensions might have been anticipated, if
not the level of unhappiness, because even the merger commission
shied away from a final decision on one ecumenical matter. The
commission said the new church should join both the National
Council of Churches and the World Council of Churches, but that
the new church should study the pros and cons of membership
for two years and make a final decision at the 1989 Churchwide
Assembly. The LCA had been a member of the National Council
of Churches. The LCA and the ALC belonged to the World
Council of Churches. The AELC belonged to neither.

Groups in some 375 congregations studied materials provided about each council by the ELCA's Office for Ecumenical Affairs. Virtually no one objected to the medical, refugee, and relief work of the councils, or their theological, education, or development efforts. At the time the NCC aroused ire because it adopted positions on virtually every social issue facing the nation. The WCC was controversial because articles in such publications as *Reader's Digest* accused the WCC of channeling funds to liberation movements in Africa, or the *Wall Street Journal* complained when the WCC condemned U.S. policy in Central America.

Some study groups were upset that the ecumenical affairs office did not include such articles in the study materials. The office acknowledged some "tilt" in the materials favorable to continuing ELCA membership, because the predecessor church bodies had positive relationships with the groups. With many of the groups deciding it was better to be a part of the councils than not being in them, 90.1 percent "agreed" or "strongly agreed" that the ELCA should continue membership in the WCC. Some 74.1 percent felt the same way about continued membership in the NCC.

At the 1989 Assembly, continued membership in both councils sailed through easily. When the WCC resolution produced no debate, Presiding Bishop Herbert W. Chilstrom asked, "Are you still awake?" The ELCA's interest in the councils has remained mild, partly because the ELCA shifted its focus to bilateral relationships with specific denominations, and did not put much energy into the council's conciliar ecumenism. Interest in the councils also declined because they became less dominant players on the ecumenical scene, and because both suffered major financial and organizational problems. Their viability remains in question; the days of the councils may be past.

Setting an ecumenical stance

Developing a statement on ecumenism for the new church set the context for the ELCA's future in the world ecumenical scene. One of the "purposes" of the church as laid out in the ELCA Constitution states: "Foster Christian unity by participating in ecumenical activities, contributing its witness and work and cooperating with other churches which confess God the Father, Son, and Holy Spirit." The Office for Ecumenical Affairs developed a draft that described the ELCA as "evangelical, catholic, and ecumenical," and said that the church "is bold to reach out in . . . several directions simultaneously to all those with whom it may find agreement in the gospel."

A draft of the statement was circulated to the eight ELCA seminaries and to a random sample of some 300 congregations. In March 1989, William Rusch, director of the Office for Ecumenical Affairs, said that more than 90 percent of the sample congregations "strongly agree" or "agree" with the statement's content. Each of the seminaries suggested changes. But 34 faculty members of what was then known as Luther Northwestern Seminary, St. Paul, Minnesota, sent a letter to each of the church's 66 bishops requesting a delay in the presentation of the statement to the 1989 Churchwide Assembly. Voting on the statement "will have destructive and divisive effects in the church rather than the unity of purpose it seeks to create," the faculty said.

The letter objecting to the statement greeted each bishop on his arrival for a meeting of the Conference of Bishops. Noting that no other seminary had asked for delay, Bishop Lowell Mays, South-Central Synod of Wisconsin, asked, "Is the Luther Northwestern faculty view a virus idiosyncratic to the Upper Midwest?" Rusch replied that the response was "a limited phenomenon in the light of the responses from the other seven seminaries. There is nothing in this document that Lutherans should fear."

Bishop Peter Rogness, then of the Greater Milwaukee Synod, asked why the statement used the term "full communion" rather than the more familiar "altar and pulpit fellowship." Rusch said "full communion is a fuller term, a recognizable goal in ecumenical theology, a term used in Lutheran-Reformed and Lutheran-Episcopal dialogues."

The following steps were listed in the statement's progression toward "full communion," which is the highest expression of ecumenism:

1. Ecumenical cooperation.

2. Bilateral and multilateral dialogues.

3. Preliminary recognition that could include eucharistic sharing and cooperation without interchangeability of ministry.

4. Full communion. This means common confessing of the faith and mutual recognition of the sacraments, mutual recognition of each others members, eucharistic sharing, interchangeability of clergy and joint efforts in such areas as planting mission congregations, publications, and the like.

Faculty members of four other seminaries—Wartburg, Pacific, Philadelphia and Gettysburg—wrote to the ecumenical office supporting Luther Northwestern's call for delay. (Gettysburg later withdrew its request.) The Wartburg letter criticized the "flawed process" that produced a document "written by a very small group and did not see the light of day with the larger church constituency" until most elements were in place.

Seminary criticism focused on three areas: the document's use of the term "catholic" to describe the ELCA, the use of "full communion " to define ELCA ecumenical aims, and its treatment of *satis est* ("it is enough"). The Latin term refers to Article 7 of the Augsburg Confession: "The church is the assembly of saints in which the gospel is taught purely and the sacraments are administered rightly. And it is enough for the true unity of the church to agree concerning the teaching of the gospel and the administration of the sacraments." The *satis est* would be raised by the Luther Northwestern faculty later to criticize both the proposal for full communion with the Episcopal Church and the support for the *Joint Declaration on the Doctrine of Justification* with the Roman Catholic Church.

The ecumenical office submitted a 30-page "working document" of the ecumenical statement to the 1989 Churchwide Assembly, with the understanding that a revised statement would be presented for adoption to the 1991 assembly.

In 1990, when representatives from the ecumenical office visited Luther Northwestern Seminary for a convocation, Lee Snook, a faculty member, charged that the revised draft of ecumenism statement was "appallingly boring" and "distressingly churchy. . . . Ordinary folk will find this so-called 'vision' to be . . . so full of language suitable only for legal documents that they will be excluded from the conversation." Criticizing the statement's content, he asked, "Once you can imagine the explosion set off by the gospel in the 16th century, how can you ever go back to thinking of unity as a return, or as a repair job?"

Rusch replied that "Snook's speech gives no quotations from the ecumenism text. He describes a document that sees unity as uniformity, ecumenism as a return to the past, and the Reformation as a repair job."

Refinement of the document, *Ecumenism: The Vision of the ELCA*, continued, with voting members at the 1991 Churchwide Assembly bursting into applause when they gave overwhelming approval (919-57) to the statement. The statement's definition of full communion was declared to be consistent with Article 7 of the Augsburg Confession, the basic doctrinal statement of Lutheranism. The article says, "It is enough for the true unity of the church to agree concerning the preaching of the gospel and the administration of the sacraments." Chilstrom said that the strong vote demonstrated that the negative reactions came from "a limited number of people." More importantly, the document gave the church a stance from which it could reach out in several ecumenical directions simultaneously.

The give-and-take over the adoption of the statement was a precursor of things to come in the ecumenical arena. Delays would be frequent, as would objections from bishops and seminaries, especially Luther Northwestern—and the ecumenical office would be criticized about the process used in developing the proposals.

Lutheran-Reformed

The first job facing the ELCA-Reformed dialogue was rebuilding trust over the uneven way two of the Reformed churches had been treated by the ELCA's predecessors. Although earlier dialogues had been held jointly by the three Lutheran churches, the churches took differing actions on *Invitation to Action*, the recommendations from the dialogue. The ALC and the AELC virtually adopted full communion with the Presbyterian Church (U.S.A.) and the Reformed Church in America as churches "in which the gospel is proclaimed and the sacraments administered according to the ordinances of Christ," approving the sharing of pastors and occasional joint services of communion. The LCA, however, was not sure about the Reformed commitment to the real presence of Christ's body and blood in the sacrament and never adopted *Invitation to Action,* choosing instead to adopt a less far-reaching statement of friendship and cooperation. When the ELCA was formed, the ALC and AELC relationship with the Reformed churches ended on December 31, 1987.

When theologians from the 5.2 million member ELCA, the 2.9 million member Presbyterian Church, and the 300,000 member Reformed Church in America sat down together in 1989, they were joined by representatives of the 1.8 million member United Church of Christ. The addition of the UCC added a new dimension to the Reformed family. UCC representative Gabriel Fackre, of Andover Newton Theological School, Newton Centre, Massachusetts, said the UCC's claim to be a "confessing church" rest on traditions, practices and a pattern of teaching as well as on "modest documents" less extensive than the confessions of other Reformed bodies. Other concerns about the UCC included whether its congregational polity precluded the national church from speaking for the congregations, and its ordination of practicing gay and lesbian people.

It took more than three years of conversations for the Lutheran and Reformed theologians to finish a document. *A Common Calling: The Witness of Our Reformation Churches in*

North America Today offered a "hopeful and new way of under-standing the relationships between these two traditions, whose mutual differences can be seen as complementary and mutually corrective." Timothy Lull, then academic dean of Pacific Lutheran Theological Seminary, Berkeley, California, and co-chair of the dialogue, said, "In the past these churches sometimes have insisted on full agreements before fellowship. Our report tries to change the dynamics between our traditions from 'if we agree on every-thing, then we can share the Lord's Supper' to 'because we have so much in common, therefore we can have full communion now, with continuing friendly discussion of our differences.'"

The proposal hinged on interpretation of *satis est* in Article 7 of the Augsburg Confession (the only things necessary for the unity of the church are the teaching of the gospel and the admin-istration of the sacraments). If there were agreement on these two things, the dialogue recommended, sufficient basis for unity existed for intercommunion, interchange of members and inter-changeability of clergy. Disagreement on other issues did not prohibit going ahead with full communion. To support this contention, the dialogue noted that Article 7 goes on to say that it is "not necessary that human tradition or ties and ceremonies, instituted by men, should be alike everywhere."

Lutheran and Reformed churches divided in the 16th cen-tury over such issues as the understanding of the Lord's Supper and the question of predestination. The report acknowledged the differences, but it did not find them a barrier to mutual recognition. The document also called for the withdrawal of any historical condemnations of one side by the other from earlier centuries. In response to the dialogue's recommendation, the 1993 Churchwide Assembly approved a four-year study that could lead to full communion with the Reformed churches.

In 1993, the ELCA Conference of Bishops and the Church Council endorsed plans for an ecumenical emphasis in 1997. That year would mark the 10th anniversary of the ELCA, the 50th anniversary of the Lutheran World Federation, and the 450th anniversary of the Roman Catholic Council of Trent that condemned the Lutheran understanding of justification by faith. Rusch noted that 1997 would be "a time when we will look more Lutheran than ever before. It allows us to be what we have always said—that Lutherans are a confessional body within the whole church, and that we can begin to put behind us, with integrity, differences with the Catholic Church while also living in full communion with other churches. It is also a commitment to the inclusiveness of the church, for we will be an infinitely larger ecclesial community and an incredibly richer one."

One needs to remember that several different U.S. ecumenical efforts were proceeding simultaneously at this time, and on an international scale as well. The ELCA-Episcopal dialogue that recommended full communion completed its work in 1991. The ELCA-Reformed group finished its deliberations in 1992. The U.S. Lutheran-Roman Catholic dialogue that said there were no impediments toward a joint declaration on justification completed its work in 1983. An international Lutheran-Roman Catholic group completed the initial draft of the *Joint Declaration on the Doctrine of Justification* in 1994. Also, 85 Lutheran, Reformed and United churches stretching from the British Isles and Portugal across Europe as far east as Greece and Latvia instituted "full mutual recognition" through the Leuenberg Agreement in 1973. The Meissen Agreement in 1991 instituted pulpit and altar fellowship between the Church of England and the 24 Lutheran, Reformed and United churches that make up the Evangelical Church of Germany. The Porvoo Agreement in 1995 brought Anglicans and Lutherans into full communion in the British Isles, Norway, Sweden, Finland, Iceland, Estonia, and Lithuania. In Norway, an agreement for full communion was accepted by Lutherans and Methodists. Eucharistic hospitality is in place between Lutherans and Mennonites in Germany.

The election of H. George Anderson as presiding bishop in 1995 brought a change in leadership in the ELCA Department for Ecumenical Affairs. The director of the department is nominated by the bishop and elected by the Church Council. Even through Rusch was widely known as the architect of the ELCA's ecumenical policy and was highly visible and respected internationally on the ecumenical scene, Anderson decided to replace him. He praised Rusch for the relationship he built with ecumenical partners and assured partner churches that the ELCA wasn't pulling back from the 1997 proposals. "At the same time, we now need to focus on the reception of these proposals in our church," Anderson said. As a former member of the Church Council, Anderson had seen Rusch in action and knew that Rusch's style was perceived, at times, as brusque or condescending. The need at the time was more for the cultivation of support for the full communion proposals *within* the ELCA Church Council, Conference of Bishops and seminaries than in maintaining ties with the partner churches. Rusch was deeply disappointed, even angered, at not being able to finish the ecumenical agenda he had begun. Anderson nominated Daniel F. Martensen, who had been the associate director, to succeed Rusch. When all the proposals were finally adopted by 1999, Anderson's calculated decision could not be second-guessed.

Anderson told the Conference of Bishops in early 1996 that the church probably hadn't taken the Augsburg Confession's view of the church seriously enough. One of the gifts we bring to the ecumenical table, he said, is this "radical simplification" of what it means to be the church (where the gospel is taught purely and the sacraments are administered rightly)." Anderson said "our ecumenical partners help us see that truth is bigger than we have seen it, not different." He also spoke of the ELCA as an "ecumenical catalyst," noting that the proposals "ask that we recognize in print what we probably all believe in our hearts— that we are not the only church body with the truth."

Responses to a questionnaire sent to congregations and individuals about full communion with the Reformed churches revealed that 57.8 percent supported the proposal. Some 82.4 percent agreed on recognizing common baptism and authorizing sharing of the Lord's Supper, 68.9 percent recognized each other as true churches, and 43.3 percent recognized ministries and orderly exchange of ordained ministers. Most questions centered on the meaning of the "real presence" in the Lord's Supper, faithfulness to Scripture and confessions, and problems with the exchange of clergy, particularly with the UCC.

In November 1996, the ELCA Church Council voted to send the historic proposals for communion with the three Reformed churches and the Episcopal Church to the 1997 Churchwide Assembly. The ecumenical officers of the three Reformed churches attended the council meeting. Each predicted enthusiastic approvals by their respective churches of *A Formula of Agreement*, the full communion proposal.

The faculty of Philadelphia Seminary endorsed *A Formula of Agreement*, noting that "although we have questions about the extent to which this document can have binding and full effect in the United Church of Christ, given its present polity, we trust that through the implementation of this formula that church's congregations will come to experience a greater level of mutual cooperation, interdependence and trust." The Gettysburg Seminary faculty said that "careful study of Calvin and our own Lutheran confessions has led us to recognize that we have more convergence on the understanding of the Lord's Supper than previously believed." Faculty of Lutheran Theological Southern Seminary, Columbia, South Carolina; and Trinity Seminary, Columbus, Ohio, also endorsed the proposal. The other four seminaries—Lutheran School of Theology at Chicago; Wartburg Seminary in Dubuque, Iowa; Pacific Lutheran Seminary; and Luther Seminary—did not respond to the document.

Writing in *The Lutheran*, Bishop Guy S. Edmiston, Lower Susquehanna Synod and chair of the Lutheran-Reformed Coordinating Committee, said he was "enthused" about *A Formula of Agreement*'s principle of mutual affirmation and admonition. Mutual affirmation is the easy part, he said, but admonishment means more than gentle reproof or caution against human error. It means to charge authoritatively, to exhort and to urge."

Bishop Paull Spring, Northwestern Pennsylvania Synod, worried that *A Formula of Agreement* said "simply that Christ is fully present and received in the supper. Is this the best we can do? Or is it the least we can say? Our churches need to reflect further, with the help of the Spirit, and seek greater consensus on the doctrine of the supper before we agree to full communion among ourselves."

Many ELCA synod assemblies during the spring and summer took straw polls on *A Formula of Agreement*. A total of 22 favored it, and seven opposed it.

The three Reformed churches met in assemblies before the ELCA assembly. Each adopted *A Formula of Agreement* with resounding votes—and some human interest stories. After only 19 minutes of debate at the Presbyterian Church (U.S.A.) gathering, 92 percent favored forwarding the *Formula* to local presbyteries for ratification. Also, 7 percent voted "no," and 1 percent abstained. In a day-long hearing on the proposal, Aurelia Fule, a member of the dialogue, described the relationship between Lutherans and Reformed as being "like sisters raised in the same family who went in different directions." She said her father was Lutheran and her mother Reformed. "They had an agreement that they would baptize their sons Lutheran and their daughters Reformed."

Attending the Presbyterian Assembly in Syracuse, New York, was Bishop Lee Miller, Upstate New York Synod. After the vote "I suddenly found my heart in my throat and tears in my eyes," Miller recalled. "While I had fully expected it to pass, I was surprised with the emotion of the moment. I couldn't talk. Here was a group of Christians who said 'let's be in full communion with the Lutherans.' It was a wonderful day."

An overwhelming voice vote from 270 delegates at the Reformed Church in America Assembly adopted the *Formula* after less than two hours of debate. "This will be heard around the world," said Rev. Wesley Granberg-Michaelson, general secretary of the RCA. James Reid told RCA delegates that when he visits his father-in-law in Leona, Wisconsin, and attends an ELCA congregation, he'd "love to come to the table, not simply as a visitor, but as a brother." Nearly all of the 700 delegates at the UCC General Synod voted "yes" to the *Formula*. About 10 voted no. The three positive actions left the ultimate result of full communion up to the ELCA.

On August 28, 1997, at 10:02 A.M., by a vote of 839-193 (81.3 percent) the ELCA Churchwide Assembly adopted the Lutheran-Reformed *A Formula of Agreement*, marking the first time U.S. confessional churches took official steps to mend the divisions between them since the 16th century.

The decision came after two days of discussions that were basically irenic. Metropolitan New York Synod Bishop William Lazareth told the assembly that "maintaining the institutional unity of the church at the doctrinal expense of the proclamation of the body of Christ" may be "too high a price to pay." Lazareth said he had five areas of concern about the *Formula*: sacramental fidelity, confessional orthodoxy, congregational autonomy, pastoral exchangeability, and ecumenical coherence—the integration of various full communion declarations. He favored interim eucharistic hospitality with the Presbyterian Church (U.S.A.) and the Reformed Church in America but not with the United Church of Christ. He said his "descriptive not pejorative" concern with the UCC was that local congregations, associations, and conferences "are all doctrinally autonomous."

President Timothy Lull of Pacific Lutheran Seminary said he supported full communion with the Reformed bodies because the proposal is "based on a fine and thorough set of theological dialogues and conversations" over 35 years. "Some want the Reformed to prove that they 'really believe' what they say. Lutherans can go on and on, like the Energizer Bunny, but on behalf of our Reformed partners, it is now time to decide whether this is enough."

Youth voting member Meredith Lovell, of the Delaware-Maryland Synod, urged support for the proposal. "Youth will be ones who will implement this. Our eyes are upon you," she told the assembly.

Grand Canyon Synod Bishop Howard Wennes referred to rejections of previous Lutheran-Reformed proposals as similar to Lucy pulling the football away from Charlie Brown. "Lucy was the Lutheran," he said. "Let's not pull the ball away this time."

John Thomas, UCC ecumenical officer and later its president, deftly handled some controversial issues. "Our three Reformed churches don't agree on ordination of gay and lesbian people," he acknowledged. "We are dialoguing, probing each other and holding each other accountable. . . . The UCC ordains people who bring us gifts and whose absence would diminish us. We feel led to this decision by the Spirit and assume that those who disagree don't consider us faithless."

On October 4, 1998, more than a year after the favorable vote on the *Formula*, some 1,500 worshipers came together in Rockefeller Chapel, Chicago, for a service that Presiding Bishop H. George Anderson called "the celebration of a miracle milestone reached" that is "only the beginning of an unfolding relationship." Entering the gothic nave from four directions and pausing at a font to acknowledge the brokenness of their separation and their oneness in baptism, leaders of the three Reformed churches and the ELCA symbolized their churches' "full communion" by forming a single procession. Heads of each church distributed the Eucharist. James Echols, president of the Lutheran School of Theology at Chicago, set up a chant among the worshipers when he used the refrain in his sermon, "And the people of God said . . . Amen!"

ELCA Secretary Lowell Almen headed a small planning committee to develop guidelines to implement the exchangeability of clergy and to prepare materials that describe the nature of full communion. A month after the festive service, the Rev. Susan Schubert was the first ELCA pastor installed in a Reformed Church in America congregation. She served for a time Hope Community Church, Scottsdale, Arizona.

And the interchangeability was portable to the world scene. Cynthia Holder-Rich, a Presbyterian pastor, and her husband, Mark, an ELCA pastor, are teaching at the graduate seminary in Ivore, Madagascar. He teaches theology, she Christian education. Both are on call by the ELCA's Division for Global Mission.

Lutheran-Episcopal—Round 1

By the time the ELCA was formed, the merging churches had enjoyed six years of "interim Eucharistic sharing" with the Episcopal Church. The LCA, ALC, AELC and the Episcopal Church in 1982 recognized each other as true churches, agreed to interim sharing of the Eucharist under certain conditions, and looked ahead to the next step—interchangeability of clergy. The ELCA's internal division over full communion with the Episcopal Church, particularly from 1997 to 1999 which saw two Churchwide Assemblies consumed by passionate speeches on each side of the issue, was considered by some to be an embarrassment because of the predecessor churches' earlier ties with the Episcopal Church. The distinguishing characteristic in the Episcopal decision was that the issue was more structural or liturgical than theological, with some of the fallout continuing to the present.

The structural issue was the "historic episcopate." The concept, one of the four pillars of Episcopal self-understanding, is the passing of authority in an unbroken line from the church's early centuries to the present by bishops being consecrated by the laying-on-of-hands by bishops who are in the historic succession. The practice is seen as a sign, though not a guarantee, of the unity of the church.

The theological issue was whether the requirement that the ELCA take on the historic episcopate added another essential element to church unity. Lutherans in the United States had always considered the historic episcopate as *adiaphora* (non-essential). The pure preaching of the word and the sacraments rightly administered were the only essentials for Lutherans. Other practices, particularly structural, could in Christian freedom be adopted by Lutherans by choice. The ELCA could accept the episcopate as a practice permitted but not required by the Lutheran confessions.

The Episcopal requirement of ordination into the historic episcopate was seen by some ELCA theologians as turning a non-essential into an essential. Another structural issue was that some areas of the ELCA did not want a requirement that a bishop must preside over all ordinations in the company of other pastors. Opponents of the episcopate feared Episcopal Church intervention into other ELCA practices. Still another complication was that Lutherans in El Salvador, Finland, Namibia, Sweden, Tanzania, and Zimbabwe practice the historic episcopate, so it was not a practice foreign to world Lutheranism.

Even though dialogues between U.S. Lutherans and Episcopalians began in 1967, impetus toward full communion came in 1988 when the once-every-10-years Lambeth Conference of the Anglican communion affirmed full communion as the goal of Lutheran-Anglican dialogues. Two years later, in 1990, the U.S. Lutheran-Episcopal dialogue began drawing up a blueprint that became the basis for full communion. That December, Bishop Herbert W. Chilstrom and Episcopal Presiding Bishop Edmond L. Browning traveled to England and Scandinavia to dramatize to Lutheran and Anglican leaders there the increasing prospects among the two U.S. churches for full communion. Winging 12,000 miles in 15 days, Chilstrom and Browning heard details of continuing discussions between the Church of England in the British Isles, the Scandinavian nations (including Iceland), and Latvia and Estonia. Browning called the trip "a foretaste of the feast to come in the church."

Early in 1991, by a 12-3 vote, the Lutheran-Episcopal dialogue team adopted *Toward Full Communion* and a proposed *Concordat of Agreement*. All three "no" votes were cast by ELCA representatives. *Toward Full Communion* said, "Episcopalians need to understand that they do not lose the historic episcopate by acknowledging the existing ministry of the ELCA as a true, gospel ministry. Lutherans need to understand that they can revise their ordination rites for the future without any hint that the integrity of their present ministries is being challenged or that their continuity with their Reformation heritage is being broken." Specific requirements of full communion were:

1. Each church would always include three bishops of the other church and three of its own in the laying-on-of-hands when a bishop is consecrated/installed.

2. Episcopal ordination candidates would study the Augsburg Confession and Martin Luther's *Small Catechism*. ELCA candidates would study *The Book of Common Prayer* of the Episcopal Church.

3. The Episcopal Church would temporarily suspend, for the ELCA only, a rule that no one can function as bishop, priest, or deacon unless ordained by a bishop in the historic succession.

4. Episcopalians would endorse the Lutheran affirmation that the gospel is the "ultimate authority" under which bishops teach.

5. The ELCA would agree to ordain bishops for life, although bishops could continue to be elected to a stated term.

6. The ELCA would agree that only bishops would ordain clergy. (As was the case in the ALC and the LCA, likewise in the ELCA, the authority to ordain or authorize an ordination rested with the synodical bishop.)

Controversy erupted almost immediately, including a remark by Walter Sundberg, associate professor of church history at Luther Northwestern Seminary, who opposed the *Concordat*. "Going to bed with Episcopalians is like ecclesiastical necrophilia," Sundberg said, referring to membership losses in the ELCA and the Episcopal Church. Sundberg said that he made the statement "while shooting the breeze with a reporter" and was "mortified" when his remark appeared in print, even in *Newsweek*.

After three days of intense debate in March 1991, the ELCA Conference of Bishops voted 45-12 to ask the Office for Ecumenical Affairs and the Church Council to delay the full communion study until "there is agreement that the doctrine and practice" of the ELCA "are not compromised." The documents "present an alarming deviation," said Bishop Harold Jansen, Metropolitan Washington, D.C., Synod. "They circumscribe our future as a national church body. Our dream as a church will now be conditioned to a long-range relationship with the Episcopal Church. We are betrothed to them when we are just out of the womb ourselves."

Bishop William Lazareth, Metropolitan New York Synod, said, "My basic complaint is that Episcopalians need not officially subscribe to the Lutheran faith while Lutherans must adhere officially to Episcopal structure. Bishop Wayne Weissenbuehler, Rocky Mountain Synod, who signed the agreement as a member of the dialogue team, said, "I voted for them because I believe they have the potential for making two major communions into closer relationships so that the mission of the church and the gospel would be enhanced in the world. Not to sign them would have sent the wrong message to our Episcopal brothers and sisters." The bishops also were concerned over adoption of an historic episcopate that is not recognized by the Roman Catholic or Orthodox churches.

The 1991 Churchwide Assembly voted to postpone official study of the *Concordat* until 1993 when the ELCA's study on ministry was completed, with the possibility of a joint meeting of the two churches in 1997 to vote on the proposals.

A lull ensued for a couple of years until a survey taken in 1995 showed that two-thirds of the respondents replied "yes" to an ELCA questionnaire about full communion with the Episcopal Church. Also, 87 percent said Episcopal ordained ministries are authentic; 64 percent supported common future ordinations of ELCA and Episcopal clergy by bishops of both churches in the historic episcopate; and 63.8 percent supported exempting future Episcopal clergy from subscribing to the Augsburg Confession.

By 1996, local efforts to understand the Lutheran-Episcopal documents helped congregations gear up for ecumenism. Some congregations were already ahead of the curve. "We don't view ourselves as maverick," said Robert Walker, pastor of the Church of the Good Shepherd in Galax, Virginia, that had been an ELCA-Episcopal congregation since 1989. Both ELCA and Episcopal bishops installed Walker in 1991 as pastor Trinity Ecumenical Parish in Moneta, Virginia, which included the Trinity Lutheran, Trinity Episcopal, and Trinity Presbyterian congregations. At Berkeley Divinity School at Yale, a seminary of the Episcopal Church, a diploma program in Lutheran studies was begun. In Chicago, six-year-old Macrina Cooper-White was called a "Lutherpalian" by her parents. Her dad, Michael Cooper-White, was executive assistant to the ELCA presiding bishop, and her mother, Pamela Cooper-White was an Episcopal priest in Park Ridge, Illinois.

In October 1996, the 66 bishops of the ELCA and 165 Episcopal bishops gathered for an unprecedented six-day joint meeting in White Haven, Pennsylvania. Edward Jones, Episcopal bishop of Indianapolis, said, "We are here to speak the truth from our 'Wittenbergian' and 'Canterburian' hearts." Among those present—Archbishop of Canterbury, George Carey. Interestingly, within a few days he told Episcopal bishops that the *Concordat* may be in trouble.

Bishop Stanley Olson, Southwestern Minnesota Synod, said that about 12 ELCA bishops, chiefly in the Upper Midwest, thought the proposal was "in trouble" in their areas. He cited worries that the proposal elevated the episcopate to being necessary for a true church. Speakers on Lutheran and Anglican identity described episcopacy as a "gift." By the end of the gathering, Olson and most hesitant ELCA bishops felt they had been heard. The ELCA bishops recommended a dozen changes in the *Concordat*, and one ELCA bishop estimated that as many as 90 percent of ELCA bishops supported full communion.

There was some fallout from the meeting, including the beginning of organized opposition to the *Concordat*. Unhappy about the amount of support for the *Concordat*, Bishop Richard Foss, Eastern North Dakota Synod, circulated a questionnaire among the bishops to ask if *The Lutheran*'s report made it appear that more bishops favored the *Concordat* than was actually true. About 40 percent of the bishops told Foss that they favored the proposals and didn't expect to change their minds; 30 percent said they favored it but with reservations.

In November 1996, the Church Council transmitted the *Concordat* to the 1997 Churchwide Assembly for action. Some clarity had been brought to the *Concordat* from the bishops' suggestions, such as the document referring to "ordinations/ installations" of bishops. The Episcopal Church could continue its practice of ordaining, and Lutherans could continue to install, even though each church acknowledges that the same setting apart of a bishop is taking place. Clergy from one church would serve in the other church only by invitation of the host church. They would teach according to the host church's doctrines and would be governed by the host church's standards.

In a Church Council meeting, Pastor Stephen Youngdahl, Austin, Texas, asked the meaning of a phrase in the revised *Concordat* that describes the three-fold ministry of bishop, pastor and deacon "as the future pattern of the one ordained ministry of Word and Sacrament shared corporately within the two churches." William Nordgren, then ecumenical officer of the Episcopal Church, replied that the "three-fold ministry is singular," likening it to the three-in-one nature of the Trinity, "There is only one ordained ministry, but there are specialized ministries flowing out from it." Youngdahl replied, "It still sounds squishy to me."

The faculty of Lutheran Theological Seminary at Philadelphia endorsed the *Concordat*, noting that "a careful reading of Lutheranism reveals consistent support for the exercise of oversight in a renewed 'historic' episcopate based on the practice and intent of the early church to serve the gospel." Supporting the *Concordat*, the faculty of Lutheran Theological Seminary at Gettysburg said, "We see no reason for fear that our voluntary adoption of the historic episcopate will either demote previous Lutheran ministry or compromise subsequent ministries, whether ordained or lay, precisely because both our communions are committed above all to the gospel of justification and the freedom it bestows in strategically advancing the gospel's mission to the world." Lutheran Theological Southern Seminary, Columbia, South Carolina, and Trinity Lutheran Seminary, Columbus, Ohio, also endorsed the *Concordat*. The presidents of the ELCA's eight seminaries adopted a statement that stopped short of endorsing the proposals. Rather, they expressed "confidence in the ecumenical relationship these proposals seek to foster," acknowledging that "whatever the outcome of the voting, our church will be a new ecumenical stage." Joe Hootman, a senior at Luther Seminary, collected 50 signatures from seminarians opposed to the *Concordat*.

The dissension that was beginning to emerge at the joint Lutheran-Episcopal bishops gathering in the fall of 1996 was gaining momentum. Writing in *The Lutheran*, Foss said that the question regarding the Lutheran-Episcopal *Concordat* is "not whether to be ecumenical; it is how to be ecumenical in such a way that we can faithfully live out Jesus' Great Commission." But "I am persuaded that the *Concordat* would fundamentally shift the ELCA's 'center of gravity.' While no one can predict how far it would shift us, we would clearly be committing ourselves to move toward a "bishop-centered" understanding of the church. . . . I do not understand myself, or other bishops, to be necessary to the church's existence. . . . Clearly, we would be establishing the office of bishops as separate from, and superior to, the office of pastor. . . . We must ask our Episcopal partners: Can't we accept each other as we are?"

Bishop Paul Blom of the Texas-Louisiana Gulf Coast Synod pointed out in *The Lutheran* that those who are unhappy about "bishops for life" need to remember that Lutherans have "pastors for life." The *Concordat* does not call for any changes in "our order of lay ministers." As for the historic episcopate, "the Lutheran reformers in the 16th century intended to uphold the orders of ministry they had known in the Roman Catholic heritage that was theirs. The *Concordat* proposes that, in the future, Lutherans will reclaim their heritage by moving into historic succession. As for pastors of one tradition serving in the tradition of another, "each pastor must honor, respect and adhere to the teachings and practices of the congregation being served. . . . The interchange of pastors in the *Concordat* is a temporary arrangement, not a permanent one."

In March 1997, only four months before the Churchwide Assembly, the Conference of Bishops spent 90 minutes in frank exchange about the full communion proposals. "The Saint Paul Area Synod is deeply divided, especially on the Episcopal proposal," said Bishop Mark S. Hanson. "It's not just an intellectual argument but a visceral one, shaped by a certain piety and a cultural context that opposes hierarchy. Those in the Midwest need to find a way to say it is OK to oppose it." Bishop Richard

Jessen, Nebraska Synod, said, "Virtually every point of opposition I have seen is based on misinformation. Nebraska is Midwest too. Why is the Upper Midwest upset about what is factual?"

Foss replied, "My opposition is mild compared to lots of clergy in my synod. I hear you say that if I'd deal with facts rather than distortions, I'd favor the proposals. I don't know whether you meant to say that, but that's how you came across."

"If people are saying their objections haven't been heard, they don't realize that both documents have been changed precisely because they have been heard," said Bishop Steven Ullestad, Northeastern Iowa Synod. "When they say you can't trust what is written or that there is a hidden agenda, then something else is going on."

"The church is in an awkward situation because this debate has never been open to the whole church," said Bishop Peter Rogness, then of the Greater Milwaukee Synod. "If we speak our minds now, we seem to be fanning division. But we need for the church to know the bishops are all over the map on this."

"I came to our meeting with the Episcopal bishops with an enormous bias against this proposal," said Bishop Peter Strommen, Northeastern Minnesota Synod. "But I came to see that the church has a lot at stake in it and will probably vote for it even though I'm not excited about it. I just hope we never get into such a managed process again."

As synod assemblies met around the church in the spring and summer of 1997, many took straw votes. A total of 30 synods favored the Episcopal proposal, and 14 voted "no."

Meeting in Philadelphia nearly a month before the ELCA was to hold its assembly there, the Episcopal Church on July 18 gave overwhelming approval to the *Concordat of Agreement*. Both the Episcopal House of Bishops and House of Deputies (priests and laity) took the action amid hymns of praise and thanksgiving.

But opposition to the *Concordat* continued to brew in the ELCA, creating some strange bedfellows along the way. For example, 20 Lutheran theologians published a "position paper" in *Lutheran Forum*, including William H. Lazareth, Princeton, New Jersey, and L. David Brown, Minneapolis (both former synod bishops), and David W. Preus, Minneapolis, and Robert J. Marshall, Chicago (heads of two ELCA predecessor bodies). Albert H. Quie, former Minnesota governor and former U.S. Congressman, gathered signatures from 260 prominent Lutherans who opposed the *Concordat*. Meanwhile, 37 synod bishops sent a letter to each assembly voting member encouraging a "yes" vote on the *Concordat*.

When the ELCA Assembly opened in Philadelphia, ELCA Presiding Bishop H. George Anderson told the voting members that he had a "duty to tell you where I stand." Dealing with the historic episcopate "is the most difficult question for me. But as I read Martin Luther and looked at contemporary Lutheran churches that have had the historic episcopacy for centuries, I discovered that there's nothing automatic or inevitable about the link between episcopacy and hierarchy." Referring to the Augsburg Confession's assertion that the only thing necessary for the unity of the church is agreement in teaching the gospel and the administration of the sacraments, Anderson said he didn't "see our acceptance of the historic episcopate as anti-confessional. We're accepting it as a gift without thereby making it a condition for unity with anyone else."

During four days of debate, three hearings were held on the *Concordat*, along with a pro and con presentation and hours of discussion during plenary sessions. At one point, 69 voting members were lined up at microphones to speak.

Outlining reasons not to adopt the *Concordat*, Michael Rogness, a member of the Luther Seminary faculty, St. Paul, Minnesota, told the assembly that "the goal of ecumenism has never been to become like me. . . . With the *Concordat*, we become Episcopalians, and they remain Episcopalian." Rogness acknowledged that "the *Concordat* doesn't require us to change our [three-fold] ministry decisions, but it moves us in that direction." He also said the *Concordat* will "separate and elevate" the office of bishop over pastors.

Speaking in favor of the *Concordat*, Walter Bouman, Trinity Lutheran Seminary, Columbus, Ohio, said that in the dialogues,

"Each of us began to see matters from the other's point of view—we need to see bishops in the historic episcopate, and they need to acknowledge the validity of our ministry now. The historic episcopate can be the outcome, not the starting point, of our work." Responding in a hearing to charges that the *Concordat* was ambiguous in parts, Bouman, a drafter of the document, acknowledged that "if we had it to do over again, we would write some things differently." The remark was repeated often by *Concordat* opponents.

"I have taught that Lutheranism is defined by our confession of faith, not by polity," said David Weeks, Southwestern Minnesota Synod. "The *Concordat* adds the historic episcopate as a necessary mark of our church. To do so is to go against Luther."

Ken Grant, North/West Lower Michigan Synod, disagreed, saying the episcopate is consistent with Lutheran tradition because it is a matter of good order, not of justification.

Saying that he was speaking with a knot in his stomach, Bishop Mark S. Hanson, Saint Paul Area Synod, and later presiding bishop of the ELCA, said he had been taught "since childhood to be suspicious of authority," but that he supports full communion because the "historic episcopate is a sign of unity."

Gary Philpy, Indiana-Kentucky Synod, said, "I have lived 23 of my 46 years as an Episcopalian. If you ask Episcopalians about the historic episcopate, you will get a blank stare. It is not part of their daily life, and it will not enter our daily life."

Pastor Brad Jenson, Northeastern Minnesota Synod, told the voting members, "I've been to three churchwide assemblies, but I've never seen a house so divided. Is it necessary to divide the church to advance ecumenism?" Jenson was one of the editors of the *Concordat Examiner* that was circulated by opponents on three occasions outside the plenary hall.

Finally, the moment came for decision. Using electronic balloting, the 1,035 voting members appeared stunned into silence when the vote flashed on the electronic screen at 10:04 A.M. on August 18, 1997: 684 "yes" (66.1 percent) and 351 "no" (33.9 percent), six votes short of the required two-thirds majority.

Not only had Lutherans turned down a wider relationship after having a more limited arrangement for 15 years, Lutherans who consider church structure to be nonessential spurned the Episcopalians largely because of fears about structure. The reversal was unprecedented in the ecumenical efforts of any of the ELCA's predecessor churches, and cast a question about the seriousness which other ecumenical partners might regard the ELCA's word.

After the vote, Anderson said he was "shocked at this narrowest of margins. I expected a more decisive vote. But we need to respect the narrow margin. We set the standard and we did not achieve it." (The two-thirds vote was used because necessary changes to the ELCA Constitution as a result of adopting full communion would need two-thirds approval).

Presiding Bishop Edmond Browning of the Episcopal Church said in a statement after the vote that "an opportunity was created, and I regret that we have missed it."

Bouman said, "Unless people of the Upper Midwest rejoice in perverse anti-institutionalism, I cannot imagine they understood the magnitude of their action."

Albert Quie acknowledged after the vote that "the majority said they would accept the historic episcopate. I would let our new bishops decide for themselves whether to take on the historic episcopate and let our church grow into it." When asked if this meant that his side that day won the battle and lost the war, he said, "Yes."

Even when the ELCA bishops met before the assembly, they talked mostly about dealing with any backlash over the passage of the proposal. After the Episcopal vote, the ELCA bishops' luncheon was full of soul-searching and deep disappointment. "I have never seen among the bishops as much sorrow, anger and outward emotional response as I did after the *Concordat* was defeated," said Bishop Kenneth Olsen, Metropolitan Chicago Synod. In reality, the opposition was more organized to defeat the *Concordat* than the ELCA ecumenical affairs leadership was prepared to promote its adoption. Neither the Episcopal representatives nor the ELCA staff was able to be sufficiently reassuring to worried voters or to diffuse controversy.

Just 29 hours after the vote, the assembly resoundingly re-committed the ELCA to seeking full communion with the Episcopalians in two years. David Perry, then the Episcopal ecumenical officer, responded, "When I meet with our presiding bishop tonight for dinner, this action will be at the top of our feast." He quipped that "the world's largest roller coaster" is in Philadelphia, a reference that Episcopalians had adopted the *Concordat* there but Lutherans didn't.

To deal with obvious divisions with the ELCA, the assembly committed the church to consult with Episcopalians in finding ways for faculties of ELCA colleges and seminaries, clergy, laity, and congregations to discuss the history, theology, and churchly nature of both churches. A second motion told the Episcopal Church that the ELCA was committed to considering a revised full communion proposal at its next assembly. The first motion was adopted 930-72, the second motion was adopted 995-15. Each was followed by a standing ovation. Quie had helped draft both motions. Nonetheless, he continued to oppose full communion to the very end.

When the motions were adopted, Anderson turned to the Episcopal representatives on the platform and said, "[You have heard] the urgent and heartfelt desire of our church to enter into full communion with your church. We ask for time to set ourselves in order and to find ways to join you in what you have already committed yourselves to, and to which we aspire."

After the assembly, various attempts were made across the church to heal the wounds. Lutheran and Episcopal bishops in the territories of the Metropolitan Washington, D.C., Synod, the Virginia Synod, and the Lower Susquehanna and Upper Susquehanna synods sent joint letters to their congregations. Members of the Episcopal-Lutheran Dialogue of Kentucky pledged daily prayer for both churches. Four Episcopal infants and one Lutheran were baptized in a joint service at Gloria Dei Lutheran Church, Bristol, Connecticut.

Lutheran–Episcopal–Round 2

Following the directive of the Churchwide Assembly and the advice of the Conference of Bishops and the Church's Council's Executive Committee, Anderson in December 1999 appointed a three-person writing team to develop a "revised and rewritten" proposal for full communion with the Episcopal Church. In addition, a 10-member panel of advisors was named. The Church Council directed that the groups "reflect the diversity of opinion on this matter in this church."

Anderson's selection of Martin E. Marty to head the writing team was seen as bringing a fresh perspective to the drafting. A well-known church historian and highly articulate spokesperson, he had not been active in the process up to this point. The points of view of the other two members of the drafting team, Michael Root (pro full-communion), a layperson on the faculty of Trinity Lutheran Seminary, Columbus, Ohio, and Dr. Todd Nichol (anti full-communion), Luther Seminary, St. Paul, Minnesota, were well-known. The team was as reflective of the 66.1 percent vote as possible, but critics of full communion said the decks were stacked against them and that Nichol was put in an impossible position. The Episcopal Church provided three drafters.

Marty's selection was seen as a coup for Anderson. Marty had not been active in any of the previous debates, and was not known as partisan on the issue. "I've never spent a moment writing a denominational document." Marty told a *Chicago Tribune* reporter. "You're not going to find many people who are more bored than I by ecumenical negotiations and official documents." Just a few weeks shy of retirement and leaving a professorship at the University of Chicago Divinity School, he took on what the reporter called "the difficult, unglamorous, and, frankly, unpromising task" of reviving the *Concordat*. Why did he agree to do it? "The bishop asked me," Marty said. Anderson had telephoned Marty and made the request. Marty did not hesitate.

Directions to the drafting team were that the new document should use "clear, down-to-earth language and include a rationale for its conclusions and recommendations." Anderson said he assumed the new proposal would include the historic episcopate.

"To go to the Episcopalians without it means it's dead on arrival because they see it as part of being in full communion," he said. That perception, though accurate, was referenced many times in the next two years by critics who said Anderson predetermined the outcome of the final draft.

Before a revised proposal could be produced, ELCA bishops in March 1998 expressed concern that debate over the proposal was already being drawn along the same lines as the 1997 vote. "We need to say something about the tone of the debate," said Bishop Mark S. Hanson, then of the Saint Paul Area Synod. "We need to get the church to see this as a new moment."

Asked if the three drafters of the revised proposal would be asked to sign it, Anderson said they "probably would not be asked." To which Bishop Rick Foss, Eastern North Dakota Synod, pleaded that the church be informed "if there is a split decision among the drafters." Anderson replied that he doesn't "keep things secret."

Daniel Martensen, director of the ecumenical affairs department, said he was often asked how the Episcopal Church reacted to the rejection of full communion. "They are patient, puzzled and gracious," Martensen replied. He added that the drafting team's Episcopal members are "present and conversing with us, but they don't sign on. It's our text, not theirs."

Bishop Stanley Olson, then of the Southwestern Minnesota Synod, asked if the 1999 Churchwide Assembly could amend the final proposal. "We can vote on it as we see fit," Anderson answered, "but we need to think carefully about amending it because of our partners. That could become a quagmire."

The revised text, titled *Called to Common Mission: A Lutheran Proposal for a Revision of the Concordat of Agreement,* produced five major changes, two of which focused on how the ELCA would receive the historic episcopate:

1. Inviting two Lutheran bishops from churches with the episcopate (Sweden, Finland, El Salvador, Tanzania, Zimbabwe, and Namibia), along with an Episcopal bishop, to future installations/ordinations of new ELCA bishops was intended

to symbolize that the ELCA is not "becoming Episcopalian" but accepting a practice that is already common among some Lutherans.

2.   The two denominations will continue to hold differing positions about the necessity of the episcopate, even when they are in full communion: "The Episcopal Church remains free to maintain its conviction that sharing in the historic episcopate, while not necessary to the being of a church, is essential to full communion; the ELCA remains free to maintain that the historic episcopate is not necessary for full communion." The revision also "endorses the Lutheran affirmation that the historic catholic episcopate under the Word of God must always serve the gospel, and that the ultimate authority under which bishops preach and teach is the gospel itself."

3.   Earlier language about the threefold ministry of bishops, pastors and deacons as the "future pattern" for ministry was eliminated. The proposal said only that "bishops in historic succession" are the future pattern. Only bishops would ordain, although pastors would assist. "Any distinction between episcopal and pastoral offices is not by divine right. Such offices are to be exercised as servant ministry, not for domination or arbitrary control," said *Called to Common Mission.*

4.   ". . . even though tenure in the office of presiding bishop and synodical bishops may be terminated by retirement, resignation, or conclusion of a term," those "installed in such offices can be called upon to carry out functions of bishops when requested, subject to regulation."

5.   The priesthood of all believers and the ministry of the laity were emphasized. "We together affirm that all members of Christ's Church are commissioned for ministry through baptism; all are called to represent Christ and his Church and to carry on Christ's work of reconciliation in the world."

Four commentaries were distributed, three by Marty and Root. The fourth was a "minority view" from Nichol, who did not recommend acceptance of the draft. Nichol said "some Lutherans couldn't support the drafting team's work because: instructions to the drafting team limited its work by saying that that the revised statement must include agreement on the historic episcopate, and 2) Lutherans who hold that right preaching of the gospel and administration of the sacraments are sufficient for the unity of the church "will object to conditions in practice asked by either church by the other." *Called to Common Mission* (or *CCM*, as it came to be known) was distributed to the bishops and the Church Council for review.

In October 1998, the Conference of Bishops raised the possibility of inserting a "conscience clause" in *CCM* that would allow the present ELCA constitutional exception that allows bishops to authorize others to ordain pastors. "People object to the image of a church saying that you can't have a pastor without having bishop," Bishop Peter Rogness, then of the Greater Milwaukee Synod, said, a member of the panel that advised the *CCM* drafting team.

"Can we urge the panel to draft language that builds unity?" asked Bishop Mark S. Hanson, then of the Saint Paul Area Synod, "something that can be heard as a conscience clause?" After the 1999 assembly approved *CCM* (without a conscience clause), the 2001 assembly approved an exception; it was the same assembly that elected Hanson presiding bishop.

Charges of mistrust flared during the Church Council's decision to forward *CCM* to the 1999 Churchwide Assembly in Denver. A show-of-hands vote among the 37-member council showed three "no" votes about forwarding the document to the assembly—the Rev. Susan Engh, Wayzata, Minnesota; the Rev. David K. Johnson, Fargo, North Dakota; and Linda Brown, Moorhead, Minnesota. The same three abstained in an earlier vote on whether to send the document to synods and congregations for study.

Martin E. Marty, chair of the drafting team, told the council, "Martin Luther would have kept the historic episcopate with all the rights attendant to it if the [Roman Catholic] bishops had not been corrupt. The confessions say that for the love and unity, we'd like to keep doing this." Marty added, "We are making this proposal for the witness to the world to do the will of God, to celebrate the central act—we share baptism but communion is broken. Functionally, in a nation where we are going to need each other's ministries, this sharing becomes evermore important."

Johnson told the council, "[The earlier *Concordat*] failed because of the inclusion of the historic episcopate. When the advisory panel and drafters did their work, they did the best they could within the guidelines that said the historic episcopate could not be re-discussed. . . . That's where the lack of trust is. The new [proposal] is like moving furniture around but the main issue is not addressed. That issue is creating more heat, more anger than before."

Engh said, "I never thought about our Episcopal friends as bad guys. Unfortunately the pain now is that I have more regard for them than I do for some in the ELCA because the [Episcopalians] have been honest with us and I do not always feel our people have been honest with us, especially about answering our questions." At a later Church Council meeting, Engh's motion that equal time and representation for pro and con expressions be given at synod assemblies and other gatherings of Churchwide Assembly voting members failed 26-5.

The council received a petition signed by more than 2,500 people from 25 states and 35 synods asking that a new agreement be drafted without the historic episcopate. The petition, spearheaded by three pastors in Washington, was not part of the council's discussion.

Before *Called to Common Mission* could be sent to the congregations, or the Conference of Bishops could discuss it, almost 200 Lutherans gathered in February 1999 at St. Andrew Lutheran Church, Mahtomedi, Minnesota, to declare that even though full communion with the Episcopal Church is desirable, *CCM* was not the way to accomplish it. Once again, the sticking point that would not go away was the historic episcopate.

The group drafted a sample resolution for congregations and synod assemblies to send the Churchwide Assembly six months later. The resolution asked rejection of *CCM* while reaffirming a "commitment to continue to work together with our Episcopal neighbors in common faith and mission, gathering at the Lord's Table and sharing in each other's ministry. We acknowledge the ordination of Episcopal clergy, and welcome them to serve in ELCA parishes or pastoral positions, preaching and teaching in a manner that is consistent with the ELCA's 'Confession of Faith.'"

Roger Eigenfeld, pastor of St. Andrew's Lutheran Church, Mahtomedi, Minnesota, said the ELCA had been flooded with materials about why *CCM* should be approved, but "you won't hear both sides of the issue here." The resolution came to be known as the "Mahtomedi Resolution" and enlisted some big-name supporters. The group also was the nascent beginning of a movement known as "WordAlone." The movement used its Web site to circulate a large number of anti-*CCM* documents, some of which were demeaning of church leadership.

"I'm disappointed—first with the *Concordat* and now with the revision—that they make it necessary for us to adopt the historic episcopate," Robert J. Marshall, former LCA president, told the Mahtomedi gathering. Lutherans and Episcopalians agree on "apostolic succession," he pointed out, as an ongoing faithful proclamation of Christ. But Episcopalians insist that the relationship have the "historic episcopate." Marshall said the historic episcopate is neither good nor useful to the church and not in the best interests of ecumenism because one church would have to become like the other.

"The Episcopal refusal to accept us 'as we are' is at the center of our disagreement," said David Preus, former ALC presiding bishop. Preus added that the historic episcopate isn't bad, but that Lutherans wouldn't be considering it if it weren't required for full communion.

"Always keep in mind that this isn't an ecumenical issue but a ministry issue," said Michael Rogness of Luther Seminary. A group of 19 people, mostly Reformation scholars, asked

Presiding Bishop H. George Anderson and the ELCA Church Council to reject *CCM* because of its content and concerns about how it developed. The letter said "the majority of Lutherans feel . . . they are hearing only the voice that favors adoption of *CCM*."

A month later, the Conference of Bishops sidestepped support for *CCM*, fearing that a resolution supporting *CCM* would be too divisive. The proposal, put forward by Bishop Paull Spring, then of the Northwestern Pennsylvania Synod, would have urged the assembly to cast a "strong, positive vote in favor of the adoption of *CCM*." "It's time for us to speak," Spring told the bishops. "It's important for the church to know where we are on this."

Bishop Rick Foss, Eastern North Dakota Synod, said, "If you want to anger the opposition, this will be a great way to do so. This is one of the most foolish things we can do."

After voting to table the resolution, the bishops endorsed a statement for use at synod assemblies that described their understandings of various elements of *CCM*, such as its omission of any reference to the threefold pattern of ministry and that bishops would not be elected for life.

The bishops also reflected on the human toll of the *CCM* discussions. Bishop Robert Isaksen, then of the New England Synod, said he expected *CCM* to pass, even though some people are saying awful, undeserved things" about Anderson, Almen and Martensen. Bishop David Olson, Minneapolis Area Synod, said he felt more than two-thirds of the bishops favored *CCM*, but predicted that "we will have a deeply divided church by the end of this spring's synod assemblies."

Anderson said he "believed God is calling us to enter into this relationship," He confessed he is "baffled by the debate over Article 7 of the Augsburg Confession, because in all Lutheran unity efforts since 1821, once fundamental doctrinal agreement was reached, structure has always been changed."

Writing in *The Lutheran*, Richard Jeske, Lutheran-Episcopal Coordinating Committee co-chair, said, "The ministry of the bishop is a sign that each congregation is connected to the greater church. The pastoral ministry of bishops is observed in moments where the faith of the whole church is expressed, such as at ordinations and installations of clergy, at baptisms and confirmations. The office of bishop serves the unity of the whole church, not only today's church but the church throughout the ages."

Writing in *The Lutheran* in favor of the Mahtomedi Resolution was Tony K. S. Stoutenburg, pastor of Chinook and Naselle Lutheran Churches in Chinook and Naselle, Washington. "Since neither the Bible nor the Lutheran Confessions speak of the historic episcopate, many Lutherans don't believe it should be required for unity. . . . Lutherans hold that the office of pastor is created by God's gift of Word and sacraments to the church. . . . Ordination is made valid by the church's call and a candidate's vow to carry out God's ministry, not by the person officiating."

As time moved toward synod assemblies, four seminary faculties—Southern, Philadelphia, Wartburg, and Trinity—and the bishops of Regions 7, 8, and 9 (the Northeast and the South) endorsed *CCM*. Four of six bishops in Region 6 signed a similar statement. The Northwestern and Southern Ohio synodical bishops in Region 6 did not sign. Actions taken at synod assemblies favored *CCM* but were mixed: 33 synods affirmed *CCM* or defeated the Mahtomedi Resolution; 19 passed the Mahtomedi Resolution or defeated affirmation of *CCM*. Heaviest support for *CCM* was solidly in the East, from New England to the Central States Synod to Oregon. Mahtomedi support came from the Upper Midwest and Pacific Northwest and parts of the Pacific Southwest. In the meantime, Mahtomedi backers met for a second time, reaffirming their intent to defeat *CCM*. Conferees discussed ways to mobilize undecided voting members through newsletters and a publicity campaign to counter the pro-*CCM* material produced by the church, and strategies for handling the vote on the assembly floor, such as making sure speakers are well-versed in rules of order.

During 1998 and early 1999, the Web site of WordAlone, named for its reference to Luther's insistence on the "Word alone" as the sole determiner of truth, became increasingly strident.

When there were accusations that Todd Nichol's dissenting opinion was not allowed to be sent to the Church Council, the WordAlone Web site trumpeted, "Free Todd Nichol. Read his dissent." Showing an illustration of Nichol in a convict uniform, the site said, "Click on Todd's leg irons and read his dissent." The charge was curious, as the summary of his dissent had already been published in *The Lutheran*.

The Web site also had a "Take the bishops or Jesus quiz," saying, "Below are seven statements that begin with 'I am . . . ' Some are taken from statements by Jesus while others are from statements made by bishops. . . . We have to decide whether the source of authority for everything we do is the living voice of Christ . . . or whether his authority is inadequate and needs to be supplemented by bishops in historic succession."

When the assembly opened in Denver, Anderson acknowledged his "fear of boiling frustrations and of misunderstood motives" among voting members. But he also called on voting members "to plunge into that wider sea" of ecumenical involvement by establishing full communion with the Episcopal Church (and the Moravian Church, also on the same agenda—see a later section in this chapter, beginning on page 149).

Three days of intense debate in plenary sessions and hearings, along with dozens of microphone speeches, occupied voting members' energies. At one point during debates, 38 speakers were lined up at microphones. By the time that plenary session ended 65 minutes later, 48 speakers were still there.

Martin E. Marty, chair of the *CCM* drafting team, told voting members that "the really distinctive feature is that this is the first time a church is bridging polity among denominations." He said the ELCA "has the enviable opportunity . . . to exemplify at the same time more Christian unity and Christian diversity." The unity would be evident in gathering around the bread and wine, and the diversity would be shown in "an unmatched variety of ways to arrange and order our own ministry."

Greeting the assembly, Episcopal Bishop C. Christopher Epting of Iowa said he was told that this "debate is not with Episcopalians but among Lutherans in which we have been invited to participate." He noted that the church's 1997 decision for full communion with the Reformed churches "clearly demonstrates your freedom in the gospel to take that step—and now, in that same freedom—to embrace, in an evangelical way, the catholic sign of the historic succession."

Pastor Norman Wahl, Rochester, Minnesota, said, "My heart is troubled. How ironic that we have stumbled into the divisiveness over an issue that was intended to enhance Christian unity. While churches with the historic episcopate believe people must be ordained in a certain way, Lutherans have never believed that ministry flowed out of certain hands. We don't need to adopt the polity of other churches to claim oneness in Christ."

Pastor Nancy Curtis, then of New Haven, Indiana, said she discussed the proposal with her congregation, and they decided that no changes would come to their worship life, and that the only addition would be a bishop in the historic episcopate at ordination services.

Timothy Lull, president of Pacific Lutheran Theological Seminary, Berkeley, California, said, "One hundred years ago no one would have expected Lutherans to lead the way in ecumenism. Now we write the final chapter [of the century]. How will it end? With a wonderful big bang into a new relationship or with a whimpering and whining that has been the dark side of Lutheranism for 400 years?

"I cannot vote yes" said David Morker, Northwestern Minnesota Synod, "because there are too many have-to's in CCM. The spirit of the Moravian document is gospel. The spirit of CCM is law."

Bishop Juan Cobrda, Slovak Zion Synod, brought relief to the discussion when he said, "I have twice received the historic episcopate. It did not change my life. Just ask my wife."

When Pastor Tom Prinz, Metropolitan Washington, D.C., Synod, asked if Episcopalians saw their bishops as hierarchical, David Perry, then the Episcopal ecumenical officer, said, "I know some bishops who are 'turkeys,' but the bottom line is that we all have leaders with different styles. My experiences with our bishops is that they are servant leaders."

The question was one of several that were planted by *CCM* proponents around the assembly floor. Although opponents said they had the votes to defeat *CCM* when the assembly opened, those favoring *CCM* were much more savvy about floor-management than during the 1997 debates when the opponents seemed to have the upper hand in getting their views to the floor. Part of the 1999 strategy was voting members asking strategic questions that Episcopal representatives on the podium were primed to answer. Another tactic was that of voting members asking the assembly for permission to yield their time to hear from ecumenical guests. John Thomas, president of the United Church of Christ, said, "In full communion, your future is our future. If it's possible for you to move with integrity to bring evangelical and catholic views together, you help solve one of the vexing issues in ecumenism. Our church is also addressing the historic episcopate. In a sense, you have anticipated what we do. Maybe Lutheran fools rush in where Reformed angels fear to tread."

Lutheran World Federation General Secretary Ishmael Noko, also invited to speak when a voting member relinquished his time, said, "I come to you from a Lutheran church (Zimbabwe) that has the historic episcopate." He said Lutherans worldwide "are watching what you do" because "65 synods here have established a partnership with other Lutherans around the globe. I had planned to send a letter of greeting to you. But I realized that I had to come here because of the tremendous interest from your sister churches."

Although floor debate was civil, tensions rose in the hearings. One panelist, Cynthia Jurisson, a church history professor at the Lutheran School of Theology at Chicago, was repeatedly called to task by ELCA bishops, Episcopal representatives and Marty, chair of the drafting team, for what they called misrepresentations of *CCM* or Episcopal Church practice. "That's not true," Marty said, jumping to his feet after Jurisson's claim in a hearing that *CCM* makes the ministry of bishops central to the church.

When it was finally time to vote, prayer was offered. And then the months of uncertainty were over when a big screen above the assembly flashed the vote 716-317, meaning a 69.3 percent approval for full communion between the ELCA and the Episcopal Church. It was 27 more votes than the required two-thirds majority. Voting members rose in applause, ELCA and Episcopal officials exchanged hugs, and people sung "If You But Trust in God to Guide You."

"This is a big step, but we're not dancing yet," Anderson told a news conference. "This is a Lutheran proposal to which the Episcopal Church will react in convention next year. But we live in hope."

After the Denver vote, Bishop Rick Foss, Eastern North Dakota Synod, who had said earlier that passage of *CCM* "would be a miracle," allowed that "it probably was a miracle. I still don't think it would get a two-thirds vote in the pews. Now the question is how to walk this path most faithfully. If I can do anything to make this a blessing, I will do it."

News of the vote was received with "joy and thanksgiving" by Episcopal Presiding Bishop Frank T. Griswold, who said, "I pray that our response can be positive" next year. It was— the House of Bishops adopted *CCM* by a hand vote of about 185-15, and the House of Deputies (lay and clergy) approved it by about 90 percent.

"God has opened a magnificent door. . . . A grand panorama of mission stretches before us," ELCA Secretary Lowell Almen told the House of Deputies after their vote. "It would be fair," Almen continued, "to characterize this as a historic step within the church throughout the world. God is doing a new thing. Where this will lead and what will happen we've yet to discover. But it is God's future, and we're optimistic." To symbolize *CCM*, Almen bought matching stoles for himself and David Perry, then the Episcopal Church's ecumenical officer.

Not every Episcopalian was so sanguine. "I have heard real hostility," said Bishop Andrew Fairfield of North Dakota. "At issue is the historic episcopate, which most Lutherans in North

Dakota view not as a gift but a threat . . . to the way they prac-tice their Christianity. They have come to see other Lutherans [who back *CCM*] as less than truthful about the implications of the historic episcopate. So they are suspicious. They see us as small and inappropriately arrogant and domineering."

Presiding Bishop Griswold took another approach. "*CCM* invites us to yield some sense of the uniqueness of our tradition to make adjustments for the sake of unity," he told the convention.

The accord formally went into effect on January 1, 2001. The soaring arches of the National Cathedral in Washington, D.C., thundered with the singing of 3,500 voices as the ELCA and the Episcopal Church celebrated. Processions into the cathe-dral included representatives from all 65 ELCA synods and nearly three-quarters of the 100 U.S. Episcopal dioceses. "We join together in Jesus' name to share in his sacraments, in his ministry and in his mission as one body in the power of the Spirit," said Anderson, as he presided at the liturgy. Before the service, the St. Olaf College Choir from Northfield, Minnesota, presented a prelude concert.

The results of the *CCM* vote did not end the debate within the church. The same issue of *The Lutheran* that reported *CCM*'s adoption included a letter to the editor from two pastors, Kathleen Lenore Anderson and Robert James Lewis of Holy Trinity Lutheran Church, Rockville Centre, New York. The letter said: "Regarding the vote in which full communion with the Episcopal Church was accepted contingent upon the ELCA accepting the historic episcopate as interpreted and claimed by the Episcopal Church, we, the undersigned, hold this vote as not binding upon ourselves, our consciences and our ministry."

In September 1999, barely a month after *CCM*'s adoption, Anderson discovered how difficult bridge-building could be when he attended forums with *CCM* opponents in Rochester and St. Paul, Minnesota. Speakers were angry that convictions they considered central to being Lutheran were betrayed by church leaders, including Anderson. Some accused Anderson of slanting the church's discussion of *CCM* against them.

Sharpest words came from Gracia Grindal, professor of rhetoric at Luther Seminary, St. Paul, Minnesota. In a strongly worded letter circulated widely on the Internet, she accused Anderson, the ELCA Department for Ecumenical Affairs and *The Lutheran* of partisanship and manipulative bias against *CCM* opponents. "We cannot submit to a practice which we, as Lutherans, believe to be contrary to the most fundamental Reformation principle of Word alone," she wrote. "Expressing your sorrow about our division, and hoping to get us to overlook what has been done, and adopt a structure in which we do not believe, simply for the sake of unity, will not work. It is like having the one who killed our mother wanting to be our grief counselor, and now wanting us to comfort him for having betrayed us."

The Minnesota meetings were "tough," Anderson told the bishops. "These are really good people, and they are really mad. We must find a way to address their underlying concerns." Anderson said people were saying "yes" or "no" to *CCM* before the vote. Now he said he heard four responses: "Yes, let's get with it"; "OK, we'll be fine, even though I didn't vote for it"; "I'm still worried, but I'll wait and see"; and "No, this is a very bad thing to do." Some people told Anderson not to talk about healing because "we're not sick."

"[Worry about the] general direction is the heart of the matter," said Peter Rogness, then bishop of the Greater Milwaukee Synod and elected in 2002 as bishop of the Saint Paul Area Synod. "People wonder what [*CCM*] means about who we are shaping ourselves to be."

Bishop Mark S. Hanson, then of the Saint Paul Area Synod, whose synod relates to Luther Seminary, St. Paul, Minnesota, said seminarians "need a signal that their conscientious objection to *CCM* won't jeopardize their certification [for rostered service]." Anderson said he would do all he could to help the seminarians.

Bishop Rick Foss, Eastern North Dakota Synod, told his colleagues, "People want to go forward, but to a lot of them this isn't going forward but backward. Asking those opposed to help with *CCM* implementation "feels like aiding and abetting something that is wrong."

Two months after *CCM's* approval, 2,200 clergy and lay-persons who opposed *CCM* came together in 45 regional meetings to find strategies to address their continuing concerns. In November 1999, 400 delegates from those meetings, coming from 21 states, gathered at the WordAlone National Gathering at Roseville Lutheran Church, Roseville, Minnesota. They discussed forming a "parallel" organization with its own roster of anti-*CCM* pastors and congregations, electing bishops who will refuse to comply with *CCM*, cutting off or redirecting benevolence, supporting seminarians who fear that their opposition to *CCM* may damage their careers, forming a nongeographic confessing synod, joining or forming a different Lutheran church body, or withdrawing their congregations from the ELCA. Also that month, the ELCA Church Council members pledged "to listen and support efforts to bring understanding and reconciliation within this church." About the same time, 12 faculty members at Luther Seminary issued a statement supporting *CCM*.

In December 1999, Roger Eigenfeld, pastor of St. Andrew's Lutheran Church, Mahtomedi, Minnesota, and steering committee leader for the WordAlone Network, met privately with Anderson. The network pledged to "actively resist and never comply with the demands of *CCM*." Eigenfeld said 85 percent of those in the network want to stay in the ELCA, but the organization must work on two tracks—to prepare to leave the ELCA even as it tries to stay, and to change *CCM's* requirement that the denomination adopt the historic episcopate. Anderson said he was pleased to meet with Eigenfeld and to "communicate the right to disagree theologically and practically" in the ELCA.

In early 2000, a letter signed by Gerhard Forde and James Nestingen, faculty at Luther Seminary, St. Paul, Minnesota, was sent to every ELCA congregation, seminary, Church Council member, synodical bishop and churchwide unit director asking for opposition to *CCM*. The cost of mailing the letter was borne by two Minnesota congregations. The letter-writers said *CCM* precipitated "a grave confessional crisis" because it strays from traditional Lutheran beliefs.

A select group of 18 pastors, lay leaders, bishops, and church-wide staff, organized primarily by Bishop Mark S. Hanson, then of the Saint Paul Area Synod, issued a "Common Ground Resolution" that made suggestions of "a possible path" to implementing the full communion proposal that could help opponents remain in the ELCA. "We believe voting members of the 1999 Churchwide Assembly did not anticipate the depth and extent of opposition that appears to exist," the statement said. It called for the Church Council to delay implementation of *CCM* until after the 2001 Churchwide Assembly to allow for certain constitutional changes, for pastors to be fully recognized even if their ordinations were irregular because a bishop was not present, or for a bishop's installation to be fully recognized even if it was constitutionally irregular because of the absence of three bishops in the historic episcopate. The resolution also suggested the possibility of a nongeographic synod within the ELCA that "may be out of conformity with certain provisions of full communion agreements."

The Conference of Bishops replied to "Common Ground" by affirming *CCM*'s adoption and invited an "exploration of possible ways" to allow a synodical bishop "in unusual circumstances" to authorize an ELCA pastor to preside at an ordination.

Michael Root, one of the drafters of *CCM*, advised against the compromise, saying that giving ordinands the right to choose whether the bishop presides over their ordination abandons the idea that it is the church's ordination. He suggested an "amicable parting of the ways" if *CCM* opponents cannot live with the Churchwide Assembly's decision.

The WordAlone Network constituted itself as a renewal movement within the ELCA in March 2000 at Mahtomedi, Minnesota, with more than 1,000 people attending. The network said it sought to "reclaim" the Lutheran confessions and uphold the priesthood of all believers," said Roger Eigenfeld, the network's president. "The churchwide office says, 'Just go away and be quiet,'" Eigenfeld said. "We aren't going to go away. . . .

This is our church. It was stolen from us August 19 [1999, the day the Churchwide Assembly approved *CCM*]. We're going to work to defeat bishops who supported *CCM* . . . and draft synod resolutions against *CCM*." The network later billed itself as "building an evangelical, confessional Lutheran future in America" and that it was "proclaiming the Word through member individuals and congregations in a mission field near you."

The Eastern North Dakota Synod voted 436-57 that it "fully supports the right of its constituent members, congregations, pastors, and bishops to freely accept or reject local implementation of a historic episcopate." When the Church Council met the following month, it rebuked the synod by saying that its support of actions "in violation of this church's governing documents are not in order."

A total of 15 synods voted in 2000 to affirm *CCM*, one voted to rescind. Eight voted to allow bishops to designate a pastor to conduct an ordination in "unusual circumstances"; 16 voted to allow exceptions to the historic episcopate for theological reasons; 10 voted not to make exceptions to *CCM*; eight voted not to rescind; and 24 synods passed no resolutions on *CCM*.

The Conference of Bishops in October 2000, looking ahead to the Churchwide Assembly in 2001, forwarded three suggestions to the Church Council recommending that 1) exceptions "be a pastoral decision of the synodical bishops . . . ; 2) the synodical bishops consult with the presiding bishop "to consider the ecumenical implications . . . ; and 3) the bishops receive the synod council's advice." The three ideas ultimately became the basis for an "exception" statement that was formulated by the Church Council—"to authorize an ordination in unusual circumstances by a pastor other than a pastor holding the office of synodical bishop."

"What is the effect on a person ordained according to an exception?" asked J. David Watrous of Richland, Washington, a member of the council. "Is that person on the regular clergy rolls or on an exceptional roll?" ELCA Secretary Lowell Almen responded, "Those ordained under the ELCA Constitution and bylaws in effect at the time are on the one roster maintained by the ELCA."

In March 2001, the WordAlone Network oversaw the formation of a new association, Lutheran Congregations in Mission for Christ. WordAlone's membership then included 166 congregations and 4,000 individuals who refused to comply with the historic episcopate requirements of *CCM*. "WordAlone doesn't ordain pastors or organize missions—LCMC will," participants at the conference were told. "It will also provide pension and health plans. Congregations would not have to leave the ELCA to join the association." Even so, by December 2001, eight congregations had withdrawn from the ELCA to join the new Lutheran church body.

The 2001 Churchwide Assembly adopted the bylaw exception 683-330. Frank Riddle, Northwestern Pennsylvania Synod, said the 1999 agreement should be honored "until there can be bilateral discussion." But Nick Olson, Minneapolis Area Synod, pleaded: "My church is split on *CCM*. We're good people, but we just don't agree. Help us. Let's not have a hardening of the categories."

After adoption, Presiding Bishop H. George Anderson said he thought the number of exceptions would be low. "This is a way to bring along as many members as possible," he said. He reminded voting members that "there will always be clergy who have joined our roster who were not ordained by a bishop. We don't reordain those who come to us from other churches."

Episcopal Church Presiding Bishop Frank T. Griswold said, "This appears to be a unilateral alteration of the mutual commitment that both our churches have solemnly made. . . . We are mindful of the pastoral realities within the ELCA but are concerned that it has seemingly created, or may create, two classes of clergy within the ELCA."

In October 2001, the Episcopal Church's Standing Commission on Ecumenical Relations said that although any provisions for exceptions to *CCM* was "a matter of serious concern," the commission said the bylaw "need not impair or hinder our relationships of full communion with the ELCA."

WordAlone's Web site continued its critical approach. When a letter from Anderson to synodical bishops gave instructions about the future installations of bishops in historic succession, Anderson included a list of bishops in historic succession from other nations. To which WordAlone replied on its Web site: "Don't breeds with the 'right' pedigrees always seem to require more expenses for their care and feeding? What you thought true of animals also seems true of the new bishop-driven ELCA. Just take Presiding Bishop H. George Anderson's recent letter to synods. When each synod elects a new bishop, it will have to pony up a hefty chunk of your benevolence dollars to fly in appropriately pedigreed bishops to perform the magic razzmatazz at the installation ceremony."

The first exception granted under the bylaw came July 20, 2002, when Daniel Shaw, a graduate of Luther Seminary, was ordained at Emmanuel Lutheran Church, Tacoma, Washington, by his pastor alone, Richard Foege, who had baptized and confirmed him. Bishop William "Chris" Boerger, Northwest Washington Synod, designated Foege to carry out the ordination. A second exception occurred September 14, 2002, when Bishop Gerald L. Mansholt, Central States Synod, gave permission for the ordination of Matthew Kuempel by Tom Hesselring, pastor of Immanuel Lutheran Church, Pflugerville, Texas. Mansholt ordained Kuempel's wife, Kristen, on September 8, 2002, under the terms of *CCM*. Both are graduates of Luther Seminary. Mansholt's decision to allow an exception for Matthew Kuempel's ordination prompted the resignation of Pastor William J. Sappenfield as one of the ecumenical representatives in the synod.

WordAlone hailed the exceptions as victories, although on the whole, neither WordAlone nor LCMC had much influence nationally. Its Web site asked for congregations to add their names to its list of like-minded congregations that were willing to call a pastor who does not conform to *CCM* requirements. The Web site also asked pastors and associates in ministry who are willing to serve with pastors not ordained by a bishop to add their names to WordAlone's list of like-minded pastors and AIMS.

Regardless of WordAlone's claims and the ordination exceptions—or perhaps because the ELCA is able to tolerate them—the Evangelical Lutheran Church in America in 2002 was a church exhibiting remarkable resiliency and strength, a church coming of age and maturity albeit with difficulty, a church able to cope positively with six years of extreme tension and even name-calling among some of its theological leadership. The future stretches favorably for a church that does not have all the answers but is seemingly able to search and give and take. There is a basic firmness in its 15 years of foundations, and still a sense of meeting expectations.

Lutheran-Moravian

After five years of quiet and non-controversial dialogue, a joint commission of the ELCA and the Northern and Southern Provinces of the Moravian Church in America recommended that the two bodies establish full communion by the year 2000. The commission concluded that there are no church-dividing issues between the two bodies.

The Moravian Church in America, a historical cousin of German Lutherans, traces its heritage to the Unity of the Brethren, organized in 1457 by Czech followers of John Hus. Hus sought to reform the Roman Catholic Church and to make worship available in people's common language. He was burned at the stake in 1415, long before Martin Luther was born in 1483. Luther was widely regarded as the "German Hus." Count von Zinzendorf, an 18th-century Lutheran, is often credited with renewing the Moravian Church.

The Moravian church has congregations in the United States and Canada, with its 50,000 members concentrated in the Mid-Atlantic states, especially Pennsylvania, and North Carolina, with a few in the Upper Midwest. Several of the 19 provinces of its global church, including one in South Africa, are member churches of the Lutheran World Federation.

After the Moravian Church's northern and southern provinces approved full communion in 1998 by nearly unanimous votes, the proposal came to the 1999 ELCA Churchwide Assembly. No one spoke against the proposal during two days of hearings and plenary discussions. The outcome, which was already a foregone conclusion, saw full communion adopted 1,007-11. "We've fulfilled our goal of reaching out in several directions at once," Presiding Bishop H. George Anderson said after the vote on *Following Our Shepherd to Full Communion.*

The Rev. Burke Johnson, president of the Moravian Church's northern province, said his church was "gratified" by the vote. "It is a further sign of our unity, and we ask that God will lead us as we move forward in our life and ministry together. We're all related by blood, but it is not our own blood."

Ecumenical conversations with Moravians are "like looking at a friend's family photos and seeing some of your second cousins," said Pastor Ronald Rinn, Augsburg Lutheran Church, Winston-Salem, North Carolina, a member of the committee that wrote the accord. Augsburg provided seed money that led to the proposal's development.

In contrast to banners and color, soaring cathedrals and dramatic surroundings, the full communion celebration between Lutherans and Moravians began quietly with a walking tour of colonial-era Old Salem, a section of Winston-Salem, North Carolina, where Moravian families still live in homes built in the 1700s. Lunch was held on the Salem College campus, followed by a panel discussion and a Moravian love feast, a ritual Moravians describe as "something between a church coffee hour and Holy Communion." Spiced buns and steaming mugs of a special blend of coffee, sugar, and cream were passed to the congregation. A festival service at Augsburg Lutheran Church concluded the day. "There's a wideness to God's mercy," Anderson told the worshipers, "and tonight we thank God for broadening our vision to match the Good Shepherd's vision."

The three full communion decisions were not the ELCA's only ecumenical efforts. In September 2001, co-chaired by Rocky Mountain Synod Bishop Allan Bjornborg, the ELCA and United Methodist Church representatives met to begin the third series of dialogues between the two churches. The most recent dialogue explores the two "churches' teachings on sanctification and the Lord's Supper" and considers the implications of the closer relationship of full communion. Other dialogues were held between the ELCA and the African Methodist Episcopal Church, a black denomination, between the ELCA and the Orthodox Church in the United States, and between the ELCA and the Roman Catholic Church. A Lutheran-Mennonite dialogue also is underway with that historic "peace church." In 2002, the ELCA accepted an invitation to become "a partner in mission and dialogue" with Churches Uniting in Christ, formerly known as the Consultation on Church Union.

On the international scene, the ELCA kept a steady pace of visitations to the centers of the world's Christian communities. Delegates, including women, went regularly to the Vatican, including audiences with Pope John Paul II, to the Ecumenical Patriarchate of the Orthodox Church in Istanbul, Turkey, and to the archbishop of Canterbury in England. Other contacts were maintained by visits to the Russian Orthodox Church in Moscow and the Coptic Church in Egypt. And the visits were reciprocated. Archbishop of Canterbury George Carey came to the ELCA headquarters and participated in a joint ELCA-Episcopal bishops' meeting. Cardinal Edward Cassidy, the Vatican's chief ecumenical officer, came to the Chicago offices, as did Ecumenical Patriarch Demetrios I. It was Demetrios's first visit to the United States, and the ELCA was the only non-Orthodox church body he visited.

Ecumenism also came home in many areas as synods signed covenants of cooperation with Roman Catholic, Episcopal, and The Lutheran Church—Missouri Synod (LCMS) judicatories. A complete list is impossible because of frequent additions. In Minnesota, there are Lutheran-Catholic agreements between the Saint Paul Area and the Minneapolis Area synods with the Roman Catholic Archdiocese of St. Paul and Minneapolis. In North Carolina, covenants exist between the synod and the Roman Catholic dioceses of Charlotte and Raleigh, and between the North Carolina Synod and LCMS district. In New England, agreements have been forged between the synod and the Roman

Catholic Archdiocese of Massachusetts. In Virginia and the District of Columbia, several covenants exist between the Virginia and the Metropolitan Washington D.C., synods and the Roman Catholic dioceses of Richmond, Arlington, and with the Episcopal dioceses of Virginia, Southern Virginia, and Southwestern Virginia. In Wisconsin, agreements have been reached between the East-Central Synod of Wisconsin, the Roman Catholic Diocese of Green Bay, and the Episcopal Diocese of Fond du Lac.

On the interfaith scene, the ELCA in 1994 publicly repudiated Martin Luther's anti-Jewish views. Another document, *Guidelines for Lutheran-Jewish Relations*, published in 1998, said:

> Lutherans need to understand the depth of Jewish concern for communal survival, a concern shaped not only by the Holocaust but built by centuries of Christian antipathy toward Judaism. Jews will thus feel strongly about topics such as the security of the State of Israel, intermarriage and conversion, in which Jewish survival is seen to be at stake. Lutherans are not obligated to adopt the same perspective on these matters, but it is vital for us to understand and respect our neighbor's concerns.

> Lutheran pastors should make it clear in their preaching and teaching that although the New Testament reflects early conflicts, it must not be used as justification for hostility toward present-day Jews.

Lutheran-Roman Catholic

Dating back to 1965, the U.S. Lutheran-Roman Catholic dialogue is the longest running "bilateral" dialogue between two denominations in the nation. Over the years, its theologians focused on such fundamental topics as Baptism, the Eucharist, the papacy, Mary, Scripture and tradition, and justification by grace through faith. Agreement on justification came in 1983. In Germany, primarily in the late 1980s, Lutheran and Roman

Catholic efforts were focusing on ways to say that the churches' 16th-century condemnations did not apply to the present churches. Combining the possibility of a common understanding of both the doctrine of justification and the removal of the condemnations, task forces from the Lutheran World Federation and the Vatican put together an initial draft of a joint statement in 1994. This became the basis for the *Joint Declaration on the Doctrine of Justification* that was signed by the Vatican and the Lutheran World Federation on Reformation Day, October 31, 1999, in Augsburg Germany. H. George Anderson was the Lutheran co-chair of the U.S. dialogue. At the time he was president of Luther College, Decorah, Iowa. He would later sign the *Joint Declaration* as ELCA presiding bishop and a vice president of the LWF.

By 1994, the ELCA Conference of Bishops was told by the then-top U.S. Roman Catholic ecumenical leader, Archbishop Oscar Lipscomb, Mobile, Alabama, that "Pope John Paul II wants this badly." He assured the bishops that the Vatican would respond positively to setting aside the condemnations that Lutherans and Roman Catholics levied against each other in the 16th century. Mutual declarations that the statements "do not apply to the present churches" was scheduled to be voted upon by the U.S. Conference of Catholic Bishops and by the ELCA Churchwide Assembly in 1997.

"If we take this step toward each other, others may follow," Lipscomb said, "but if we do not take it, other steps will not. We are both mutually embarrassed and mutually ready to go beyond the condemnations. You are considering full communion with two other groups, and at least maybe we can stop cursing each other." That same year, the German Conference of Catholic Bishops praised the U.S. Lutheran-Roman Catholic document.

Discussion continued until 1996, when the Lutheran World Federation's Council said that revisions to about six paragraphs—out of 45—were all that remained before a joint declaration on justification could be accepted by the Lutheran World Federation and the Roman Catholic Church. The key agreed-upon section states: "Together we confess: By grace alone, in faith in Christ's saving work and not because of any merit on our part, we are accepted by God and receive the Holy Spirit, who renews our hearts while equipping and calling us to good works."

The revisions dealt with four paragraphs dealing with the Roman Catholic view that sin is overcome by baptism, whereas Lutherans say that the baptized remain simultaneously both saint and sinner. The final language that would finesse this dilemma was a commentary that explained the differences and said the churches would acknowledge the validity of the other's views, even though the churches did not share identical views.

The necessity of the revisions meant that the *Joint Declaration* was not ready for acceptance at the LWF Assembly in July 1997 in Hong Kong. The delay, however, meant that the ELCA could act on the document at its August 1997 assembly, which was scheduled after the Hong Kong assembly. Once again, the Luther Seminary faculty recommended that the ELCA postpone action on the *Joint Declaration* because of questions about its authority, and saying it is "surely unwise for an assembly to seek to legislate doctrine, and it is probably constitutionally not permissible to vote on such matters."

With breathtaking speed—and no debate—the 1997 ELCA assembly affirmed the *Joint Declaration* with a vote of 958-25. Not only had the two traditions agreed on an understanding of the basic issue that divided them in the 16th century, they agreed also that the condemnations each church hurled at the other were no longer applicable to today's churches.

Voting members rose to prolonged applause. Anderson quickly led the assembly in singing "Now Thank We All Our God." Even though the Vatican had not yet given its approval to the document, the Vatican's chief ecumenical officer, Cardinal Edward Cassidy, was quoted as saying that the Roman Catholic Church may approve the document "by 1998 or certainly by the end of the century."

Final votes on the declaration came in quick succession in 1998—June 16 by the LWF Council and nine days later on June 25 by the Vatican. The LWF Council had circulated the document to its 124 member churches, with 80 responding "yes" and five responding "no." The affirmative answer represented

54.7 million Lutherans around the world. ELCA Presiding Bishop H. George Anderson, who was presiding over the council at the time, declared the council's vote unanimous. Again, he led in singing "Now Thank We All Our God."

The Vatican's five-page response created some initial confusion. Cassidy indicated that of the declaration's 44 points, Roman Catholics were in full agreement on all but three (which were later covered by the commentary). But he said that there would be a "formal signing of the *Joint Declaration* and a celebration of the consensus achieved." Anderson said simply, "We have an agreement."

Some irony exists over the agreement. In 1963, the Lutheran World Federation's Fourth Assembly tried to adopt a common understanding of justification by grace through faith. They adjourned in failure. But with the *Joint Declaration*, Lutherans who were unable to agree among themselves, finally were able to do so in the context of, and in conjunction with, the Roman Catholic Church.

On a day that began with leaden skies but gave way to crisp sunshine, Lutheran World Federation and Vatican leaders met in Augsburg, Germany, on October 31, 1999. Beginning the service at Augsburg's Roman Catholic Cathedral, they marched in procession through the city's streets to St. Anna Lutheran Church. Sustained applause by the overflow crowd greeted the signing of the *Joint Declaration* as 10 signatures on two leather-bound documents laid aside nearly 500 years of arguments and condemnations between the two churches. After the signing, Anderson said, "In the United States we think of the declaration as a coming together. We have been walking with this theological stone in our shoe, but now we can take out the stone and it's easier to walk together."

William Rusch, former head of the ELCA Department for Ecumenical Affairs who was in Augsburg, remembered after the signing that he approached the Vatican in 1993 about the possibility of a worldwide statement on the meaning of justification. He took his idea to Pope John Paul II, who, Rusch said, replied, "We can do it. Can you?"

Nonetheless, Cassidy had the quote of the day. When asked about the role of faith and works in salvation, he smiled and said, "When the Lord asks me, 'Did you do any good works in your life?" I can say, 'I signed the *Joint Declaration.'"

Two months after the signing, 14 Lutheran theological professors from the United States, Germany, Denmark, Sweden, and Norway sent Cassidy a statement of their opposition to the *Joint Declaration*. Included were five professors from Luther Seminary, St. Paul, Minnesota, and one from the Lutheran Theological Seminary at Gettysburg. They said the declaration is not reconcilable to the confessions of the churches.

In some areas, the *Joint Declaration* was a matter of the churches' official documents catching up with congregational and individual practice. In Beavertown, Oregon, Mission of the Atonement Church, an ELCA–Roman Catholic congregation, symbolized the growing unity among Christian groups long divided by diverse doctrines and practices. Father Matt Tumulty serves the congregation with Laurie Larson Caesar, an ELCA pastor. In Des Plaines, Illinois, a covenant between St. Mary's Roman Catholic Church and Trinity Lutheran Church helps Janelle and Paul Sammarco and their children, Chelsea and Charlie, participate in both of the couple's religious traditions.

ELCA and LCMS

The ELCA's ecumenical advances widened its already considerable gap with The Lutheran Church—Missouri Synod (LCMS). Some of the distance came with LCMS's increasingly conservative bent, which began in the late 1960s and continued with increased intensity during the presidency of Dr. A. L. Barry. Another contributor to the distance was the ELCA's willingness to move ahead on several ecumenical fronts, even though LCMS warned against the breaches that would be set up, even to the point of calling the ELCA "no longer an orthodox Lutheran Church."

The ELCA's consideration of full communion with the three Reformed Churches brought a warning from then LCMS

President Ralph Bohlmann in 1992. Bohlmann said dialogue participants "overstated the accomplishments" to reach consensus, especially on the meaning of the Lord's Supper. Moving ahead toward full communion "is to imply that the doctrinal differences are not that significant, an assumption that I would have to challenge very strongly."

In 1994, LCMS theologians said that the ELCA "would formally and officially become part of a union church" if the ELCA entered into full communion with the three Reformed churches. The theologians said that in *A Common Calling* the "life-giving truth of God's word is lost" when they compared the report with *The Book of Concord* (Lutheranism's chief doctrinal book). "What is finally important about this is not merely that the truth is lost, but that in losing the truth, salvation is lost."

In 1997, when Barry addressed the ELCA Churchwide Assembly, he said that the LCMS considered the ELCA's full communion decision with the Reformed churches "most unfortunate." Later he would write in the LCMS *President's Newsletter* that the ELCA's ecumenical decisions "represent a contradiction of essential doctrinal truths that Lutherans have confessed as points that cannot be compromised or surrendered, under any circumstances, or at any cost. . . . Our synod needs to reach out to those within the ELCA who are now feeling as if they have lost their church. Winsomely, yet clearly, we need to help them understand our position on these issues. More than talk, we need also to welcome any ELCA congregation, pastor, or layperson who now recognizes that their church body has made a decision that compromises what it means to be a fully Lutheran church." The LCMS prepared bulletin inserts that outlined its differences with the ELCA. In response, the ELCA developed inserts that articulated its beliefs without mentioning the differences with LCMS.

A year later, 94 percent of delegates at the LCMS triennial convention passed a resolution stating, "In faithfulness to God's Word and the Lutheran Confessions, and motivated by our love and concern for the people and pastors of the ELCA, we express our deep regret and profound disagreement with these actions taken by the ELCA." Perhaps in ironic contrast to his statement six years earlier, former LCMS president Ralph Bohlmann asked delegates, "Why do we so often act as though we are the only boat on the sea, always quick to label and condemn mistakes that occur on other boats, but remaining too isolated and aloof to appreciate progress?"

When the ELCA adopted full communion with the Episcopal Church and the Moravian Church, Barry issued a statement expressing the LCMS's "profound regret and deep disagreement. . . . These decisions have only pushed our two churches further apart."

After the signing of the *Joint Declaration*, Barry's office placed a full-page advertisement in *USA Today* and 15 other newspapers in cities with significant Lutheran population, using the page to explain why the LCMS did not support the joint declaration. Six ELCA bishops and eight Roman Catholic bishops in Wisconsin responded, with the Roman Catholic bishops saying they "could not recognize their beliefs as expressed" by Barry. The LCMS president also claimed that 45 percent of the world's Lutheran church bodies did not support the declaration. Of 61.5 million Lutherans in the world, 58 million are represented by the LWF. The LCMS is not a member of the LWF.

In July 2001, the LCMS convention declared, "We can't consider [the ELCA] to be an orthodox Lutheran church body." The sentence came from a report written by Barry before his death in the spring of that year: "The LCMS indicated to the ELCA that in light of its theological direction we cannot consider them to be an orthodox Lutheran church body, and they expressed their feeling that precisely because we do not agree with their ecumenical agreements they regard us in a similar manner."

Expressing regret on the day before the orthodoxy vote, Anderson told LCMS delegates, "I deeply regret the distance that has grown between us. We share a common heritage and ought to bear a common witness."

A Lutheran Committee on Cooperation, composed of five representatives each from the ELCA and the LCMS, meets twice a year. It rarely reports any agreements, except in its common concerns about military chaplaincy and the two churches' joint participation in some social ministry organizations. In November 2002, Presiding Bishop Mark S. Hanson told the Church Council that a recent meeting had a "different tone" and was "positive" compared to other meetings.

In retrospect

In looking back over the ELCA struggle toward ecumenism, particularly in the groundbreaking action over full communion with the Reformed churches and the Episcopal Church, it becomes clear that some unusual alignments and strange bed-fellows were created.

In the Reformed proposal, the theological issue was the meaning of "real presence" in the Lord's Supper. The ecclesiological issue arose about the nature of the UCC, namely whether it was so congregational that its national organization could not speak for its congregations. Both of these issues were primarily concerns to the old East Coast LCA. They were not an issue in the ALC-dominated Midwest, particularly the ecclesiological issue, because much of the Upper Midwest supports congregationalism.

By contrast, the structural issues of the historic episcopate loomed large, primarily in the Midwest and the Pacific Northwest and Southwest, while the LCA-dominated East Coast was not too concerned about the episcopate and had experience with many Episcopalians from colonial times forward. The Midwest had little experience in dealing with the Episcopal Church, whereas the LCA had long been accustomed to the Episcopalians, going back as far as Old Swedes' Church in Philadelphia in 1700. Nowhere was the give-and-take on the episcopacy so noticeable as in the Conference of Bishops.

The seminaries tended to be predictable. Philadelphia, Southern, and Trinity endorsed all the proposals, Gettysburg, Wartburg, and Pacific agreed publicly with some of them, while Luther and LSTC never endorsed any of them. Luther was a hotbed of resistance to the Episcopal proposal, both as a strategic nerve center and with several faculty members often speaking at conferences, including James Nestingen, Gerhard Forde, Michael Rogness, Paul Berge, Walter Sundberg, and others. It was unusual in the predecessor bodies to have theological faculties so opposed to directions that their churches were taking. Luther Seminary faculty also criticized the Episcopal proposal on ministry grounds, saying that the ELCA did not need Episcopal interference in the ordering of ELCA ministry, especially after the ELCA adopted a unitary office of ministry in 1993.

Robert J. Marshall, former LCA president who was a leader in the LWF and the WCC, actively opposed the Episcopal proposal, speaking at various conferences including WordAlone gatherings. He was joined there by David Preus, former ALC presiding bishop, with whom Marshall often disagreed on other subjects during the years. It was Preus's reluctance to look ahead to an ALC-LCA merger that was a factor in Marshall's decision in 1978 not to continue as LCA president. Others who were normally ecumenically minded, Bishop William Lazareth, Metropolitan New York Synod, and Kenneth Sauer, former LCA Ohio Synod bishop and then ELCA Southern Ohio bishop and chair for a four-year term of the Conference of Bishops, lined up against the Reformed and Episcopal proposals. The collection of notables from the predecessor churches who opposed the proposals quickly got the attention of voting members in 1997 and 1999 assemblies.

Nonetheless, the ELCA emerged as a world leader in ecumenism, showing not only that it could sustain serious internal convulsions, but also that it was flexible enough for disparate views to live together after decisions were made. Its ecumenical decisions allowed enough room for differing theological views, and managed to bring structural patterns together in full communion, such as congregationalism and episcopal orders, that had never been partnered before this era. The ELCA stood apart as unique in having such a stance as the next century began.

CHAPTER 6

FOUR BIG SUCCESSES

"Being at the gathering strengthened my Christian
voice because I saw so many thousands of other young
people just like me who believe what I believe."

Michelle Kravec, Little Falls, New York,
at the ELCA Youth Gathering, July 2000

A mid the growing pains, the controversy over sexuality and
the struggle for ecumenism, the new Evangelical Lutheran
Church in America also was doing some things exceedingly well.
Several very large and very public activities were successes beyond
what might be expected. They range across the spectrum from
enormous gatherings of youth, to being the largest church-related
health and human service network in the United States, to a
World Hunger Appeal that annually brings in about $15 million,
to Global Mission Events that tell the church's international story
like nothing else the church does. Each has been a part of the
ELCA since its inception, some getting little notice from day to
day, but all are making a major impact on millions of people in
the ELCA and in society around the world.

Youth are seen and heard

The ELCA has more than 50,000 youth in its 5.1 million
membership. In congregations around the United States, youth
ministry efforts focus mostly on fellowship and service. "Service
projects outrank pizza," said Presiding Bishop H. George
Anderson in 1996. "Our youth want to count for something."

They also like gathering in large groups. In 1988, more than
21,500 youth gathered in San Antonio. In 1991, 23,000 youth
came together in Dallas. In 1994, 35,000 youth came together in
Atlanta. In 1997, 35,000 went to New Orleans. However, so many
youth registrations were turned away from New Orleans that in

2000 two national youth gatherings were held on successive week-ends in St. Louis, with about 22,000 youth at each. Two gatherings were planned for Atlanta in 2003. The gatherings continued traditions from the American Lutheran Church and the Lutheran Church in America, but the ELCA gatherings were larger.

The Lutheran Youth Organization, working within the Division for Congregational Life (later called the Division for Congregational Ministries) focuses on youth between 15 and 18, bringing them together at all levels, from congregational groups to the triennial nationwide gatherings. (Lutheran Men in Mission, which has units organized in 42 synods, men's ministries in about 3,400 congregations and a mailing list of 7,000 men, also is part of the Division for Congregational Ministries. In January 2003, Lutheran Men in Mission shipped 5,800 "Master Builders Bibles for Men" to congregations across the United States and the Caribbean.)

From the beginning, the Lutheran Youth Organization found a formula for the huge gatherings that appealed to youth—rock music, inspirational speakers, Bible studies, skits, monologues, clowns, high-tech visual presentation, service projects, and free time for the thousands of kids to learn to know each other.

Meg Nesbitt, Golden, Colorado, who attended the San Antonio gathering, put it this way: "It's overwhelming here. We're all here to express faith in Christ. Here you see your faith more and what it means. It's no problem to say how we feel." The preacher at the closing worship told of a conversation she had ridden with a San Antonio cab driver: "There are 20,000 Lutherans teenagers in town," the driver said. "They are so happy. I never believed Jesus was God, but after seeing these kids, I might have to rethink some things."

Offerings during the San Antonio event totaled $100,000 and were designated for projects in El Salvador, South Africa, the Lutheran World Federation, the Middle East, and the former East Germany. Participants also donated 10 tons of canned goods to the San Antonio food bank.

The gatherings elected members to the LYO board and urged the church's nine regions to organize region-wide youth gatherings. Also from the outset, the national gatherings included two special groupings, the Multicultural Youth Leadership Event, and a Differently Abled Youth Leadership Event. The LYO board asked for a teenage voice and vote on ELCA decision-making bodies. The Church Council was sympathetic but did not feel comfortable mandating youth representation to the entire church. In 1998, the council added two youth advisory members with voice but not vote.

When 23,000 youth and 4,000 adults gathered in 1991, they made a big impression on the Dallas business community: 29 hotels were needed to house them, and 250 chartered buses were used to get participants to the two main arenas, with closed-circuit television between them, the 9,000-seat Dallas Convention Center and 18,000-seat Reunion Arena. The throng dropped an estimated $9.7 million into the Dallas economy. They also brought 13.5 tons of food to the opening worship service that was donated to 30 Dallas-area food pantries. Each afternoon, small groups went out into the community to work on various projects, including the construction of a playground at an apartment complex for people with AIDS and their families. Its $165,000 closing worship offering went to eight projects at home and abroad. They cheered the Jay Beech Band and inspirational speaker Tony Campolo.

In 1994, under the theme "2 B Alive," 35,000 youth descended on Atlanta. The total was more than the number of ELCA members in all of Georgia! Communion for two worship services needed 3,900 pita loaves and 14 cases of wine, and 800 communion assistants. Youth brought more than 2,500 boxes of linens, towels, and hygiene kits for Atlanta's poor—almost 19 tons. Former President Jimmy Carter sent a taped message. A format of workshops with more than 140 options occupied part of the five days, as did 44 Atlanta agencies where the crowd transformed a warehouse into a shelter, cleaned a house for homeless people, and packed food at a pantry. Even so, the real attraction was speakers, music, dancing, clapping, and singing—and 519 people attended the multicultural event and 19 the Differently Abled event.

Planning for the 1997 gathering brought a good news/bad news scenario. On the first day of registrations, 39,000 requests came in. Unfortunately, the New Orleans facilities could only handle 35,000. Youth gathering staff blindfolded themselves and drew the number of names that could be accommodated, and sent apologies to those not chosen. Some congregations, such as St. Mark, Salem, Oregon, protested the one-day registration date. "Why are people subjected to what is virtually a lottery situation when you must adjust to the vagaries of the U.S. Postal Service for a letter to arrive on exactly the right day?" asked Daniel Schlewitz of the Oregon Synod's youth committee.

The 35,000 who went to New Orleans under the theme, "River of Hope," trickled down Bourbon Street, gathering more marchers at each intersection, until the throng flooded the street and stopped traffic at the Superdome, home of the gathering. Worship services centered around a Holy Week motif—with a New Orleans twist. On "Good Friday" a 40-foot cross on stage was shaded red. A 15-foot puppet of Jesus traveled around the Superdome, surrounded by dancers wearing Mardi Gras masks. The "Easter" service, with Presiding Bishop H. George Anderson preaching, opened with fireworks as dancers threw confetti in the air and on the crowd.

Learning from the 1997 disappointments, two youth gatherings were held on consecutive July weekends in 2000 in St. Louis, Missouri. Using the theme, "Dancing at the Cross Roads," each attracted 22,000 youth. Michelle Kravec, Little Neck, New York, said of the closing worship: "We started reading the Apostles' Creed quietly. We read each sentence louder than the one before it. It was incredible. Communion with 22,000 people was something else too. . . . The experience also strengthened my relationship with God. Usually I don't like to talk in front of people, but during the service [after I went back] home, I got up to tell people about the event. I wasn't nervous at all because I had so much to say!"

The two Atlanta gatherings in July 2003 are focusing on the theme *Ubuntu*. The term, which literally means "humanity," was lifted up by Archbishop Desmond Tutu, retired Anglican archbishop of Cape Town, South Africa, in his keynote address for the 2000 youth gathering in St. Louis. As many as 45,000 youth are expected to gather in Atlanta. In all, nearly 160,000 youth over a 13-year period learned, in the words of Drew Blasingame, Latrobe, Pennsylvania, that "the church is a much bigger place than I thought."

In 2002, the ELCA Conference of Bishops adopted a strategy proposed by a steering committee for youth and family ministry to "recognize the urgency and create passion within synods and among bishops, for the evangelical task of youth and family ministry." The proposal calls upon "the church to embrace a vision, mission, and core values which support faith formation in children, youth, families and young adults." In the Texas–Louisiana Gulf Coast Synod alone, the number of people serving as youth and family ministers grew from three to 42.

Provider of care

The legacy of Lutherans being the largest private provider of care in the United States goes back to 1849 when William A. Passavant opened the Pittsburgh Infirmary, the first Protestant hospital in America. He opened an orphan's home three years later. Then came the Emigrant House in New York City. When Passavant died in 1884, he was planning a home for epileptics. His followers built it the next year.

From these beginnings has come Lutheran Services in America, an alliance of 280 social ministry institutions and services of the ELCA and The Lutheran Church—Missouri Synod that make up the largest nonprofit social and health services network in the United States. Through this network of services annually (all figures 2000-2001):

- Nearly 128,000 children receive foster care services.

- More than 1,400 clients receive adoption services, resulting in 2,768 adoptions.

- More than 25,000 clients served with permanent housing; 12,729 units available with elderly occupying 8,974 units.

- More than 106,000 people receive counseling services.

- More than 104,000 individuals live in 1,440 residential facilities that provide 24-hour care.

- Nearly 200,000 received emergency services; 277,195 received non-residential food services with 5.1 million meals served; 9,852 were provided temporary shelter; and 8,862 received disaster response services.

- Nearly 250,000 hospital admissions for acute care.

- More than 4 million people receive care through outpatient visits.

When the ELCA began in 1988, the Lutheran social ministry associations ranked second in income among 100 top U.S. charities, according to the *NonProfit Times*. The ranking changed to No. 1 in 1993 and has hovered there ever since, being first in 1999, 2000, and 2001, with more than $7.6 billion in annual income. The National Council of the YMCAs and the American Red Cross ranked second and third in 2001, followed by Catholic Charities USA, United Jewish Communities, Goodwill Industries International, Salvation Army, Fidelity Investments Charitable Gift Fund, Boys & Girls Clubs of America, and the American Cancer Society. Branches of Lutheran social ministry organizations serve in every state, the District of Columbia and the Virgin Islands. "LSA is one of the best kept secrets in our land," said Presiding Bishop Mark S. Hanson. "One in 50 people in the United States have been served by a ministry of LSA."

The statistics are staggering. More than 5.7 million people are served yearly—8,784 people with developmental disabilities, 4.3 million in inpatient and outpatient hospital care, 104,930 elderly, children, youth, and adults in residential care, 593,175 with short-term assistance (crisis, food temporary shelter, disaster response), and 780,708 with social services. Of LSA's $7.6 billion income, $3.7 billion comes from service fees, $2.8 billion from federal, state, and local government sources, $157 million from the United Way, private foundations, corporate contributions and non-Lutheran church support), $16 million from the Lutheran church, and $958 million from other sources. Expenses total $7.56 billion, with $6.4 billion going to services, $510 million to capital expenditures and $22 million for fund-raising (less than 1 percent). Employees total 144,468; 93,796 volunteers donate 4.1 million hours.

The statistics, of course, are not the whole ministry story. For example, The Wartburg Home, Mt. Vernon, New York, was opened originally in 1866 as a home and farm school for children orphaned by the Civil War. Another 30 years later, its doors opened to people at the other end of life also. Now Wartburg's services include a hospice program, a unite for people with Alzheimer's disease, retirement homes, assisted living and home health care.

- In San Francisco, a nine-unit apartment building provides women living with HIV/AIDS and their children a safe and affordable home complete with supportive services from Lutheran Social Services of Northern California.

- In Chicago, Bethel New Life Community Development Corporation has developed more than 1,000 units of affordable housing in an urban community, building or rehabbing 30 units a year.

- The Lutheran Medical Center in Brooklyn began as a center to care for the health and social needs of Norwegian sailors who settled along the Brooklyn waterfront. The center's 520-bed hospital in a renovated factory is the main site of four health centers, forming the largest federally funded community health-care center in the United States. Sister Elisabeth Fedde, the Norwegian deaconess who founded the hospital and insisted on its openness to immigrants, surely would have been pleased to see how the hospital's ministry has grown to include Spanish, Chinese, Russian, Arabic, Hindi,

and Yiddish—not to mention the Shabbos Room, an overnight room so visiting patients don't have to travel on the
Sabbath, and the prayer room for Islamic employees and
patients. As far back as 1994, George Adams, then president
of the medical center, emphasized, "Health is speaking a
language. . . . If you don't speak English you're not in a state
of well-being in this country."

- Bethphage, headquartered in Omaha, Nebraska, serves more
  than 1,400 people with developmental difficulties in 13
  states. Between 1980 and 2002, its budget grew from $4 mil-
  lion to $93 million. Likewise, the Martin Luther Home
  Society, based in Lincoln, Nebraska, serves 2,300 people in
  23 synods plus Latvia and Great Britain, and has a budget of
  $74 million. In July 2003, Bethphage and Martin Luther
  Homes will merge.

- In Cleveland, the "red coats" are ex-offenders who help the
  homebound who live in public housing to have groceries,
  garbage disposal, and a host of household chores. "Red
  coats" have served time for such crimes as assault, receiving
  stolen property, and auto theft. They are part of the Lutheran
  Metropolitan Ministry association.

Helping the hungry

In 1974, in the midst of famine in sub-Sahara Africa, and the
harsh realities of urban unrest and a rural crisis at home, the
American Lutheran Church and the Lutheran Church in
America each launched world hunger appeals. As the years passed,
the appeal grew both in strength and in visibility, taking deep
root in congregations that now raises more than $15 million
annually, over and above all other giving to the ELCA. Since
1974, gifts to the appeal have totaled more than $200 million.

Lita Brusick Johnson, director for the appeal since 1995,
described the appeal as an expression of the "holy imagination"

of those who created it. "Holy imagination," she said, "inspires our work with others of good will to strengthen what is life-giving in our society, in our economy, and to change the systems and structure that rap people in a deadly cycle of poverty and hunger. We walk with those who are hungry for the length of the journey, not just when it is convenient or when the road is easy. We fight hunger and poverty at its bud and its stems and its root, using all the tools at our disposal through relief, sustainable development, education and advocacy."

In contrast to other financial experiences in the new church, contributions to the World Hunger Appeal increased yearly during the church's early days—$10.6 million in 1988; $10.9 million in 1989, $11.0 million in 1990, and $12 million in 1991. In 1999, the appeal's 25th anniversary, total gifts were $16 million. In 2001, $15.6 million was received. In 2002, income declined slightly, and the ELCA Church Council reaffirmed the goal set by the 1999 ELCA Churchwide Assembly of reaching a $25 million goal by 2005. The goal could be met with $5 from each ELCA member.

Of the $15.6 million received in 2001, 72 percent was spent on international hunger relief and development, 11 percent on domestic hunger relief and development, 10 percent on hunger education and advocacy, and 7 percent on administration of the appeal, including fund-raising and communication.

Even though most of the hunger appeal monies are spent internationally, 244 domestic hunger relief grants totaling $1.1 million, were channeled through synods to local relief, development, or community organizing projects in 2001. Hunger appeal funds spent overseas primarily go through such channels such as Lutheran World Relief, the overseas relief arm of the ELCA and the LCMS, and through the Lutheran World Federation. (According to 1988 figures in *Money* magazine, Lutheran World Relief was fifth on a list of "the 10 best charities that watch their pennies best.") The Lutheran World Federation, operating out of Geneva, Switzerland, is widely known and saluted by the United Nations as a can-do agency that gets food, relief materials and self-help development projects to where it is needed. Food is distributed according to need and never according to creed; it goes to whoever needs it without regard for the nationality, political stance, or religious belief of the recipient.

Such was the case when the Muslim-dominated government in northern Sudan refused to let LWF food get through to Christian-dominated southern Sudan. The Sudanese government was using food as a weapon against their own people, an example of hunger being caused more by political regimes than by natural disasters such as drought and wind. The LWF rented Hercules aircraft to get the food into the south where it needed to be. Similarly, when the LWF was sending food into Muslim-controlled areas during the disintegration of the former nation of Yugoslavia, LWF officials realized that they could not get clearance into some disputed areas. Consequently, they food was turned over to the Red Crescent Society, a Muslim humanitarian agency. The final leg of the delivery of food from Lutheran sources reached its destination through a non-Christian agency.

The Lutheran Immigration and Refugee Service, another cooperative agency of the ELCA and the LCMS, assists in the resettlement of refugees, usually in congregations. In 2001, 8,961 refugees were resettled by LIRS's 27 affiliates. That same year, 18,392 adult and 1,939 asylum seekers in detention facilities of the U.S. Immigration and Naturalization Service received legal orientation consultations by the network of LIRS-supported legal service providers.

The ELCA Domestic Disaster Response, a part of the World Hunger Appeal, provides million of dollars in assistance to those affected by domestic disasters, such as hurricanes, tornadoes, floods, and terrorism. In 2001, ELCA members gave $10.8 million in disaster response, with nearly $7 million designated for response efforts of the church following the September 11, 2001, terrorist attacks in New York City, Washington, D.C., and rural Pennsylvania. Disaster contributions usually total about $2 million a year.

By the end of 2001, $2.7 million was forwarded to Lutheran Disaster Responses—New York, an inter-Lutheran response in that city coordinated by ELCA Bishop Stephen Bouman and LCMS District President David Burke. Among various ministries, Lutheran Disaster Response began providing assistance to those easily overlooked in the September 11 tragedy—people whose immigrant status is undocumented, workers whose service industry jobs have been terminated, and others with little or no support systems. In an obvious reference to Ground Zero, where the World Trade Center Towers stood, "Camp New Ground," a weeklong day camp was hosted by Lutherans to help children deal with their feelings from the terrorist attacks. Lutheran Disaster Response provided funding, along with matching funding from two Lutheran fraternal insurance societies. The LCMS response brought total Lutheran contributions for New York to $20 million. The Disaster Response's long-term response could go on for five or more years.

When Hurricane Hugo struck the Virgin Islands, Puerto Rico, and South and North Carolina in 1989, ELCA members gave $1.1 million to the Disaster Response Fund to help victims of the hurricane and an earthquake in Northern California a month later. In St. Croix, Queen Louise Home for Children received an estimated $50,000 in structural damage. Hope Lutheran Church, a mission congregation in Holly Hill, South Carolina, went ahead with its charter service the Sunday after the storm, even though the funeral home chapel it used had no power. Approximately 60 people came to the altar to sign the charter by candlelight.

Leon Phillips, then director for both the inter-Lutheran Disaster Response and the ELCA Domestic Disaster Response at the time, noted that $200,000 was spent in the emergency phase, but $500,000 was spent in the "repairing damage and 'getting back to normal' stage." Phillips said that in disaster relief circles, Lutherans are known as the people who stay after the TV cameras leave—stages two and three, getting life back to normal and counseling services. After the 1999 devastation in eastern North Carolina from Hurricane Floyd, some disaster volunteers periodically were on the job as long as three years later, including work teams organized by Lutheran Men in Mission of North Carolina.

Relief efforts after horrendous floods in the Red River Valley in 1997 involved clean up and resettlement of people whose homes were damaged beyond repair. Eleven church buildings in North Dakota were damaged, plus 10 more in Minnesota and two in South Dakota. Oak Grove Lutheran School in Fargo, North Dakota, the ELCA's only residential high school, was closed for a time to recover. A five-foot wall of water broke an earthen dike and raced across the campus. For three days, the campus's only occupants were the turtles that surfaced from time to time. Trees along the school's football field, which was under-water for about six weeks, had foliage on the tops but none below.

Among the thousands of people who were aided by Lutheran Disaster Relief was Vicki Schmidt, wife of the pastor of Faith Lutheran Church, West Fargo, North Dakota. She said that when she received a check from Lutheran Disaster Response, "it was as if the church had put its arms around me and held me." A year after the floods, some $20 million had been given through the disaster funds of the ELCA, The Lutheran Church—Missouri Synod and the two Lutheran fraternal benefit societies. "Long after FEMA (the Federal Emergency Management Association), the Red Cross and the Salvation Army are gone," said Gilbert Furst of Lutheran Disaster Response, "your church will still be here. The body of Christ is rolling up its sleeves for the long haul." In time, 750 congregations across the ELCA became partners with churches and people in need in the flooded areas. Camp Noah, a program developed in the area to help children make sense of flood disasters and other traumas, is now used in other settings, including being translated into Spanish for use in New York and Puerto Rico.

The world comes home

Beginning in the summer of 1988, and continuing a tradition of the merging churches, Global Mission Events became a mainstay of the new church's interpretation of its overseas mission involvements. Following what was to become an annual pattern, the Division for Global Mission sponsored two, three, or four virtually identical four-day GMEs in different sections of the nation, usually using ELCA college campuses as sites. In 1989, for example, GMEs were held at Muhlenberg College, Allentown, Pennsylvania; Concordia College, Moorhead, Minnesota; and Texas Lutheran College, Seguin, Texas, attracting 3,718 people. The following year, GMEs were held at Pacific Lutheran University, Tacoma, Washington; Carthage College, Kenosha, Wisconsin; and Adrian [Michigan] College. Between 1988 and 2002, 41 GMEs have been held with 40,000 people attending. The ELCA Division for Outreach also is a part of the GMEs, telling the stories of mission outreach around the United States.

In addition to inspiring worship services, the core of GMEs popularity is the "global university" that usually offers more than 120 different seminars on subjects from the church in modern China to Christian ministry in a war zone such as Lebanon. Most GME-goers complain that there are many more "courses" they want to take than there is time to take them. In addition, conversations between participants who came from various parts of the world and from diverse occupations and lifestyles bring not only learnings but also friendships. Some participants link the events with annual family visits and vacations. Sylvia Jerdee, Frankfurt, West Germany, said in 1990, "This is my third GME, and it has been a life-changing experience."

The GMEs became especially valuable in telling the story of ELCA overseas involvement as the role of missionaries changed in the last third of the 20th century. In 1955, for example, 125 Lutheran missionaries served in the central area of the Evangelical Lutheran Church in Tanzania. Today there are only two ELCA volunteers in what is now called the Central Diocese because that church now has trained its own pastors, bishops, and teachers. More than 481 international church leaders—327 men and 155 women who now serve their home churches—have completed studies in the United States or other nations at the ELCA's expense.

In 1988, the ELCA had slightly more than 500 adult missionary personnel, but budget restrictions and changing overseas needs reduced the total to slightly less than 400 by 1992. By 2001, because of finances and increases in indigenous leadership, more ELCA volunteers, and the sending of short-term specialists, the ELCA had 305 missionaries in 45 nations. Among them are 164 long-term missionaries, 31 two-year missionaries, and 40 self-supporting volunteers serving from three to 22 months. Also, 70 percent of the missionaries are laypersons who work as teachers, medical personnel, computer technicians, hospital administrators and librarians. Clergy serve as parish pastors in some areas, but most pastors teach at seminaries and colleges. Nearly half of DGM's $28.3 million budget in 2002 was spent on sending missionaries and volunteers in response to requests from companion churches and agencies. The other half was devoted to development, justice, relief, and health care projects. The division's budget was 27.9 percent of the church's operating expense in 2002.

Among the division's special concerns are the support of Palestinian Christians in the Middle East, particularly through the six congregations of the Evangelical Lutheran Church in Jerusalem (serving in Palestine, Jordan, and Israel); support of the church's five schools for Christian and Muslim students in such cities as Bethlehem, Ramallah, Beit Jala; relating to the LWF-operated Augusta Victoria Hospital on Mount of Olives, and continuing ministry in Palestinian refugee camps.

Another major component of the ELCA's global outreach is the Companion Synod program that links each ELCA synod with a church or a synod in 50 overseas nations. Development of the Companion Synod program was part of Mission90, the church's "see, grow, serve" emphasis. Over the years, hundreds of ELCA synodical leaders and members have visited their companion synod territory, and representatives from the companion synods have come to the United States in return. In 2001, for example, some members of the Northwest Synod of Wisconsin experienced the daily life and customs of Malawi when their companion synod, the Evangelical Lutheran Church in Malawi, hosted a three-day camping event for the Wisconsin visitors.

Members of the Virginia Synod went to the Islands District of the Evangelical Lutheran Church of Papua New Guinea. In spite of civil war in Liberia, the Upper Susquehanna Synod and the Lutheran Church in Liberia exchanged several visits.

In tandem with the companion synod program, the Division for Global Mission entered the 21st century lifting up the philosophy of "accompaniment," a "walking together in Jesus Christ of two or more churches in equal companionship in service in God's mission." The philosophy is a refinement of mission principle of interdependence from the latter decades of the 20th century, as well as an obvious evolution from the mission philosophy of the mid-1900s of "sending" and "receiving" churches. The division's documents state that "accompaniment emphasizes relationship before resources. Development of programs and allocation of resources flows from how companions relate, rather than vice versa. . . . More practically speaking, accompaniment is time shared to spend the time together to get to know one another—the strengths, weaknesses, gifts, and abilities. It is sharing the work, where the larger partner in companionship shares the work of the smaller partner; where one partner shares the joys and pains of the other; sharing the work through prayer and sharing information. Companionship is the sharing of similar interests: in areas of our common life on this planet, in economic and political spheres, in the ongoing evangelism mission of the church. It is about living with each other and speaking the truth."

An early example of "accompaniment" came in 1990 when Bishop Medardo Gomez of El Salvador, who had been forced to leave his country because of death threats from some elements of his country's military forces, returned to El Salvador accompanied by three ELCA bishops, including Bishop Herbert W. Chilstrom. The Evangelical Lutheran Church of El Salvador's aid of refugees in the nation's civil war was interpreted by the Salvadoran government as support for the government's enemies. At the time, the United States supported the Salvadoran government. The presence of U.S. bishops provided a measure of safety for Gomez because the Salvadoran government was unlikely to create a disturbance against bishops from a nation that supported the government, even though the Salvadoran government was suspicious of Gomez.

DGM also began to express accompaniment by appointing Area Program Directors who have ethnic ties with the geographic areas they now oversee. Rafael Malpica-Padilla, former bishop of the Caribbean Synod, became the division's program director for Latin America and the Caribbean. Pastor Said Ailabouni, a native of Nazareth, Israel, became program director for the Middle East and Europe. Margrethe Kleiber, with Japanese American heritage, became program director for South Asia. Benyam Kassahun, originally from Ethiopia, became program director for southern Africa.

More examples of outstanding ventures—beyond those of youth events, social services, hunger and disaster relief, and global missions—might be cited. Every church tries to be "all things" to all its members, but invariably a church will distinguish itself in some areas. These ELCA areas of distinction harken back to some of the roots of the faith—evangelism and service. Through them the ELCA reflects not only the Great Commission, but also the admonition to love one another.

CHAPTER 7

DIVERSITY AND OUTREACH

"We will double our people of color
membership in 10 years."

Fred Rajan, director of the Commission for Multicultural Ministries,
in January 1999, responding to the church's inability to meet its goal of
10 percent minority membership during its first 10 years.

The new church's emphases on diversity and outreach
seemed on the surface to be part and parcel of each other.
Both were heavily evangelistic; both were highly laudable. Only
1.85 percent of the membership of the ELCA in 1988 was non-
white and non-West European. The diversity of the predecessor
churches, by and large, remained in those "special interest groups"
that were European in background, but some of whom had not
fully assimilated into the church's culture—Hungarians, Germans,
Danes, Finns, and Slovaks. If the ELCA were to be at the forefront
of 21st-century American culture, it obviously would need to
broaden both its vision and its membership.

For Lutherans, growth often meant establishing new congregations in communities that were different from the location of
their established churches. This did not come easily. Both the
Lutheran Church in America and the American Lutheran
Church also had an uncertain history of integrating already existing congregations. The Association of Evangelical Lutheran
Churches, through its roots in The Lutheran Church—Missouri
Synod, had a more impressive track record of ministry among
black members.

But in the ELCA's beginning years, despite vigorous efforts
by the Commission for Multicultural Ministries to sensitize the
church to the needs and opportunities of what were then called
the African American, Asian, Hispanic, and Native American
communities, issues of diversity tended to devolve into debates
about quotas. Outreach—the starting of new congregations—

foundered because funds were not forthcoming to start as many new congregations as had been anticipated. These two "partner" efforts, diversity and outreach, could have augmented each other's efforts, but they languished, both individually and jointly, until the mid-1990s. By then, quotas were basically accepted and attention to multicultural efforts began to bear fruit, especially in the Hispanic communities, and in the newer immigrant communities from Southeast Asia and the Middle East. The fortunes of the Division for Outreach changed about the same time that enough funding was available for 20 percent or more of new congregations to be ethnic-specific, and for the church to talk about developing 2,000 new congregations between 2000 and 2020. Evangelism, though, remained a challenge.

Another churchwide unit that promotes diversity is the Commission on Women. Almost 600 people, including 16 men, attended the first ELCA Women's Leadership Roundtable in 2001, celebrating the growing number of women in positions of leadership across the ELCA, including 30 years as clergy. The gathering's "Lift Our Voice" theme, which saw participants gathered around more than 70 round tables, emphasized worship and song, mentoring, leadership development, and Bible study. "Women in leadership in the church is a theological issue," Pastor Barbara Lundblad, New York, told the gathering. Women and men are both created in the image of God, and spiritual gifts are granted regardless of gender or ordination, she said. "To deny the gifts of God is to dry up the waters of our baptisms."

From 1.85 percent to 2.6 percent

The ELCA's documents specifically singled out four minority groups as a focus for the new church—African Americans; Hispanics, later referred to as Latinos; Asians, later grouped with Pacific Islanders, and Native Americans, later changed to American Indians and expanded to include Alaska Natives. When the church began, its 5.2 million members included 48,261 African Americans, 22,766 Hispanics, 19,985 Asians, and

5,418 Native Americans, for a total of 96,403—or 1.85 percent of the ELCA's membership.

The interests and concerns of these four groups were brought together in the Commission for Multicultural Ministries. The commission was charged with seeing that issues related to the ethnic groups, along with the perspectives of these groups, became part of the agenda of every churchwide unit and synods. Headed by Craig J. Lewis, an African American pastor, the commission began its life aggressively. In his report to the 1989 ELCA Churchwide Assembly, Lewis said that the commission's work "progressed well in spite of or perhaps because of these challenges." He enumerated the challenges as "the lack of a clearly articulated churchwide vision of a multicultural, multi-ethnic church; the complexity of understanding and interpreting the role and function of a 'commission' in the ELCA churchwide organization, particularly the prophetic role of the commission as a social change agent for church in society; the inexperience of staff members who were underrepresented on the executive staff of the predecessor church bodies, and the failure of the ELCA constitutions, bylaws, and continuing resolutions to address adequately critical commission organizational issues and operating procedures." Lewis also said the combining of the concerns of African American, Asian, Hispanic, and Native American populations into one commission was unique among major Protestant denominations.

Each of the minority groups formed their own independent ethnic association with funding by the commission (originally at about $40,000 yearly)—United Lutherans for Black Concerns, later the African American Lutheran Association; Association of Asians—ELCA, later Association of Asian/Pacific Islanders—ELCA; Asociacion Luterana de Ministerios Hispanos de la Iglesia Evangelica Luterana en America (Association of Hispanic Ministries in the ELCA); and Native American Lutheran Association, later the American Indian/Alaska Native Association. In 1993, a fifth group was added, the Association of Lutherans of Arab and Middle Eastern Heritage.

When European-language groups asked to be included as the commission's "fifth desk," the commission's board said that the definition of "persons of color and/or persons whose primary language is other than English" did not include European-language groups. The German Interest Conference of North America, speaking on behalf of the German, Finnish, Danish, and Hungarian interest conferences, said these conferences serve immigrants not yet assimilated, as well as European students, business people, government representatives and tourists. The commission referred the request to the Church Council for clarification, which later said that the European-language groups were recognized by the Department for Ecumenical Affairs, not the multicultural commission. In 2002, the Church Council recommended a fifth special interest conference—the Batak conference, composed primarily of Batak (Lutheran) immigrants from Sumatra, Indonesia, who are part of congregations primarily in the states of California, Colorado, New York, and Washington but who wish to maintain their heritage and relationships with their homeland.

The Church Council turned down a request by the deaf community to become affiliated with the commission in 1994, saying that the responsibility for that group's concerns lay with the Division for Church in Society. (The first culturally deaf person to be ordained by the ELCA was Beth Lockard in 1999.)

Even before the ELCA officially began, sensitivity to the church's multicultural goals was being noticed. In August 1987, after the Constituting Convention elected three white officers (and the Church Council added a white treasurer), and after Presiding Bishop Herbert W. Chilstrom had selected three white assistants, the ELCA Conference of Bishops asked that the next assistant to the bishop be a member of a minority group or someone whose primary language wasn't English. Chilstrom explained that the original ELCA budget allowed for four assistants to the bishop, but early cuts in funding removed one of the positions. The bishops asked the Church Council to restore the funding in 1988, and that "this position be left open" until a minority person could be selected for the position. (The "fourth" position was never filled, and a minority person was not appointed as an assistant until one of the original assistants retired in 1993. That new assistant was Craig J. Lewis.)

Also in 1987, a multicultural gathering, "Celebrating Cultural Diversity as God's Gift for Ministry," drew more than 500 African American, Asian, Hispanic, Native American, and white congregational leaders for three days of meetings in Chicago. Three-day Multicultural Mission Institutes began in 1989 and held yearly thereafter except for 2001. The 13th and last institute was held in 2002 because the commission is combining the institute with a new Multicultural Music Festival and the biennial assemblies of the five ethnic associations to create a single biennial Multicultural Gathering beginning in 2004.

The teaching theologians of the church worked with the commission during the church's early years in exploring a vision of a multicultural church. Churchwide units sought the services of the commission to help integrate the commission's concerns into their programs. The Lutheran Youth Organization held a Multicultural Youth Leadership Event in conjunction with each Youth Gathering. The Women of the ELCA began sponsoring a multicultural gathering of women prior to each of the Women of the ELCA triennial conventions. In 1999, the Women of the ELCA considered dropping the gathering in favor of folding its activities into the main meeting with "cross-cultural, multicultural, and cross-community sharing." The convention asked the Women of the ELCA board to consider proposing a constitutional amendment "to include anti-racism as a principle of the organization."

In 1989, the commission started a series of ethnic writers workshops designed to produce ethnic writers for ELCA publications. The workshops continued yearly with 15-20 participants each workshop. That same year, Lewis told 650 participants at a Multicultural Gathering, "The ELCA is the whitest so-called mainline Protestant church in America. Our theological affirmations do not square with our sociological realities." Bishop Sherman Hicks, Metropolitan Chicago Synod and the ELCA's only black bishop at the time, cautioned the group against taking a "we-they" stance toward the church. "The reality is, you and I are the ELCA," he said.

In other early actions, the commission said that because 50 percent of ELCA Asian ministries are conducted in Chinese, churchwide units should plan on translating publications into Chinese. The commission's steering committee also asked for the church to employ Spanish and Chinese translators. A full-time Spanish translator was hired in 1993. The ELCA published three *fotonovelas*, photo stories presenting Christian themes in comic book style, a popular form of literature among some Hispanics. The commission opposed legislative efforts that would make English the official language of the United States. The commission applauded the 1989 decision when a Buffalo, New York, congregation changed its name to Christ Evangelical African-American Lutheran Church, the first ELCA congregation to change its name to reflect is racial makeup.

The commission also faced the challenge of resolving disputes within different ethnic groups. For example, the "Gathering of Reconciliation" was held to resolve a dispute over the leadership and direction of ELCA ministries among Native Americans. The issue was not resolved until mid-1989, when the Native American Lutheran Association decided by one vote to limit membership to Native Americans who are members of ELCA congregations. Similar inter-group dynamics came into play between Caribbean, Central American, and Texan-Mexican Hispanics.

In 1998, the commission brought together native Africans and African Americans for the first time. Meeting at Tuskegee University in Alabama, youth at the gathering reenacted being put on a slave ship, and took a bus trip that followed the civil rights freedom trail. The African American Lutheran Association decided to restructure in 2001 after only 119 people attended the association's assembly. Eric Campbell, director for the commission's African American ministries, said it was "evident that the organization isn't fully representative of people from across the board," referring to tensions between African Americans, Africans, and Caribbean blacks. Another sensitive point was the role of the four white members on the commission's governing body, an issue that the commission asked the Church Council to clarify.

A mandatory, two-day "multicultural training" workshop was attended by 453 ELCA staff in 1990 at a cost of $55 per person. "This church decided to become an inclusive, multicultural church, and the staff has a higher percentage of 'persons of color' and a different social fabric than previous Lutheran churches," Lewis said. "Everybody on staff was expected to reflect that commitment to inclusivity, and yet there was no training or orientation to help them meet that expectation." The spending of $24,915 for anti-racism training drew criticism because the church had ended the previous year well in the red.

ELCA Secretary Lowell Almen later said he was "convinced that the training events represented a good investment. . . . The assumption that ethnic groups are or must behave as enemies, the political and social processes that promote divisions and suspicions, the perpetuation of racial and ethnic stereotypes both by those within and outside a particular group, unwillingness to accept accountability for one's actions and attitudes—all of these are factors that in our experience had demonstrated clearly needed attention for the effectiveness of this work place." Beginning in 2003, new churchwide staff members and elected and volunteer leaders would attend a two-day anti-racism training program.

In time, the ELCA expanded its multicultural efforts in 1993 to include a group of Lutherans that said it felt "unrecognized"— the Association of Lutherans of Arab and Middle Eastern Heritage. Estimating that there were between 15,000 and 50,000 Arab and Middle Eastern Lutherans in the United States, the group asked the ELCA for a commitment to start mission work among such groups. In 1998, Salem Danish Lutheran Church in Brooklyn was reborn as Salam Arabic Lutheran Church. Salam was the first Arab Lutheran Church organized within the ELCA.

After the September 11, 2001, terrorism attacks, Pastor Khader N. El-Yateem, a native of Beit Jala on Israel's West Bank, feared hate crimes would come to his community. The congregation was featured in a PBS documentary that showed how it became a haven for both Christian and Muslim Arabs who lost their jobs and were harassed after September 11.

An increasing stream of immigrants from Southeast Asia did not ask to form a separate association, but they added to the mixture of new ELCA members. Kansas Lake Lutheran Church, Butterfield, Minnesota, which was founded in 1871 and worshiped in Swedish for its first 50 years, found in 1994 that "over half of our confirmation class is Laotian," said the Rev. Jan Hartsook. In 1998, 158 Laotians and other Southeast Asians were baptized in a swimming pool in Sioux City, Iowa. Tom LoVan, a native Laotian, had spent eight months establishing ministries at Morningside Lutheran Church in Sioux City, and at Salem Lutheran Church, just across the Missouri River in Dakota City, Nebraska. At the time the ELCA had 20 Southeast Asian ministries—seven Laotian, eight Hmong, one Cambodian, three Vietnamese, and one Thai. Another typical new congregation was La Resureccion Lutheran Church in Garden City, Kansas, an area that by 1995 was 40 percent Hispanic because of immigrants coming to work in the feed lots and meat-processing plants. A Salvadoran, Tony Mendez, was the founding pastor.

Not all the multicultural efforts were aimed at worship. Barrios Unidos, a Santa Cruz, California T-shirt production shop that helped keep kids off the streets, received a loan from the ELCA for $100,000. By 1997, the shop had annual revenue of $180,000 and, more importantly, was training youth with a skill. Based on the original ELCA loan, the director, Daniel Alejandrez, put together a revenue base from private foundations and government that brought in $1.7 million and employed 40 people on staff.

Some of the multicultural efforts became international. In 1999, the Asian Lutheran International Conference was initiated and organized by the Association of Asians—ELCA. That same year, the African American Lutheran Association participated in the Conference of International Black Lutherans that met in Wittenberg, Germany. Additionally, 100 Lutherans of African descent nailed 38 theses to the door of Castle Church titled, *Confession for the Third Millennium: Black Lutheran Experiences.*

Increasing members of color

Since the ELCA's governing documents set a goal that "within 10 years of [the church's] establishment its membership shall include at least 10 percent people of color and/or primary language other than English," the Multicultural Mission Strategy Task Force was appointed in 1988. The goal meant that 440,000 African American, Asian, Hispanic, and Native American members would be needed by 1997 to meet the goal. Presiding Bishop Herbert Chilstrom noted that the ELCA would need to add almost 1,000 ethnic members a week to reach the goal. In working with synods about their plans for multicultural ministries, the commission told the Church Council in 1990 that "only 28 synods reported that they had adopted plans to meet the mandate of the governing documents. An additional 18 synods said they either already nearly meet the goal or have an interim strategy that will lead to a long-term strategy. Nineteen synods reported that they had not yet adopted a plan."

When the ELCA turned five years old, it became obvious that the 10-year goal of 10 percent ethnic membership would not be reached. In 1992, only 2.05 percent of the church's membership was African American, Latino, Asian/Pacific Islander, or American Indian/Alaska Native—107,210 of the church's 5.2 million members. Even so, the gain represented a 22.1 percent in the increase of minority members between 1987 and 1992. African Americans totaled 51,818, for 0.99 percent; Asians/Pacific Islanders were 20,964, for 0.40 percent; Latinos were 25,023, for 0.48 percent; American Indian/Alaska Native were 6,418, for 0.12 percent. Whites totaled 5,127,358, for 97.65 percent. At this five-year juncture, the commission reported:

- There are 215 congregations with 30 percent or more African American membership. Of those 215 congregations, 30 are 100-percent African American.

- Spanish is used in worship in 158 ELCA congregations, and 54 are totally Spanish-speaking congregations.

- The ELCA has 23 "Asian/Pacific Islander specific" congregations.

- Of the ELCA's Asian and Pacific Islander members, 22 percent worship in those congregations.

- 20 ELCA congregations had 10 percent or greater American Indian/Alaska Native membership; of these, 12 had 50 percent or greater American Indian/Alaska Native membership.

By the ELCA's 10th year, 1997, movement toward the 10-percent goal still lagged far behind. Between 1988 and 1995, African American membership in ELCA African American congregations declined by 6,000. Latino membership in Spanish-speaking congregations went down by 2,000; Asian/Pacific Islander and American Indian/Alaska Native membership in their congregations remained unchanged. Even though more than 20 percent of the ELCA's new mission starts were in ethnic communities, they added only small numbers of ethnic members —African Americans, 840; Asians/Pacific Islander, 895; Latino, 2,585; American Indian/Alaska Native, 242. The only real growth in minority membership during the 10 years came in mostly white congregations. African American membership was up in these congregations 4,164; Asian/Pacific Islander, up 3,744; Latino, up 4,904; American Indian/Alaska Native, up 1,811. Pastor Frederick E. N. Rajan, who succeeded Lewis as director of the multicultural commission, pointed to social class, upward mobility of ethnic people and programs offered by white congregations as reasons. Rajan, a naturalized Indian, was president of the Association of Asians—ELCA before he became part of the commission's staff.

In 1999, Rajan predicted, "We will double our people-of-color membership in 10 years." He based his prediction on trends that the church was beginning to make real progress. ELCA worship, he pointed out, is conducted in 33 languages other than English, up dramatically from the 20 reported when the church began. "The ships are not coming from Europe," Rajan said.

Current immigrants are coming from Asia, Africa, and the Middle East, with additions of worship services in such languages as Laotian, Thai, Arabic, Amharic, Oromo, and Urdu.

A total of 60 new Spanish-speaking congregations were organized between 1991 and 1999, for a total of 207 Spanish-speaking congregations in the ELCA. Rajan noted that the church is adding congregations that worship in Spanish, Asian, African, and Middle Eastern languages faster than it is losing congregations of Northern European languages. Iglesia Luterana Principe de Paz, a 1,500-member, Spanish-speaking congregation in Miami, is the largest ELCA congregation in the city and the ELCA's largest Spanish-speaking congregation. Moreover, Rajan continued, along with the increase in ethnic churches, more than half of ELCA people of color belong to predominantly white congregations, a sign that intentional welcoming of people of color has worked.

The 2001 Churchwide Assembly adopted evangelism strategies for Latino and Asian ministries. The Asian proposal called for establishment of 40 more Asian congregations in the next eight years. Development of "A Vision: The Evangelical Lutheran Church in America's Plan of Action for Ministry in the African, African American, Black, and Caribbean Community," due in 2003, has been delayed until 2005.

Producing new music resources became a cutting-edge item for the church. In 1989, the Spanish-language hymnal *El Pueblo de Dios Canta* (*The People of God Sing*) became available. The liturgical section of *Lutheran Book of Worship* also was translated into Spanish, *Liturgia Luterana*. A major Spanish worship book, *Libro de Liturgia y Cancion*, 640 pages of liturgies, rites, services and hymns from South American, Central American, Mexican and Caribbean traditions, was published in 1998, 20 years after *Lutheran Book of Worship*. Intended for use in both Spanish and English-speaking congregations, the hymnal was a cooperative effort of the Division for Congregational Ministries, Augsburg Fortress and the multicultural commission. The ELCA Church Council shared via conference call in the excitement of the hymnal's first use by Iglesia Luterana Divino Salvador, Catano,

Puerto Rico. "We are watching a miracle happen," said Evelyn Soto of the congregational ministries division. "I can barely talk because the emotion is so great." Three boys were baptized during the service, using the new baptism liturgy. The hymnal went into its third printing in 1999.

In 1999, the ELCA published the first Lutheran hymnal reflecting African American faith and heritage, *This Far by Faith*. The 520-page worship book included more than 250 hymns, including spirituals and traditional gospel, contemporary choruses and gospel songs, and songs from Africa and Cuba. The book also contained liturgical settings for communion and other worship services for special occasions such as a Martin Luther King Jr. observance and Kwanzaa. *This Far by Faith* went into its second printing after less than six months.

By 2001, 2.6 percent of the ELCA's membership was African American, black, Asian, Pacific Islander, Latino, American Indian, Alaska Native, Arab, and Middle Easterners. African American membership was 52,848; Latino, 38,706; Asian or Pacific Islander, 22,994; and American Indian or Alaska Native, 7,161. Another 10,281 ELCA members identified their race or ethnic heritage as "other."

During its first 15 years, top ELCA leadership from the African American community included the ELCA vice president, an assistant to the presiding bishop, two synod bishops, a co-director of the Division for Congregational Ministries, a director of the multicultural commission, two presidents of Women of the ELCA, two presidents of the Lutheran Youth Organization, and two interim directors of churchwide units. From the Hispanic community came four bishops, all in the Caribbean Synod. The Asian community provided a director for the multicultural commission. A member of the American Indian community was president of the youth organization.

Perhaps the ELCA's greatest learning in its first 15 years is that its ethnic membership increase occurs largely through the welcoming of people of color by predominantly white congregations. For a church in which its predecessors had difficulty integrating congregations, this is a significant step forward, and one that seems, thus far, more promising than the founding of ethnic-specific mission congregations.

Increasing congregations

Under a colorful carnival tent along Martin Downs Boulevard in Palm City, Florida, Immanuel Lutheran Church on January 3, 1988, became the ELCA's first new mission congregation. The congregation worshiped in a converted real estate office but used the tent for the organizing service because of the size of the crowd. Charter members totaled 240, including about 118 families and 40 children.

Unfortunately, the type of experience at Immanuel Church did not occur in as many new congregations as the ELCA founders had hoped. The lower figures were made even worse because the predecessor bodies in 1986 and 1987 together started almost 200 new congregations. The intention for 1988 was 110, but the reality was 34. The Division for Outreach also closed down five missions that showed that they were unlikely to become self-supporting congregations.

In all fairness, a rumor that that the church would start 1,200 congregations by 1995 gained far too much credibility and put the church at a disadvantage. That figure was part of a resolution passed during the merger commission's late stages, who passed it on to the Transition Team who said it would be considered in the budgeting process. But the "1,200 by 1995" was never funded or adopted as a goal. As years passed, the ELCA averaged 24 new congregations a year, for a total of 335 new congregations between 1988 and 2001.

Of course, the division had other items on its agenda than starting new congregations. In 1990, about half of its $17 million budget supported existing ministries—134 congregations under development from previous years, ongoing support to 177 urban and 84 rural ministries, assisting 400 new organized ministries. In 1993, the ELCA Churchwide Assembly affirmed a commitment to rural ministry, largely through the Division for Outreach, that pledged the church to use its seminaries to develop pastors and trained laity for rural ministries, to provide resources to assist multi-point congregations, and to advocate for those hurt by economic and social conditions in rural America. In 1997, the ELCA, through the work of the division, approved an urban initiative titled "In the City for Good." Lutheran Brotherhood, a fraternal benefit society (now Thrivent), gave a $1 million grant to the effort.

During the years 1988-2001, the Division for Outreach took on a diversity of its own, partly in its outreach to ethnic communities, but more through a variety of ways of starting mission congregations. The creativity was born largely because of economic need, but the fresh strategies also responded to the needs of people who had no church experience and the population shifts in the United States. Outreach efforts included crossing some social boundaries such as extending the church's hand to gays and lesbians, and mission starts aimed at baby boomers and other generational groups, such as the Spirit Garage in Minneapolis, which was started by an existing congregation.

The upshot was that the ELCA moved from a majority of mission starts that were strategically planned by the churchwide organization to a variety of other strategies. In 1991, facing the reality that it could fund only 19 new ministries during the year, the Division for Outreach expanded its Mission Partners program to include Mission Founders, an emphasis that encouraged strong mission-minded congregations to provide full support for a new ministry until it became a self-supporting congregation.

In Fargo, North Dakota, Hope Lutheran Southpointe, an extension of Hope Lutheran Church, began as a ministry to Hope's 110 families in south Fargo and to the unchurched in that fast-growing area, but the congregation soon found its own niche by averaging 260 worshipers per Sunday.

In Middletown, Maryland, a worshiping community came together that was entirely lay-led. In Minneapolis, 90 local parishes funded partnerships in 1994 to aid the synod's urban congregations because funds from the ELCA were not available. By 1997, 1,700 congregations had contributed $5 million through Mission Partners to help support new congregations.

In 2001 alone, approximately 2,200 congregations provided almost $6 million directly to other congregations to strengthen outreach in those communities.

Mission Builders, a group of about 108 retired carpenters and construction workers from 28 states, go to new sites and spend months helping with the construction of new buildings. During its first decade, builders completed 69 construction projects in 29 states. Some new congregations were funded almost entirely by Lutheran Brotherhood (now Thrivent) that contributed nearly $1 million a year for new missions and developing congregations. In other places a combination of churchwide and synod funding started new congregations, such as in North Carolina with the synod's Loan and Gift Fund.

In many congregational starts, the division provides nearly $60,000 annually for two to three years for salaries of mission developers. But with congregational starts requiring from $250,000 to $1 million each for land and for construction of a first unit, the infusion of deposits into the ELCA Loan Fund became a critical element of mission starts. A revolving fund that lends money to new and developing congregations at a low interest rate, deposits in the Mission Investment Fund, as the Loan Fund came to be called, reached $251 million in 2001 and provided loans to 501 congregations. Finally, in 1998, the Division for Outreach heard the news for which it had waited a decade: Because of increased giving to the ELCA, the division's budget for that year was boosted by $900,000. The Division for Outreach budget for 2002 was $15.3 million, 15 percent of the church's total operating expense.

Eventually the Division for Outreach employed some 60 models for mission, including regional, ethnic, and tent-making ministries, focusing primarily on using the best style for a given location. In northern Michigan, a clergy couple started two congregations as worker/priests. The congregations are 100 miles apart in Michigan's Upper Peninsula—Christ Lutheran Church, Shingleton, and Paradise Lutheran Mission, Paradise. Pastor Kurt Kovanen was an accountant at a nursing home and Pastor Mary Beth Kovanen was the director of a day-care center.

In 1992, the ELCA made its only foray into the megachurch style. Aimed primarily to baby boomers, the effort was located in east Yorba Linda, California, in highly mobile and affluent Orange County. The effort was a joint effort of the Division for Outreach, the Pacifica Synod, local congregations and Lutheran Brotherhood. Malcolm Minnick, then the executive director of the Division for Outreach, said much of the impetus for the megachurch model came not from boomers, but from older Lutherans who want "revitalized congregations so they can reach the spiritual needs of their children and grandchildren." Officials expected the first service in Yorba Linda to attract 500 adults, with a church membership there between 3,000 and 5,000 member in five to 10 years.

The experiment in "mega" starts was unsuccessful. "We don't use the term anymore," said Richard Magnus, executive director of the Division for Outreach in 2002. "It sets up too many expectations that are not guaranteed just because we entered in a more costly way. We found that it was difficult to put a team together. Our pastors are not trained well to work in teams—too often competition develops that undermines the goals. We also learned that we need to enter with strong leadership and then encourage that leadership to find the rest of the team of leaders from the group that is assembling. In other words, the answer is not more clergy to start a large congregation, but visionary clergy that can empower laity to use their gifts to do ministry. Some of those laity, in areas that grow rapidly and reach significant size, will become part of a paid staff." In time, Messiah Lutheran Church in Yorba Linda became a significant congregation (1,340 members in 1999) because they came together with another congregation and answered some of the challenges that way, Magnus said.

Elsewhere, new congregations were funded that seemed reminiscent of earlier days. German multicultural corporations sent staff in such numbers to Atlanta and Charlotte that German-speaking missions sprang up in both cities. A Russian-speaking mission congregation began in Philadelphia, and a Finnish-speaking pastor became the pastor-in-residence at St. Andrew

Lutheran Church, Lake Worth, Florida. Distinctive language services were frequently the focus of a mission start—Portuguese, Polish, Sri Lankan, Korean, Ethiopian, Vietnamese, and Hmong. A Chinese ministry began in Philadelphia. Truth Lutheran Church flourished in Naperville, Illinois. A Thai congregation became part of the ELCA in 1995, an outgrowth of St. Paul Lutheran Church, Forest Park, Illinois.

New congregations inside prison walls developed in South Dakota and Iowa. The division's involvement in the Lutheran Association for Maritime Ministry expanded with a congregation to fisherfolk in Providence, Rhode Island. The division affirmed "Ecumenical Shared Congregations" that outlined operating principles for churches composed of two or more denominations and served by one pastor. In 1996, the division's board directed the staff to "develop outreach strategies to gay and lesbian people, especially in communities where there are large populations of homosexual persons," to ensure that they hear "the basic gospel message of salvation" (see chapter 4). The result was "Congregational Hospitality to Gay and Lesbian Persons," a notebook shared with interested congregations.

In 1998, a decade after the church's founding, the division launched a major campaign to boost the founding of 2,000 congregations between the years 2000 and 2020, an average of 100 per year. Key to the initiative was the division's challenge to all ELCA congregations "to participate in parenting a new congregation during the first 20 years of the new millennium. Congregations would be asked to recruit potential pastors and pastor/developers from their membership, to recruit lay volunteers to be trained in evangelism who will serve for a limited time in the new mission, and to cover mission development costs for three years, including a pastor/developer's salary and setup costs for marketing, office and worship materials. These projects may be done cooperatively by more than one congregation.

Part of the challenge focuses on congregations sponsoring new churches not in their vicinity, but in growth areas of the United States that may be thousands of miles from the congregation. For instance, Immanuel Lutheran Church, Thomasboro, Illinois, celebrated its 125th anniversary by financing a congregation 400 miles away in Georgia. St. Andrew Lutheran Church, Eden Prairie, Minnesota, committed $150,000 to found Spirit of Grace Lutheran Church, Surprise, Arizona. National demographics make this cross-country support mandatory. Seven states—Pennsylvania, Ohio, Illinois, Iowa, Wisconsin, Minnesota, and North Dakota—have 57 percent of the ELCA's baptized membership and 50 percent of the ELCA's congregations. But the states with the fastest growing populations by percentage from 1990 to 1996 were Georgia, Texas, New Mexico, Colorado, Arizona, Utah, Nevada, Idaho, Oregon, and Washington. In most new congregations, 60 to 80 percent of the charter members have never been a church member or have been inactive for at least two years.

The congregations organized since 1988 (272 reporting) have 82,290 baptized members, average 252 baptized members, and contribute $2.8 million in mission support (2000 figures). The Southeastern Synod has seen the greatest number of congregations organized since 1988—25. This is followed by the Florida-Bahamas Synod, with 20; the Grand Canyon Synod, with 17; the Rocky Mountain Synod, with 15; the Metropolitan Chicago Synod, with 13; and the Central States Synod, with 11. In January 2002, 120 congregations were under development, 24 of which were started in 2001. Between 1988 and 2001, the ELCA averaged 24 new congregations a year.

Late in 2002, Magnus said it was "music to our ears" that the evangelism strategy (see below) and Presiding Bishop Mark Hanson's strategic planning process were prompting questions about what starting 100 congregations a year would cost. "That's been the problem up to now," Magnus said. "We've said we want to do it, but we haven't come close to funding it. At least this time the church will know what it would take to do it."

Growth and evangelism

The diminishing number of new congregational starts is unfortunately reflective of the ELCA's track record in evangelism.

The 1991 Churchwide Assembly adopted a 10-year evangelism strategy, "A Telling Witness of God's Good News." When a report on the effectiveness of the strategy was given at the 2001 Churchwide Assembly, the news was sobering, if not shocking, in its assessment.

The report noted, for example, that during that decade, the churchwide organization produced or conducted 280 distinct evangelism resources or events. The ELCA developed a comprehensive set of print, video, audio, and Web site congregational evangelism resources. The ELCA churchwide organization launched a four-point strategy to equip congregations for effective evangelism in hospitality, discipleship/incorporation, intentional community outreach and communication. Grants to synods encouraged synodical evangelism ministry. Nonetheless, a March 1996 report showed that both clergy and congregation council members ranked "proclaiming the Gospel to the unchurched" as one of the three areas of 24 congregational activities in which they were least effective. Another report indicated that during the 1991-2001 decade, no more congregations, based on clergy reports, organized programs for membership recruitment than in 1977.

On a more optimistic side, a five-year study of growing congregations found that they grew because of a primary understanding of the Great Commission as the congregation's mission, and movement from maintenance ministry among members to a focus on mission among the unchurched. Growing congregations also engaged in cross-cultural evangelism, active neighborhood outreach, diverse and multiple worship services, strategic future planning, shared leadership between church staff and lay leaders, intentional hospitality to guests, relational evangelism among members, and multiple forms of disciple-making ministries.

The report noted that between 1991 and 1999, 25 of the ELCA's 65 synods grew, led by the Saint Paul Area Synod with 17,462 members and Grand Canyon Synod with 13,474 members. The greatest losses—3,000 or more members—came in three Pennsylvania synods, the metropolitan synods of New York and Chicago and the Southern California (West) Synod.

But the report's historical perspective was the most revealing. The steady stream of immigrants from Scandinavia and Germany throughout the 19th century provided Lutheran churches with new adult members without needing to proselytize. The report recalled historian E. Clifford Nelson's observation: "The high rate of immigrating had the effect of establishing and institutionalizing on American soil the Lutheranism of 19th century Europe." Furthermore, Nelson noted, the movement also had an "isolating and introverting effect upon Lutherans in their relationships to each other and to other American Protestants" and "provided for membership growth despite the isolation and introversion." In other words, Lutherans did not need to work at being overtly evangelistic; they relied on growth that came naturally from within.

Immigration from Scandinavia and Germany slowed at the beginning of the 20th century. Lutherans did not experience significant growth in their membership until after World War II, as did virtually all churches in America. The American Lutheran Church and the Lutheran Church in America added 1.5 million members, a 42 percent increase, between 1950 and 1970. During these years, the Roman Catholic Church grew by almost 20 million members, and the fastest growing Protestant body, the Southern Baptist Convention, grew by 4.5 million members. Also during these years, the Assemblies of God grew by 98 percent and the Church of Jesus Christ of Latter-day Saints increased its membership by 87 percent.

In 1965, the membership of the predecessor bodies of the ELCA peaked at 5,650,137, about 3 percent of the total population of the United States. By 1970, the members in the ALC and the LCA decreased about 30,000 and the downward trend continued into the 1980s. Between 1970 and 1980, the ALC and the LCA lost about 26,000 members per year.

Between 1990 and 1999, church membership stabilized. Losses were not as severe among the mainline denominations and gains by the conservative and Pentecostal groups moderated. Instead of growing at 10 percent a year, the growth rate among Assemblies of God congregations is now about 2 percent per year. Most established religious denominations in the United States, including the ELCA, are still losing members, but at a rate of about 1 percent per year or less. Most of the growing groups are gaining less than 1 percent per year. Between 1998 and 1999, the ELCA lost about 28,500 members. ELCA membership dropped by 36,937 in 1988 and by 12,736 in 1989 before gaining 1,959 members in 1990. By 2001, the church had two years of statistical growth and 12 years of losses, with membership at the end of 2001 standing at 5,099,877.

The most chilling commentary about membership comes in the unvarnished language of a 1991-2001 evangelism review: "From this simple but bottom-line point of view—that membership growth is evidence of progress in evangelism—the conclusion is straightforward. Lutherans have never embraced evangelism as a central part of the mission of the church. Despite an enormous amount of recent effort at reorienting this church, the ELCA has lost members every year since it adopted an evangelism strategy in 1991 (and well before). While accounting for the losses with some confidence is difficult, they appear to come

ELCA Baptized Membership

1988	5,251,534	1995	5,190,489
1989	5,238,798	1996	5,180,910
1990	5,240,739	1997	5,185,055
1991	5,245,177	1998	5,178,225
1992	5,234,568	1999	5,149,668
1993	5,212,785	2000	5,125,919
1994	5,199,048	2001	5,099,877

Net loss: 151,657 baptized members

from two primary sources—decline in child baptisms and fewer transfers from and to other ELCA congregations. The number of members who are dying also has increased somewhat, but this increase is moderate. The number of people transferring to non-ELCA Lutheran and non-Lutheran congregations is down. On the gain side, the number of adult baptisms averages about 8,300 per year and has varied little since 1991. Adult affirmations of faith also vary little and average about 62,000 per year.

"In short," the review continues, "this church is baptizing fewer children and a larger and larger proportion of existing members are leaving ELCA congregations with little evidence that they are becoming active again in other churches. Without adult conversions to Lutheranism to offset the decline in child baptisms, or without considerable attention to why people are leaving, the ELCA will continue to lose members and a voice in the American dialogue on religion."

ELCA Secretary Lowell Almen remarked that the "report essentially listed a number of things that had been done during the decade related to evangelism and between the lines acknowledged that none of them had worked all that well. All that activity took place, and yet the congregations of this church still lost members—not nearly as many as some mainline churches, such as the Methodists and the Presbyterians, but we still lost members."

The 2001 assembly adopted 965-9 an evangelism strategy that invites the entire church to reflect on evangelism, inviting individual congregations to clarify their sense of purpose and mission, to seek ways to be open to innovation and change, and to share new or existing evangelism plans with the whole church. A 33-member "blue-ribbon" task force was assembled to develop a comprehensive evangelism strategy for the 2003 assembly, including a multiplicity of models for congregational growth along with the "best practices" of evangelism in the church, and a continuation of the ELCA-wide Call to Discipleship. Four objectives were listed at the heart of the strategy—to help the ELCA become a praying church, to develop evangelical lay and clergy leaders, to begin and renew congregations, and to teach discipleship.

Colleges and seminaries

The ELCA's 28 colleges and eight seminaries support the church's diversity and outreach efforts in a variety of ways, some of them unique. Beginning in 1986, 25 of the ELCA's colleges gave tuition, room, and board to 70 students from Namibia as a way of helping the nation have college graduates who would become the nation's leaders when it received its independence from South Africa in March 1990. The program was developed because Namibia—nearly 50 percent Lutheran—had no colleges or universities. The Namibians presence gave them insight into "seeing whites in a new way," and "opened the eyes" of U.S. students at the colleges. At one time, Dana College, Blair, Nebraska, had six Namibian students.

In 1989, enrollment of African American, Asian, Hispanic, and Native American students in the ELCA's 29 colleges (later 28) reached a then-all-time high of 2,770, representing 6.3 percent of the colleges' full-time enrollment. Upsala College, East Orange, New Jersey, the church's most urban college, reported that ethnic minorities made up 49 percent of its student body, while Augustana College, Sioux Falls, South Dakota, had fewer than 1 percent. (Upsala College closed its doors in 1995.)

In 2001, the ELCA's 28 colleges served 48,500 students, with 6,900 students of color, 13 percent of the colleges' total enrollment. There are also some 1,200 international students. Remarkably, 55 percent of the young seminarians are graduates of an ELCA college or university. The ELCA also has campus ministries at 160 public and private colleges and universities. In the Council of Ecumenical Christian Ministry, the colleges cooperate with the colleges of several of the ELCA's full communion partners.

Other college and seminary activities related differently to diversity. Midland College, Fremont, Nebraska, where athletic teams are nicknamed the Warriors, banned the "tomahawk chop." In Northfield, Minnesota, the heavily Norwegian-background St. Olaf College, named a liaison to the student senate to advocate for the school's 2.7 percent ethnic enrollment. During the 500th anniversary of Christopher Columbus landing in the Americas, the students and staff of Wartburg Seminary, Dubuque, Iowa, apologized for the treatment of Native Americans. The apology was read during a radio interview with Wartburg student Joe Brown Thunder. The seminary invited elders from the Sac and Fox Nation in Stroud, Oklahoma, for an overnight visit with entertainment, singing, a potluck supper and presentation of gifts.

A major outreach into ethnic communities, particularly in urban areas, comes through the 200 elementary and 30 secondary schools sponsored by ELCA congregations. There are also 2,000 preschools, serving 25,000 children with 20,000 teachers. The number of schools related to congregations grew by 25 percent since 1995.

With increasing number of ethnic-specific congregations, developing leadership for congregations of people of color became a key issue for seminaries. In 1989, Craig J. Lewis, director of the Commission for Multicultural Ministries, said that Lutheran churches in the United States suffer an "alarming and discouraging shortage" of African American pastors, noting that of the 15,000 ELCA clergy at that time, only about 200 were African American. The shortage meant that white pastors would serve a majority of predominantly black Lutheran congregations for at least another decade.

The Theological Education for Emerging Ministries (TEEM) program, known until 1999 as the Alternative Route program, initially was intended for developing minority pastoral candidates. Begun by Pacific Lutheran Seminary, Berkeley, California, it allowed participants to continue their employment and support themselves and their families. As the years passed, the program become part of all eight ELCA seminaries, with most students working with the Lutheran School of Theology at Chicago. Courses are taught by seminary faculty through intensive three- to four-week classes and through on-line courses. In a shift from earlier days, the greatest number of students are now preparing for rural ministries, nearly half of them Caucasian. From 1996 to 2002, 70 persons were ordained through TEEM—30 Caucasians for rural ministries, 13 African Americans, 14 Latinos,

11 Asians, and two American Indians. In early 2003, 81 people were preparing for ordination through TEEM, 35 Caucasians, 20 Latinos, 18 African Americans, seven Asians, and one Arab.

In 1988, the ELCA had 270 pastors of color, as well as 32 African-American, 13 Hispanic, six Asian, and one Native American seminarians. In 2001, the ELCA had 473 pastors of color—172 African American, 157 Latino, 120 Asian and Pacific Islander, and 24 American Indian and Alaska Native. In addition, 26 African-Americans, 14 Latinos, 13 Asian and Pacific Islanders, and one American Indian were Master of Divinity candidates in the church's eight seminaries.

Another source of help for all seminary students is the Fund for Leaders, which provides full tuition scholarships yearly for seminarians. In 2000-2001, the fund supported 24 students; 16 more were added in 2002. The fund, administered by the Division for Ministry, responded to the trend in the 1990s toward more second-career students who often completed seminary with a significant debt load. In the late 1990s, the average age of an ordinand was 39. An unusual ordination in 1993 was the ordination at age 76 of Pastor John O'Neal Sr., an ex-convict. By 2001, the number of seminarians under the age of 35 increased sharply. Also in 2001, women accounted for more than half of ELCA seminarians—615 out of 1,211 students in Master of Divinity programs. Total ELCA seminary enrollment reached a high of 1,465 in 1994, but declined each year afterward.

A similar option for alternative leadership, especially for small congregations with few finances, is "lay presidency" in which a bishop may authorize a layperson to perform official functions. The Conference of Bishops in 2002 asked the ELCA's ministry and worship staffs for advice on laypersons presiding at communion and preaching, as well as concerns related to education, standards and accountability. Practices now vary from synod to synod. The ELCA has 575 synodically authorized lay ministers.

In 2003, an element of full communion agreements came into play when McCormick Theological Seminary of the Presbyterian Church (U.S.A.) and the ELCA's Lutheran School of Theology at Chicago completed the construction of McCormick's new offices on the LSTC campus.

In 1988, ELCA 10,030 pastors served 11,120 congregations; a decade later both figures decreased—9,583 pastors serving 10,862 congregations. But the number of ordinations remained steady at an average of 322. Difficulties arose, however, because in 1988, 21 percent of congregations with 175 or fewer members had no called pastor, while 10 years later 38 percent of congregations that size had no called pastor. At the same time, more ELCA active pastors leave the roster each year than are added.

In 1998, 379 ministers were added to the ELCA roster, but 490 left. In 2001, the ELCA had 17,686 pastors (active and retired), 1,058 Associates in Ministry, 53 diaconal ministers and 71 deaconesses. Thirty-one years after the beginning of the ordination of women, 20.4 percent of ELCA pastors are women. In 2000, the oldest active pastor is age 84, and the pastor serving the same call for the longest time is 52 years. A 2002 study on clergy health and wellness found the following:

1. More ELCA clergy and rostered lay leaders report job-related stress than the population average.

2. That 68 percent of ELCA clergy report they are in the over-weight to obese range, compared with 61 percent of the U.S. population.

3. That 18 percent of clergy and rostered lay leaders report elevated blood cholesterol, which is similar to the U.S. population.

4. Clergy are in the top 10 occupations dying from heart disease, with Lutheran clergy have a higher rate of heart disease than other clergy.

CHAPTER 8

2001 AND BEYOND

"I do not regard this an election won,
but a call received."

*ELCA Presiding Bishop Mark S. Hanson,
accepting election August 11, 2001*

The new millennium has arrived, and with it unimaginable challenges and changes. The church as the ELCA has known it, both through its predecessors' history as well as it own first 15 years, will rapidly recede into the past. The future is arriving and the ELCA may not be ready to meet the looming challenges. Early in 2002, the ELCA's director for research, Kenneth Inskeep, pointed out some new trends in the ELCA— smaller congregations with fewer worshipers, small congregations losing members and not able to afford a full-time pastor, richer congregations getting richer, and the number of congregations and pastors decreasing.

More specifically, regular attendees in ELCA pews are older adults, families with children ages six to 12, married people, widows and widowers, and college graduates. Not-so-regular attendees in ELCA pews are high school students, young mobile adults, families with young children, empty nesters, single people, divorced or separated people, couples living together before marriage, people of color, immigrants, gays and lesbians, people with disabilities, high school dropouts, and high school graduates who did not graduate from college.

The lists are breathtaking, as in taking one's breath away. Thus the ELCA's own research not only assesses the present but lays down in graphic language a path that lies ahead, a path fraught with more difficulty than most churches or church members are ready to admit or actively trying to meet. Those who stay away from church do so mainly because their needs aren't being met, analysts say. Inskeep notes that roughly two-thirds of singles stay away from churches. "Many singles put their energies into their education and careers. But once they marry and have children, about one-third come back."

An ever-mobile and busy society, Inskeep adds, has created "weak ties"—people participate in social structures, such as the church, at their convenience and on their terms. ELCA research also shows that 41 percent of members have belonged to their congregations for more than 20 years, compared with a national survey that found that one in every three worshipers is new to their congregation. When ELCA members were asked what aspects of their congregation they valued the most, the majority of answers were "sharing in Holy Communion." Although some congregations have been split by the so-called "worship wars" that exist when congregations struggle move from a traditional way to a contemporary style worship, the church as a whole has taken changing worship practices in stride. The adoption in 1997 of a *Statement of Sacramental Practices, The Use of the Means of Grace,* was widely appreciated and helpful to those involved in local worship planning.

"There are signs that the debate is shifting away from battles over style," said Michael Burk, ELCA Director for Worship, "making way for conversations about more central things. There is interest all across the church in the 'quality' of worship. People want worship to embody what we claim to believe. This churchwide interest may add to the intensity, but it need not distract us from deciding together that there really are some things we hold in common, some practices we ought to share."

Based on *The Use of the Means of Grace,* Burk continued, these convictions are that Sunday is the primary day for worship, that the assembled gathering is the church and the entire assembly participates in proclaiming the Word of God, that worship is enhanced when lay assisting ministers serve in various roles, that baptism takes place in the midst of the faith community, that the Eucharist is celebrated every Sunday and festival, and that believers gathered around Word and sacrament are led into mission by these very means of grace.

Renewing Worship, a process that will continue through the summer of 2005, encourages the whole church to participate in the development of the next generation of worship resources to succeed *Lutheran Book of Worship*. An early gathering of materials focused on the four dimensions of ELCA worship: language, music, preaching, and worship. Congregations and members are asked to share their creations in word, song and art. A series of provisional materials will be developed and tested in a variety of worship settings. The materials are intended to be "newly developed, ecumenically shared, and recently revised texts, rites, and music." "We're listening for what works and what doesn't work locally," Burk said. "There is a desire for freedom in how we worship locally, and a desire to worship in ways that can legitimately and with integrity be called 'Lutheran.'" Significant input is coming from the church's full communion partners—the Reformed, Episcopal, and Moravian traditions.

Still another survey of ELCA members said that 80 percent felt their congregation clearly expresses its Lutheran heritage, 82 percent said their congregation's worship services are spiritually uplifting; 99 percent said the sermon always or often focused on God's love and care; 86 percent said that Scripture is "absolutely foundational" as a source of authority for congregational worship and teaching; 49 percent said their congregation has a clear sense of mission; 30 percent reported conducting a growth or evangelistic campaign within the past year; and only 18 percent said they were doing "very well" or "quite well" in trying to increase the racial diversity of their congregation.

Other research, especially the study of young people by Roland Martinson of Luther Seminary, St. Paul, Minnesota, deals with "whether our children will have faith, and whether our faith will have children." Martinson's study suggests that although high percentages of ELCA baptized children participate in children's ministries and confirmation, if these same youth cease participation in worship and congregational ministries by age 21—and do not return to the faith community by age 35—they have an anemic, distorted faith and theology.

Shockingly, Martinson found that only about 10 percent of baptized children and youth continue in the life of the church.

A total of 17 ELCA congregations were singled out in 2001 in a nationwide study as among 300 "outstanding Protestant churches" in the United States. Traits of such congregations, the study showed, were "having faith in God and faith in the people," "relying on people in the pews—not just the staff and the clergy," "accepting people as they are—jeans or suits," being a "place to elevate the spirit," and looking "at their areas as a mission field." The size of the congregation does not matter, the report continued. "What matters is imagination or lack of it," not the amount of resources or a beautiful building. "It takes work," the report continued, "constantly asking if there is a better way to do things."

An ELCA survey on worship attendance revealed that "a clear sense of mission and purpose" is the most "important factor associated with a change in average worship attendance." The next most important factor associated with a change in average worship attendance is the congregation's willingness to welcome innovation and change. Other important "predictors of growth" in average worship attendance are that the congregation is "spiritually vital and alive," " the congregation is excited about its future," the congregation is a place where new members are easily "incorporated" into the life of the church, and the congregation deals openly with disagreements and conflicts.

Partially because of the ELCA Identity Project, a multimedia advertising campaign aimed at raising awareness for the ELCA, recognition of the Lutheran church name between 1996 and 2001 increased from 25 to 30 percent in a random sample of the U.S. population, according to a study commissioned by the ELCA Department for Communication. "The increase from 25 to 30 percent in 'unaided' awareness of the Lutheran Church represents more than 14 million people who now know the name 'Lutheran,'" said the department's director, Eric C. Shafer.

In addition to the almost overwhelming challenges to the ELCA that emerge from these statistics, some philosophical trends arise that present still other issues for the church to face.

Despite Gallup Polls showing how an overwhelming number of Americans believe in God, American culture is generally indifferent to religion—turning often to a superficial piety that has virtually no understanding of sin and grace, repentance and renewal, or doctrines and dogma, of depth and substance. An increasing disinterest in denominations is difficult for a denomination like Lutheranism for whom doctrine is foundational. "Pop culture" reflects whatever is popular at the moment and is an unlikely conveyer of the meaning of timeless issues. Young people don't seek absolutes because they don't believe there are any; rather, they tend to give all choices equal weight. A disinterest in art, music, and history adds to the shallowness, and although there is some interest in spirituality, much of it is highly personal and inner-directed, a private matter that disdains an institutional framework and rejects organizational interference in the religious experience. While Generations X and Y value personal relationships and the desire for community, these staples of organized religion somehow do not connect with them.

Against these daunting projections of the future and still grappling with divisiveness in the church over ecumenical decisions and issues related to gay and lesbian people, the 2001 Churchwide Assembly gathered in Indianapolis for what turned out to be a different assembly than any in the ELCA's past. The assembly format was the same and the 1,039 voting members worked long and hard. The agenda was varied and full. *The Lutheran* heralded on its cover, "Assembly moves church forward." On its inside pages, the magazine reported that "this was an activist and multifaceted assembly . . . revealing a church hungry for unity, anxious for outreach and eager to work together to heal its divisions and strengthen its witness. Voting members breathed confidence that the future holds promise and blessing, even as they moved forward on controversial issues, which they have now set squarely before the entire ELCA."

The 2001 assembly was the first assembly to be a multiple-issue assembly—election of a presiding bishop, tidying up the aftermath of *Called to Common Mission*, and setting a time line for making a decision about gay and lesbian ordinations in 2005.

In 1989, the Churchwide Assembly met in a dark Chicago warehouse where little happened other than the confrontation between voting members and the Board of Pensions over divestment from South Africa. In 1991, the abortion statement was a significant decision and a time that showed the church was coalescing significantly except in Region 3 (Minnesota and the Dakotas) and part of Region 5 (Iowa, Illinois, and Wisconsin). In 1993 in Kansas City, the ministry study was concluded, which turned out not to be such a momentous decision after all. In 1995 in Minneapolis, H. George Anderson was elected presiding bishop, setting a different tone in the Office of Presiding Bishop. In 1997 in Philadelphia, there was the split-decision on full communion, with the Reformed churches up and the Episcopal Church down by six votes short of the two-thirds requirement. In 1999 in Denver, the vote for Episcopal full communion passed by 27 votes more than the two-thirds requirement (716-317).

"The overall tone of the 2001 assembly seemed to be positive," recalled ELCA Secretary Lowell Almen. "I am tempted to characterize the assembly as the Chihuahua assembly, with nipping at the heels of Bishop Anderson from one time or another by three or four voting members." David L. Miller, editor of *The Lutheran*, said, "Voters took control of this assembly more than at any ELCA assembly I have attended, even turning the Memorials Committee recommendations on their head on several occasions. By inserting an extra question-and-answer session with the finalists in the presiding bishop election, the mood of the assembly was, 'I don't care what the assembly planners have in mind, this [election] is our decision, and we need as many chances to hear nominees as we can get.'"

The assembly might have seen more political activity than previous assemblies—maneuvering by those wanting an exception to ordination in the historic episcopate, the gay ordination issue and the secretary's vote, which needed four ballots as some candidates appeared to posture for the future. Regardless of the various dynamics, however, the election of Saint Paul Area Synod Bishop Mark S. Hanson as presiding bishop gave both the assembly and the church a sense that a new day was coming in the ELCA.

Mark Stephen Hanson—a new breed

The ELCA's third presiding bishop is the first to have spent as much of his ministry in the ELCA as in one of the predecessor churches. The first two presiding bishops had LCA roots, but Hanson—and six of the seven finalists in the 2001 voting—were ALC in background. His election marked the first time that the church's chief executive came from the smaller of the churches involved in the ELCA, LCA, or ALC mergers.

The fourth ballot, which included the names of Hanson, Bishop Donald McCoid, Southwestern Pennsylvania Synod, and James Nestingen, a faculty member at Luther Seminary, St. Paul, Minnesota, reduced the field for the final ballot to Hanson and McCoid. "I'm as happy as a clam to go back to the classroom," Nestingen told the assembly. On the final ballot, Hanson was chosen over McCoid by a vote of 533-499, a 34-vote margin. In his acceptance speech, Hanson reminded voting members that a two-thirds vote is required in congregations to call a pastor. "This [vote] is a stark reminder that this church has raised up seven people—all of whom could have served you well."

With no clear front-runner when the assembly opened, the election placed more emphasis than usual on the nominees' "performance" in their five-minute addresses and in the two question-and-answer periods. The format seemed to play to Hanson's strength. He was articulate and telegenic on the assembly hall's big television screen, charismatic and fearless, warm and inviting, casting a rather different vision of what the church could be. One observer said that "Don seemed diffident about being presiding bishop, but Mark looked like a guy who saw the Office of Bishop as a potent expression of his own deep sense of call. He was the more convincing of the finalists, and clearly relished the opportunity to speak to the assembly and tell them about his grasp of the mission of this church, and voters began to get on board." By contrast, McCoid seemed uncomfortable and cool, and had trouble identifying the center of the questions.

Hanson's ecclesiology (the nature of the church) gained him votes and lost him votes. He seemed to know that if the church is to be in mission, then the church has to have some breathing room on some issues. He doubtless had the support of those who felt strongly that the positions of the church related to gay and lesbian issues must change in significant ways. Former LCA members feared his leanings toward congregationalism when he said before the assembly that the church may need to consider ordaining certain people for certain places, referring to ordinations of gay persons to serve in churches that serve gay communities. Others, including a number of former ALC voting members, did not object to such suggestions.

Voting proceeded largely along both regional and predecessor church body lines. The Conference of Bishops tried hard to elect McCoid who had served as their chair the previous four years. The support backfired at least once when a voting member told his bishop, "I hear you about McCoid, but I've been listening to the speeches and I have to vote for Hanson." Highlighting the politicizing that lay behind the voting, some members of the WordAlone network and some individuals including James Nestingen and Bishop Rick Foss, Eastern North Dakota Synod, lobbied voting members before the final ballot to vote for McCoid. Hanson's perceived liberality on gay issues overrode a concern for electing someone from their region.

Without question, Hanson earned voting members' confidence with the speeches and the question-and-answer sessions, gaining in votes with each ballot. His passion for the church came through repeatedly. "Can we have a sense of urgency for God's mission without becoming so frenetic with activity that we fail to remember this is the Lord's church, not ours, that we live each day as forgiven sinners, bathed in God's grace, marked with the cross of Christ, sealed with the Holy Spirit?" he challenged.

Responding to his vision for the church, Hanson told voters that we are a "missionary church. . . . I think for a few generations that we became lazy about that because the culture started seemingly producing Christians for us. That does not happen any longer. I sense within the ELCA an awakening desire among laity to learn how better to have the courage to invite others into the faith."

Regarding how he would facilitate decision making to help the church address difficult issues, Hanson said, "We must make sure we are listening to each other rather than talking about one another. I am afraid that we have divided this church with so many in special interest groups, that we only talk with people who agree with us about those other people who are not in the room. Most of us were not raised in families where we learned to have lively discourse and fierce debates, but we were utterly certain that at the end of them, we still belonged to each other in a bond of love." He lamented the inability of many people in the ELCA to debate issues and still maintain a sense of unity.

Hanson even asked the voting members a question: "Will we permit the one whom we call to his office to be a servant leader and not just a lightning rod for this church? Yes, continuing to lead us in conversation about the important questions of ministry, authority, sexuality, and unity, but also calling us to a time of prayer and discernment regarding what God can do when the members of 11,000 congregations are brought together in mission and in Christ's name, and then bring a vision of that mission to the 2003 assembly so that we might debate it and revise it and embrace it and begin to restructure this church around it, remembering always that we have already been given to the power of the Holy Spirit, and we are already sent into the world to bear witness to God's love and grace and mercy in Christ Jesus, our Lord. Ahhh, what a holy calling it is that we all share."

At a news conference Hanson made perhaps his most remembered declaration: "I don't plan to spend most of my time reacting to crises. Differences and conflict don't scare me. I will define my call not on the basis of conflicts but mission."

Throughout the assembly, Hanson was accessible to voting members. Hanson, McCoid, and their wives showed their genuine regard for each other by worshiping together on the night of Hanson's election.

Fifty-four at the time of his election, Hanson is a native of St. Paul, Minnesota, the son of a Lutheran evangelist. He graduated from Union Seminary, New York, attended Luther Seminary, St. Paul, Minnesota, and was a Merrill Fellow at Harvard

Divinity School in 1979. He was pastor of two congregations in Minneapolis, and one in Edina, Minnesota. In 1995, he was elected bishop of the Saint Paul Area Synod in an area where his late father-in-law, the Rev. J. Elmo Agrimson, served as an ALC district president. Hanson and his wife, Ione, have six children, four adopted. In addressing the churchwide staff about three weeks after his election, Hanson said, "I will enter this church-wide office remembering that it is God's mission for which I am being called, not mine." He said the close vote for presiding bishop was not a sign of a divided church, but that it signifies a "very balanced church." Disagreements and live debates in the ELCA are the sign of a healthy church, he said.

At his installation October 6, 2001, in Rockefeller Chapel on the campus of the University of Chicago, he heard the Rev. Heidi Neumark's sermon challenge him: "Mark, people will be watching your feet—where you walk, where you visit, where you lead and where you allow yourself to be led. . . . Mark, please lead the stampede. Lead us to Ground Zero. Take us to the waste places of disconnect from each other, from other nations, from our earth, from God—that we too may be able to be made new all together."

In his first year, Hanson met with the ELCA synods, and in 2002 he was elected a vice president of the Lutheran World Federation. ELCA Secretary Lowell Almen, who served in his capacity with each of the ELCA's three bishops, noted after Hanson's first year, "Mark is doing an outstanding job, certainly a worthy successor to George Anderson and the knowledge, perspective and gravitas that George brought to that office."

Hanson initiated several efforts to help the church commit itself to the breadth and depth of God's mission in the world. Hanson also wrote *Faithful Yet Changing: The Church in Challenging Times*, a booklet intended to inspire congregational groups and to elicit discussion in eight specific areas: being a witnessing, worshiping, engaging, equipping, inviting, connecting, changing, and a praying church.

Hanson also began developing a strategic planning process. The process includes several continuing emphases—ministry among people in poverty, ecumenical partnerships, leadership development, ethnic ministry strategies, renewing worship including conferences about new primary worship resources designed to succeed *Lutheran Book of Worship*, developing a vision for evangelism and organizing studies on sexuality.

"It is important that we address each one and see their inter-relatedness," Hanson said. To assist in this process, he asked every 2002 synod assembly to discuss the three most important factors in the larger society in the last three decades that continue to have the greatest impact on the mission and ministry of the ELCA as a whole. The assemblies were then asked what three things are most essential to do so the ELCA can move effectively into the future. The 2003 Churchwide Assembly will receive the results.

Hanson also found his public voice, speaking out sharply against potential U.S. military involvement in ousting Saddam Hussein from power in Iraq, and publicly supported the United Nations resolution to disarm Iraq by peaceful means. He joined other church leaders in meeting with President George W. Bush's national security advisor, Condoleezza Rice. Earlier, Hanson affirmed the President Bush's call for an independent Palestinian state, for Israel to remove its military forces from Palestinian-controlled areas, and supported Israel's right to exist.

In March 2003, Hanson criticized the White House for declining to meet with 40 religious leaders on Iraq. The group was informed that the president's staff questioned why President Bush should meet with a group opposed to his policy. "I say that would be a reason in and of itself," Hanson said. "If the president severs himself from moral leaders in society and hears only the voices that are advising him in terms of what is strategically the right military response, then we have essentially had our president turn his back on moral leaders."

In October 2002, when bishops, vice presidents, secretaries, and treasurers from the 65 synods, along with leaders of church-wide units—nearly 500 in all—gathered in Chicago, Hanson spoke candidly about potentially divisive issues in the church. "We run the risk that we become a church that is focused on what divides us versus the mission we have," he said. "Some people feel disengaged from the larger church. We need a broad conversation grounded in Scripture and the Holy Spirit."

Hanson also expressed concern that many people seem unwilling to discuss matters related to sexuality and the church. "There is beneath the reality of this issue a deep, deep reservoir of avoidance," he said, fearing that any decisions made at the 2005 Churchwide Assembly will be interpreted by many members as decisions made by a few people and imposed on the church. He acknowledged that the strategic planning process "feels messy" because the church has made a deliberate effort to invite thousands of people into the process.

Hanson repeated some of his concerns in March 2003 at the Conference of Bishops, especially that one his "deepest fears" is that the "vast middle of this church is becoming more and more disengaged from the wider church."

These members lack a passion for the wider church, and there is a lack of trust for church leadership. It is difficult to reestablish trust when some members are not engaged in wider relationships with the church, he continued. Unfortunately, his comments were a kind of commentary on all of the ELCA's early years.

But Hanson's most ambitious early undertaking was spelling out a vision for the ELCA for 2012, an interesting 10-year vision for a bishop with a six-year term. It marked the first time a presiding bishop had outlined such a vision. Herbert Chilstrom put together studies that focused on the Lutheran confessions and the Bible. George Anderson outlined initiatives about which congregations could pick and choose. But Hanson has laid out a vision.

Calling the ELCA "a reforming movement within the church catholic," he said, "We cannot see with any clarity where God is leading us if we do not know from whence we have come and to whom we belong." To look ahead, Hanson said the church must look through the "lenses" of God's grace, through Christ's death and resurrection, through the work of Martin Luther, and through the ELCA's predecessor church bodies. He said that one issue that "haunts" him more than any other—

the unity of the church around strong, central themes. He is concerned that disenfranchised groups may be forming around specific issues.

The presiding bishop identified five strong "currents" that flow from "the waters of baptism." They are that the ELCA: is called to live among God's faithful people; will hear God's word and share in the Lord's Supper; is called to proclaim the good news of Jesus Christ through word and deed; will serve all people following the example of the Lord Jesus; and is to strive for justice and peace in all the earth.

Under each theme, Hanson cited a number of visions that might become reality 10 years from now in the ELCA. For example, he suggested that the Lutheran World Federation and the Vatican could be involved in "eucharistic sharing" and preparing jointly for the celebration "of the gifts of the Reformation" on the 500th anniversary of the Reformation in 2017. Or, in 10 years he visualized that "justice and peace will be the vocation in this church of all the baptized." Or, that in 10 years, "we could we look back on the sexuality studies and wonder why we were so anxious?"

High expectations

Thus the ELCA settled into its 15th year, in 2002, with its third bishop and with high expectations. There is every reason to believe that the expectations can be met, perhaps with less internal, organizational turmoil than at the ELCA's advent 15 years ago. But storm clouds are on the horizon, because the issues are getting tougher, not easier. The ELCA will continue to face debate over issues related to homosexuality and ordination, and learn how to live into its ecumenical agreements. Also, the ELCA's need for evangelistic zeal, consistency in worship practices, growth in diversity, and continuing financial stability will present challenges. Overarching these matters is a need for the church to determine its theological center over against the various voices and forces that historically have, and still continue, to try to tug it one way or another, often with influence beyond their size. The ELCA's largely silent theological center is the ballast to keep the ship of the church on an even keel, and needs to assert itself more clearly.

The legacy of the 2001 Churchwide Assembly may reflect, perhaps unwittingly, the need for this strong center. The assembly's actions may have signaled the decline of the uniformity of practice in congregations, synods and the churchwide expression. The exceptions for ordinations outside the understandings of *Called to Common Mission* may be the beginning of various exceptions to practice. Some voices suggest that, for the breadth of the church's ministry in some areas, it might be advisable to ordain gay and lesbian persons for service in specific geographic areas of the church. Both are examples of polity by exception, which may nibble at the center.

In its early years, the ELCA tried to be a uniform church in its ecclesiology, but culture tends to erode rather than salute uniformity, and some church members have such broadly diverse, and sometimes uninformed backgrounds, that tradition and uniformity do not hold much sway. To maintain unity, the church's own organizational needs are beginning to reflect the growing diversity of opinions in society, giving rise to a freer structural style. This will not be without some tension. Consistency of practice, informed by the church's confessions, long has been the hallmark of Lutherans who take comfort in feeling at home in virtually any congregation they visit across the United States.

This is a challenging time for the ELCA, both with its mission and how it melds its organization into an effective delivery system of that mission. The ELCA's future challenges come from a new set of expectations, borne not of newness as in 1988, but of its coming of age, of maturing, of its learning precisely in 2003 and beyond who it is theologically and where it is going organizationally.

INDEX

A

Aamodt, Gary, 52-54
Abortion, 77, 81-83, 96, 208
Adams, George, 168
Adrian College (Adrian, MI), 173
AELC, *see:* Association of Evangelical Lutheran Churches
African American Lutheran Association, 182, 184
African-Americans, *see:* Minority issues and groups
African Methodist Episcopal Church, 151
Agrimson, J. Elmo, 212
AIDS, 96, 167
Ailabouni, Said, 176
Aker, George, 35, 36, 39, 40, 43, 44
ALC, *see:* American Lutheran Church
Alejandrez, Daniel, 184
Almen, Lowell, 4, 11, 14-16, 18, 25, 39, 43, 56, 67, 70, 117, 136, 141, 146, 183, 198, 208, 212
American Indians, *see:* Minority issues and groups
American Lutheran Church, 4, 7-12, 15, 16, 22, 30, 31, 39, 40, 45, 50, 57-59, 64, 68, 105, 110, 117, 120, 162, 168, 177, 196
    Mergers, 7, 9-11, 37, 160, 209, 210
    Regional domination, 7, 12, 64, 159
Anatomy of a Merger, 4
Anderson, Albert, 10, 50-53
Anderson, Hugh George, 54, 57, 61, 63-69, 73, 102, 104, 105, 113, 117, 126, 128-131, 136, 138, 141-144, 147, 148, 150, 153-155, 158, 161, 164, 212
    Election as presiding bishop, 112, 208
Anderson, Jutta, 64
Anderson, Kathleen, 142
Anderson, Kenneth, 25
Andover Newton Theological School, 110
Anglican Church, 112, 119, 122, 164
Apartheid, 26, 61
Asians, *see:* Minority issues and groups
Assemblies of God, 196
Association of Asians—ELCA, 179, 184, 186
Association of Evangelical Lutheran Churches, 4, 8, 10, 15, 30, 31, 39, 40, 45, 59, 105, 110, 117, 120, 177
    Mergers, 7, 9, 37
Association of Lutherans of Arab and Middle Eastern Heritage, 183
Augsburg Confession, 108, 109, 111, 113, 119, 121, 126, 136
Augsburg Fortress, Publishers, 10, 16, 23, 26, 36, 50-56, 103, 187
Augsburg Publishing House, 16, 50
Augustana College (Sioux Falls, SD), 199

B

Bacher, Robert, 27, 44, 58-60, 66
Baerwald, Kathryn, 69
Baldorioty, Hector, 14

Baptismal language, 72, 73
Baptism and ELCA membership, 197-198, 204-206
Barry, A. L., 156, 158
Basting, Paul, 99
Berge, Paul, 160
Bergquist, James, 40
Berkeley Divinity School, 121
Bethel New Life Community Development Corporation, 167
Bethphage, 168
Bishops, 33, 65, 72, 120
    Consecration of, 119, 120, 122
    First Lutheran woman bishop, 71
    Length of term, 32, 33
    New bishops in new church, 30
    Synodical bishops, role of, 11, 70, 73, 79, 93, 120, 145, 146
    See also entries for individual presiding bishops
Bjork, Elvin, 24
Bjornborg, Allan, 150
Blasingame, Drew, 165
Blevins, Tom, 85
Blom, Paul, 124
Bloomquist, Karen, 86, 87, 90-92, 95, 96
Board of Pensions, 24, 25, 50, 70, 208
Board of Publication, 50
Boerger, William "Chris," 148
Bohlmann, Ralph, 157, 158
Book of Common Prayer, The, 119
Book of Concord, The, 157
Bouman, Stephen, 71
Bouman, Walter, 126-128
Braaten, Carl, 19, 20
Bradosky, John, 94
Briggs, David, 91
Browning, Edmond, 61, 119, 128
Brown, L. David, 125
Brown, Linda, 133
Brown Thunder, Joe, 200
Bruggeman, Ronald, 55
Buffalo Synod, 7
Burk, Michael, 204, 205
Burtness, James, 81
Bush, George W., 213
Bussert, Joy, 82
Butler, Addie, 69

C

Cabinet of Executives, 4, 39, 43
Caesar, Laurie, 156
Called to Common Mission, 67, 131-133, 136-141, 145, 148, 207, 216
    Disagreement about, 134-137, 140-147
Call to Discipleship, 198
Call to Faithfulness conferences, 19, 20